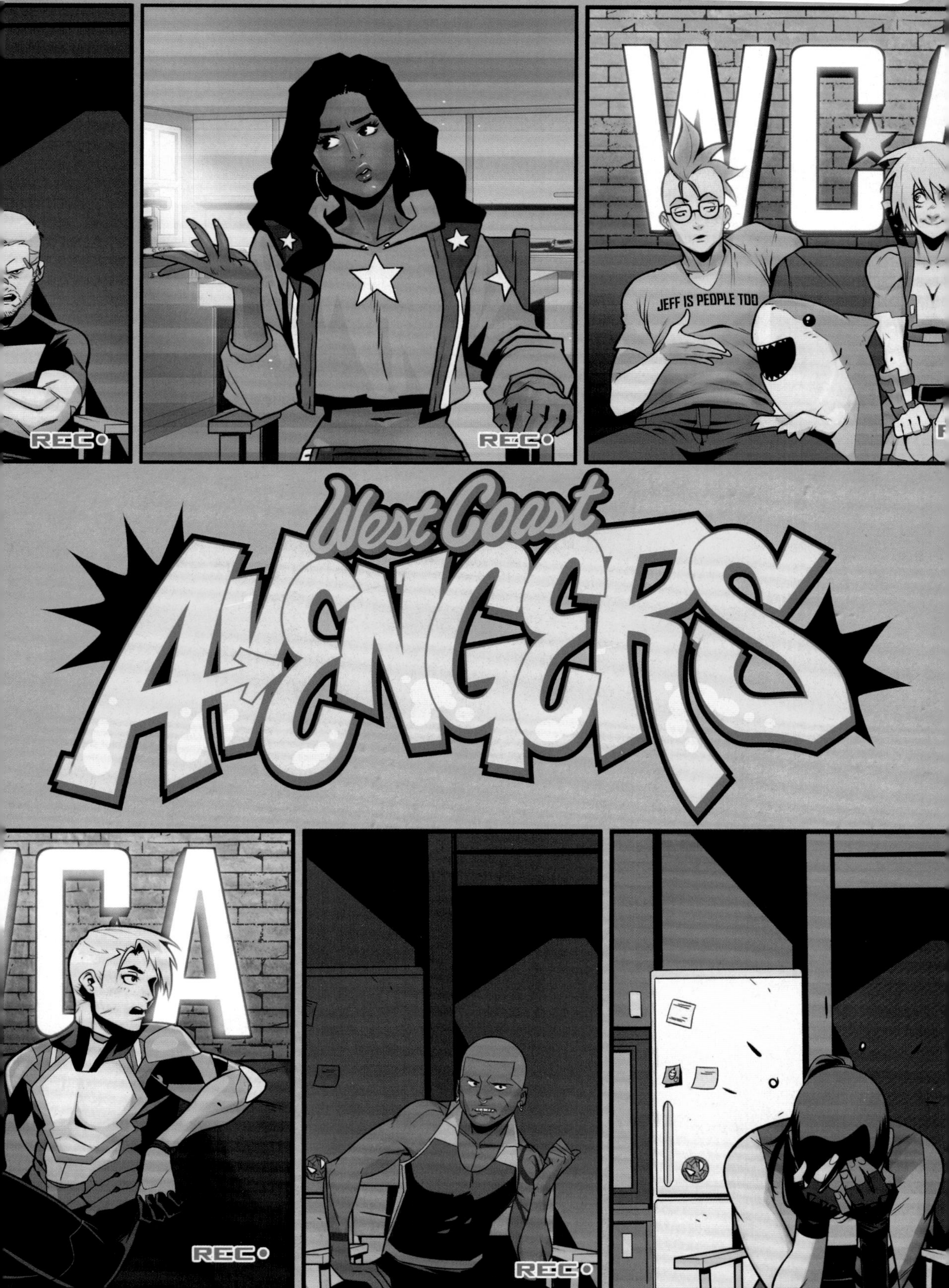
REC
REC
WC
JEFF IS PEOPLE TOO
West Coast
AVENGERS
CA
REC
REC

KATE BISHOP, A.K.A. HAWKEYE, HAS RECRUITED A TEAM TO PROTECT THE VULNERABLE
WEST COAST, BUT FUNDING IT CAME WITH A CATCH: THEY ALL HAD TO MOVE IN TOGETHER
AND LET A FILM CREW FOLLOW THEM AROUND.

THE TEAM RECENTLY SCORED A BIG WIN THAT GOT THEM IN BIG TROUBLE WITH CAPTAIN AMERICA,
WHO WASN'T THRILLED THAT THEY WERE USING THE AVENGERS NAME. AND HE'S NOT
THE ONLY ONE WHO'S UNHAPPY THAT THE WEST COAST HAS A NEW SUPER-CREW...

West Coast AVENGERS
CITY OF EVILS

KELLY THOMPSON
WRITER

DANIELE DI NICUOLO (#5-7),
GANG HYUK LIM (#8-9) & MOY R. (#10)
ARTISTS

TRIONA FARRELL (#5-7 & #9-10)
& GANG HYUK LIM (#8)
COLOR ARTISTS

STEFANO CASELLI & NOLAN WOODARD (#5-6),
EDUARD PETROVITCH (#7-8) AND GANG HYUK LIM (#9-10)
COVER ART

VC'S JOE
CARAMAGNA
LETTERER

SHANNON
ANDREWS
ASSISTANT EDITOR

ALANNA
SMITH
EDITOR

TOM
BREVOORT
EXECUTIVE EDITOR

AVENGERS CREATED BY STAN LEE & JACK KIRBY

COLLECTION EDITOR JENNIFER GRÜNWALD · ASSISTANT EDITOR CAITLIN O'CONNELL
ASSOCIATE MANAGING EDITOR KATERI WOODY · EDITOR, SPECIAL PROJECTS MARK D. BEAZLEY
VP PRODUCTION & SPECIAL PROJECTS JEFF YOUNGQUIST · BOOK DESIGNER JAY BOWEN

DIRECTOR, LICENSED PUBLISHING SVEN LARSEN · SVP PRINT, SALES & MARKETING DAVID GABRIEL
EDITOR IN CHIEF C.B. CEBULSKI · CHIEF CREATIVE OFFICER JOE QUESADA
PRESIDENT DAN BUCKLEY · EXECUTIVE PRODUCER ALAN FINE

WEST COAST AVENGERS VOL. 2: CITY OF EVILS. Contains material originally published in magazine form as WEST COAST AVENGERS #5-10. First printing 2019. ISBN 978-1-302-91346-5. Published by MARVEL WORLDWIDE, INC., a subsidiary of MARVEL ENTERTAINMENT, LLC. OFFICE OF PUBLICATION: 135 West 50th Street, New York, NY 10020. © 2019 MARVEL No similarity between any of the names, characters, persons, and/or institutions in this magazine with those of any living or dead person or institution is intended, and any such similarity which may exist is purely coincidental. Printed in Canada. DAN BUCKLEY, President, Marvel Entertainment; JOHN NEE, Publisher; JOE QUESADA, Chief Creative Officer; TOM BREVOORT, SVP of Publishing; DAVID BOGART, Associate Publisher & SVP of Talent Affairs; DAVID GABRIEL, SVP of Sales & Marketing, Publishing; JEFF YOUNGQUIST, VP of Production & Special Projects; DAN CARR, Executive Director of Publishing Technology; ALEX MORALES, Director of Publishing Operations; DAN EDINGTON, Managing Editor; SUSAN CRESPI, Production Manager; STAN LEE, Chairman Emeritus. For information regarding advertising in Marvel Comics or on Marvel.com, please contact Vit DeBellis, Custom Solutions & Integrated Advertising Manager, at vdebellis@marvel.com. For Marvel subscription inquiries, please call 888-511-5480. Manufactured between 5/3/2019 and 6/4/2019 by SOLISCO PRINTERS, SCOTT, QC, CANADA.

10 9 8 7 6 5 4 3 2 1

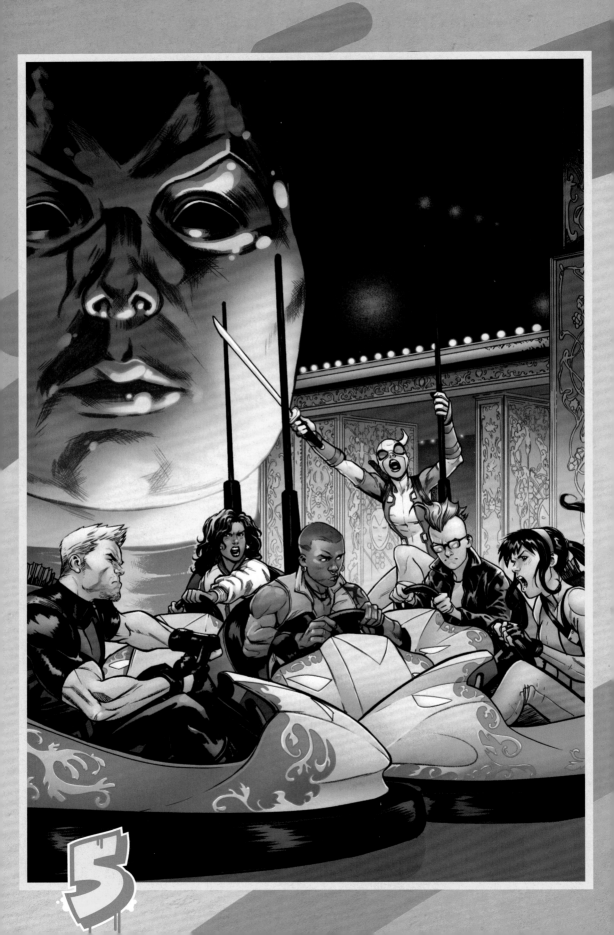

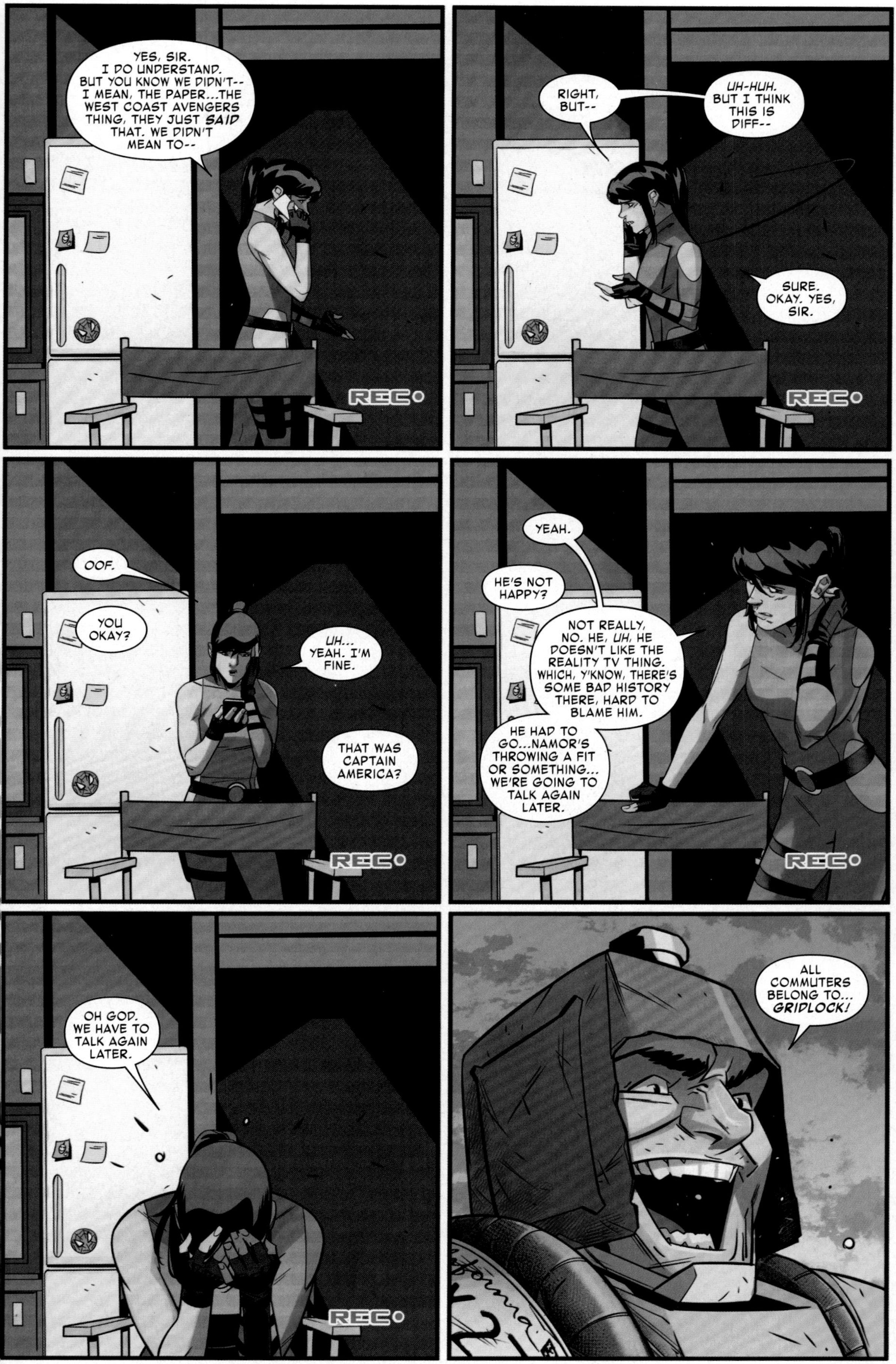
YES, SIR. I DO UNDERSTAND. BUT YOU KNOW WE DIDN'T-- I MEAN, THE PAPER...THE WEST COAST AVENGERS THING, THEY JUST SAID THAT. WE DIDN'T MEAN TO--
REC
RIGHT, BUT--
UH-HUH. BUT I THINK THIS IS DIFF--
SURE. OKAY. YES, SIR.
REC
OOF.
YOU OKAY?
UH... YEAH. I'M FINE.
THAT WAS CAPTAIN AMERICA?
REC
YEAH.
HE'S NOT HAPPY?
NOT REALLY, NO. HE, UH, HE DOESN'T LIKE THE REALITY TV THING. WHICH, Y'KNOW, THERE'S SOME BAD HISTORY THERE, HARD TO BLAME HIM.
HE HAD TO GO...NAMOR'S THROWING A FIT OR SOMETHING... WE'RE GOING TO TALK AGAIN LATER.
REC
OH GOD. WE HAVE TO TALK AGAIN LATER.
REC
ALL COMMUTERS BELONG TO... GRIDLOCK!

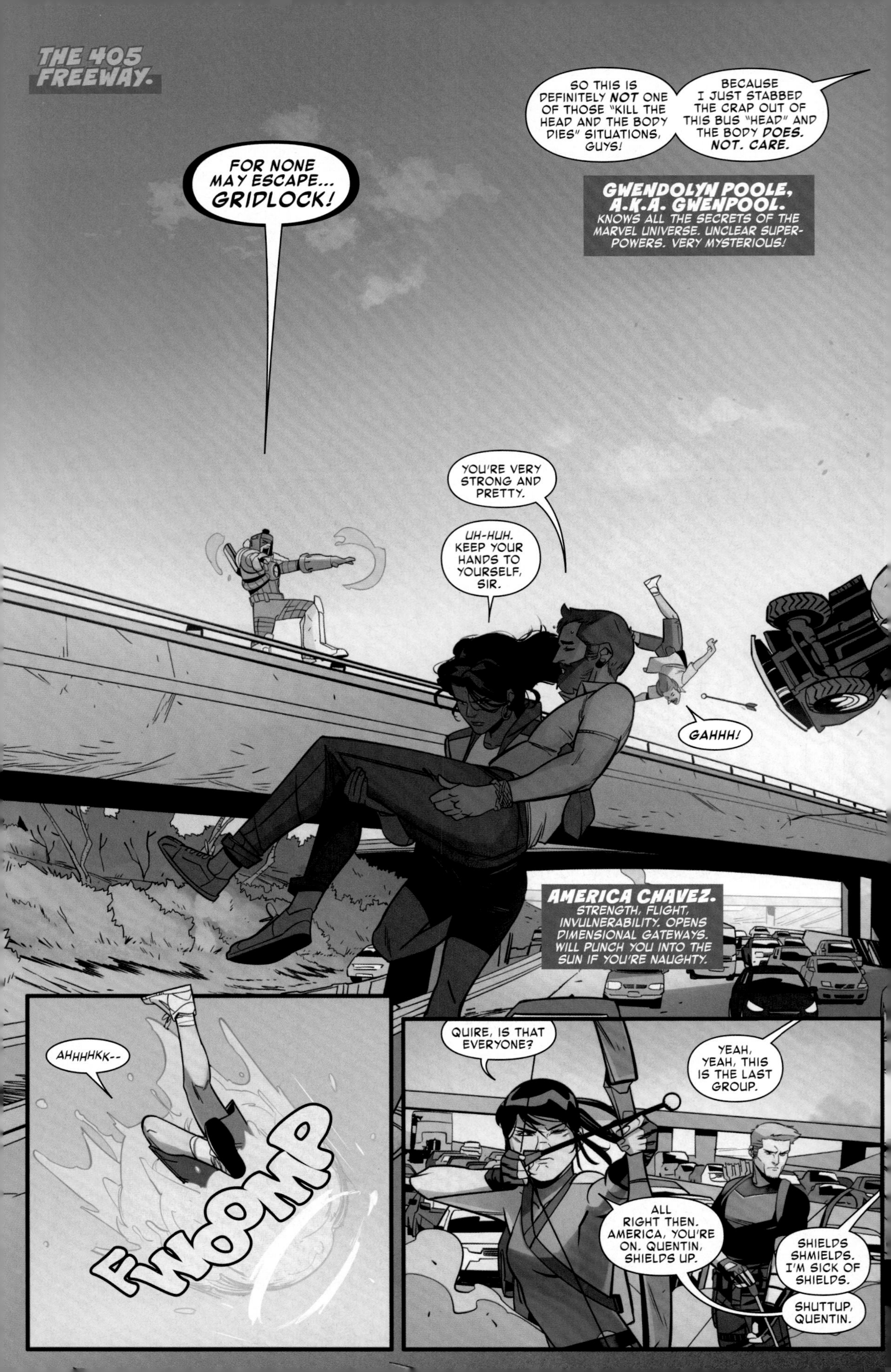
THE 405 FREEWAY.
FOR NONE MAY ESCAPE... GRIDLOCK!
SO THIS IS DEFINITELY NOT ONE OF THOSE "KILL THE HEAD AND THE BODY DIES" SITUATIONS, GUYS!
BECAUSE I JUST STABBED THE CRAP OUT OF THIS BUS "HEAD" AND THE BODY DOES. NOT. CARE.
GWENDOLYN POOLE, A.K.A. GWENPOOL. KNOWS ALL THE SECRETS OF THE MARVEL UNIVERSE. UNCLEAR SUPER-POWERS. VERY MYSTERIOUS!
YOU'RE VERY STRONG AND PRETTY.
UH-HUH. KEEP YOUR HANDS TO YOURSELF, SIR.
GAHHH!
AMERICA CHAVEZ. STRENGTH, FLIGHT, INVULNERABILITY. OPENS DIMENSIONAL GATEWAYS. WILL PUNCH YOU INTO THE SUN IF YOU'RE NAUGHTY.
AHHHHKK--
FWOMP
QUIRE, IS THAT EVERYONE?
YEAH, YEAH, THIS IS THE LAST GROUP.
ALL RIGHT THEN. AMERICA, YOU'RE ON. QUENTIN, SHIELDS UP.
SHIELDS SHMIELDS. I'M SICK OF SHIELDS.
SHUTTUP, QUENTIN.

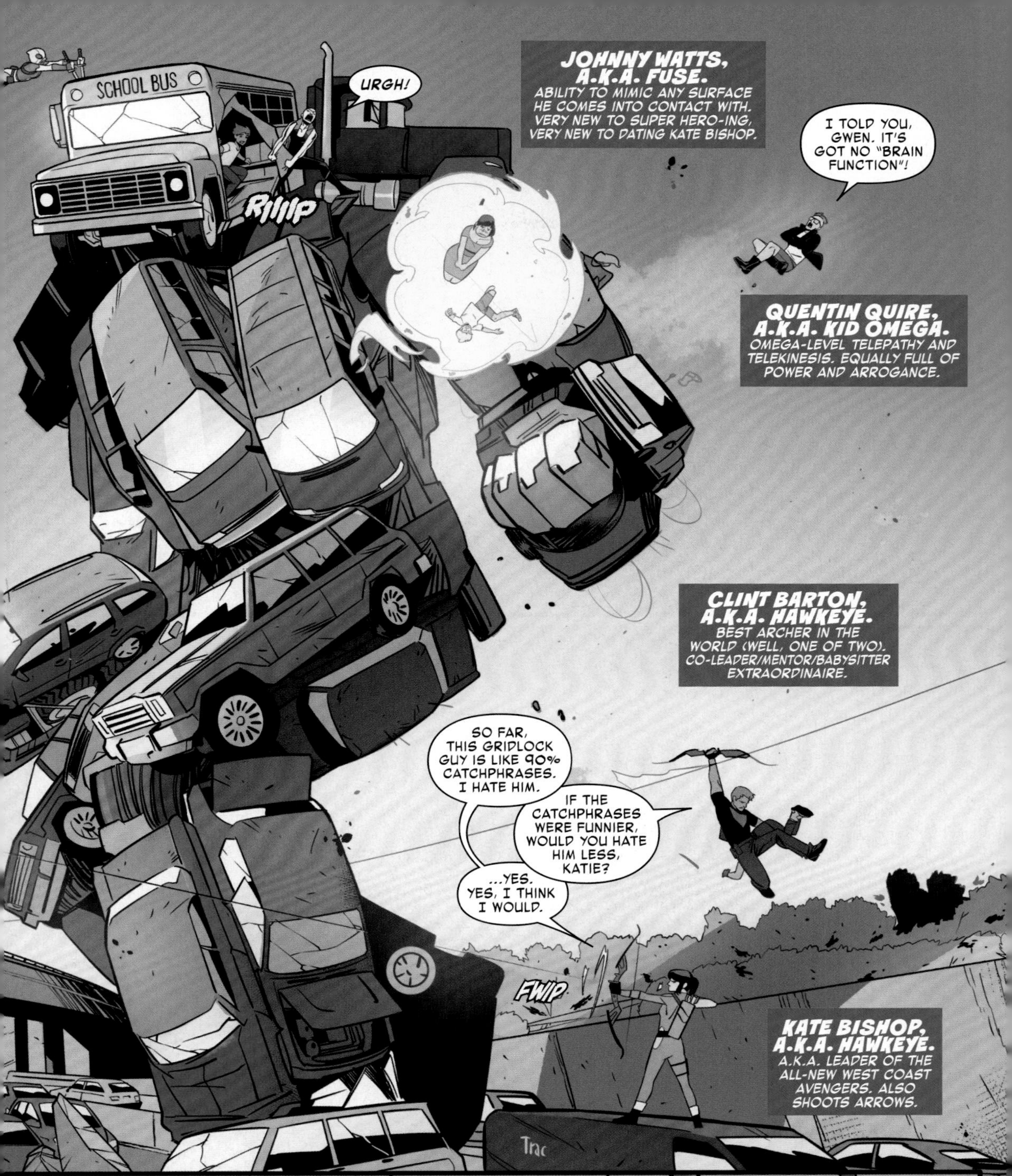
SCHOOL BUS
URGH!
JOHNNY WATTS, A.K.A. FUSE.
ABILITY TO MIMIC ANY SURFACE HE COMES INTO CONTACT WITH. VERY NEW TO SUPER HERO-ING, VERY NEW TO DATING KATE BISHOP.
RIIIP
I TOLD YOU, GWEN. IT'S GOT NO "BRAIN FUNCTION"!
QUENTIN QUIRE, A.K.A. KID OMEGA.
OMEGA-LEVEL TELEPATHY AND TELEKINESIS. EQUALLY FULL OF POWER AND ARROGANCE.
CLINT BARTON, A.K.A. HAWKEYE.
BEST ARCHER IN THE WORLD (WELL, ONE OF TWO). CO-LEADER/MENTOR/BABYSITTER EXTRAORDINAIRE.
SO FAR, THIS GRIDLOCK GUY IS LIKE 90% CATCHPHRASES. I HATE HIM.
IF THE CATCHPHRASES WERE FUNNIER, WOULD YOU HATE HIM LESS, KATIE?
...YES. YES, I THINK I WOULD.
FWIP
KATE BISHOP, A.K.A. HAWKEYE.
A.K.A. LEADER OF THE ALL-NEW WEST COAST AVENGERS. ALSO SHOOTS ARROWS.
Trac

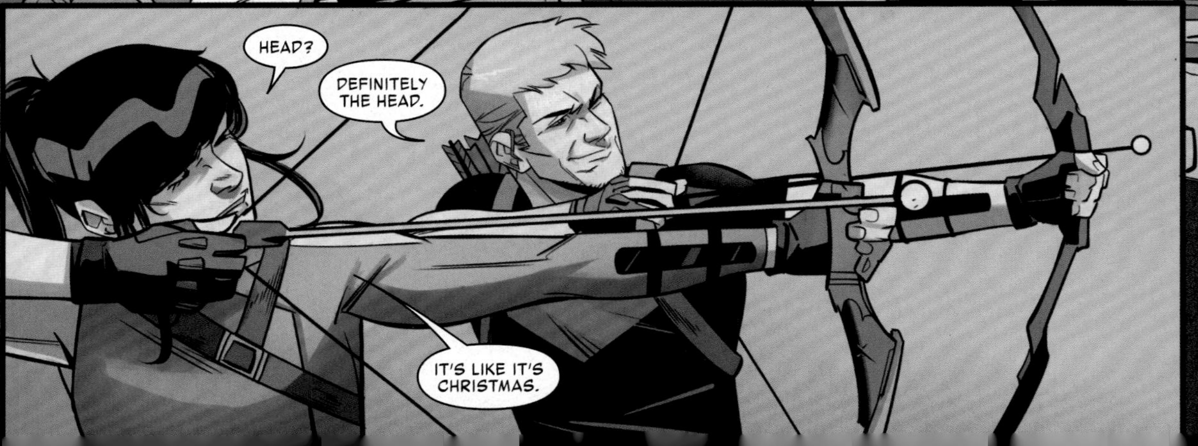
HEAD?
DEFINITELY THE HEAD.
IT'S LIKE IT'S CHRISTMAS.

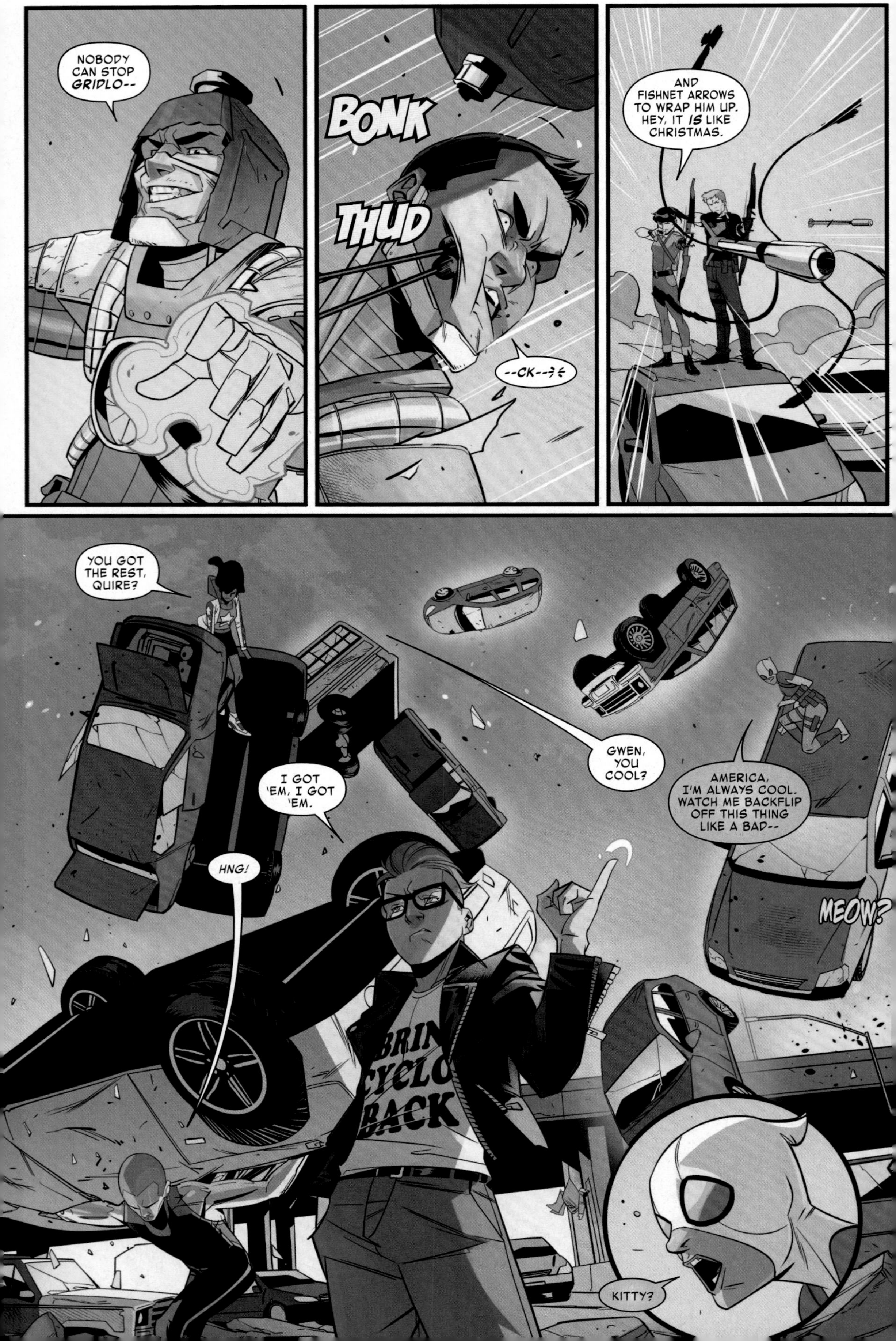
NOBODY CAN STOP GRIDLO--
BONK
THUD
--CK--
AND FISHNET ARROWS TO WRAP HIM UP. HEY, IT IS LIKE CHRISTMAS.
YOU GOT THE REST, QUIRE?
GWEN, YOU COOL?
AMERICA, I'M ALWAYS COOL. WATCH ME BACKFLIP OFF THIS THING LIKE A BAD--
I GOT 'EM, I GOT 'EM.
HNG!
BRIN CYCLO BACK
MEOW?
KITTY?

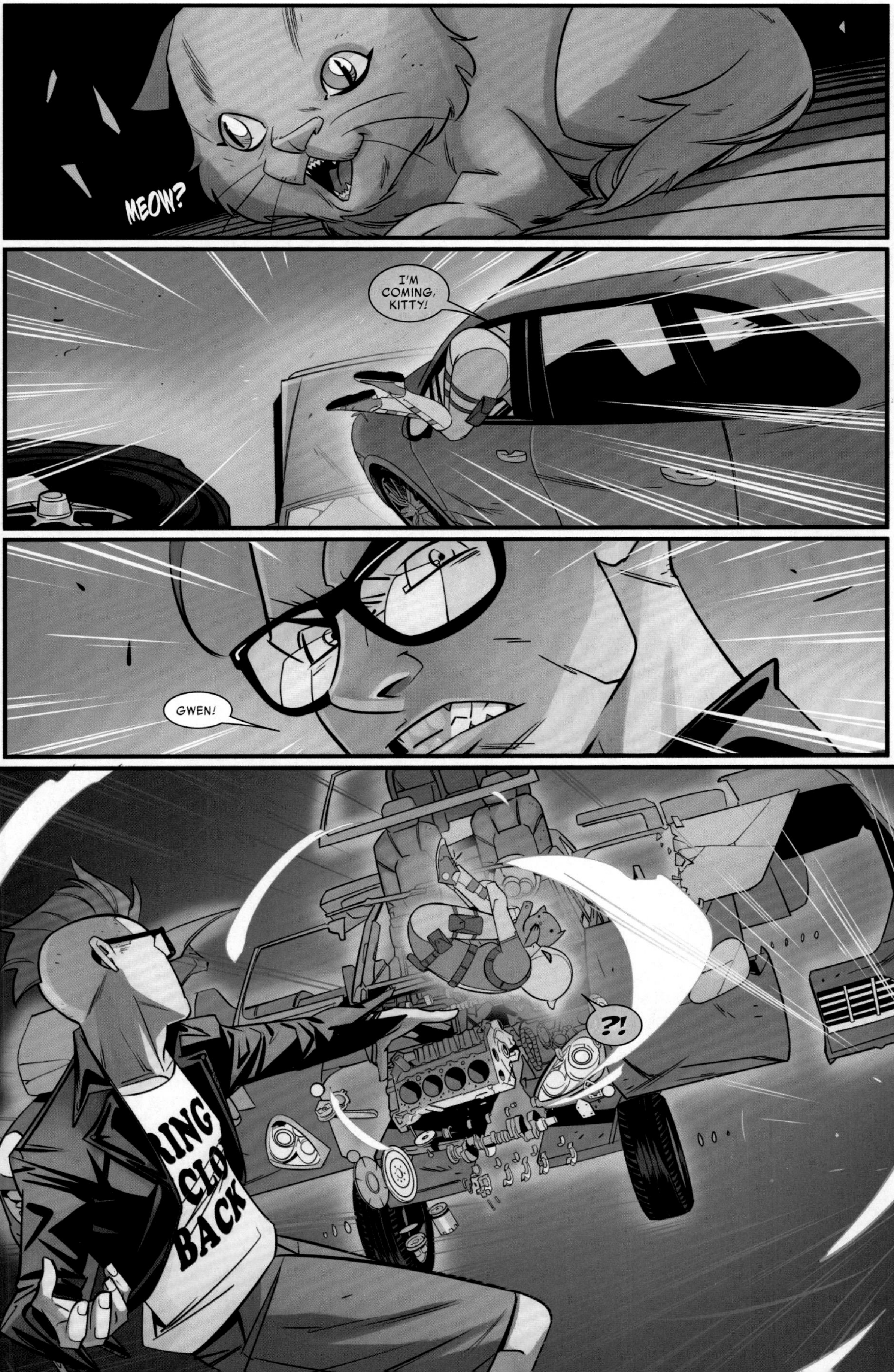
MEOW?
I'M COMING, KITTY!
GWEN!
?!

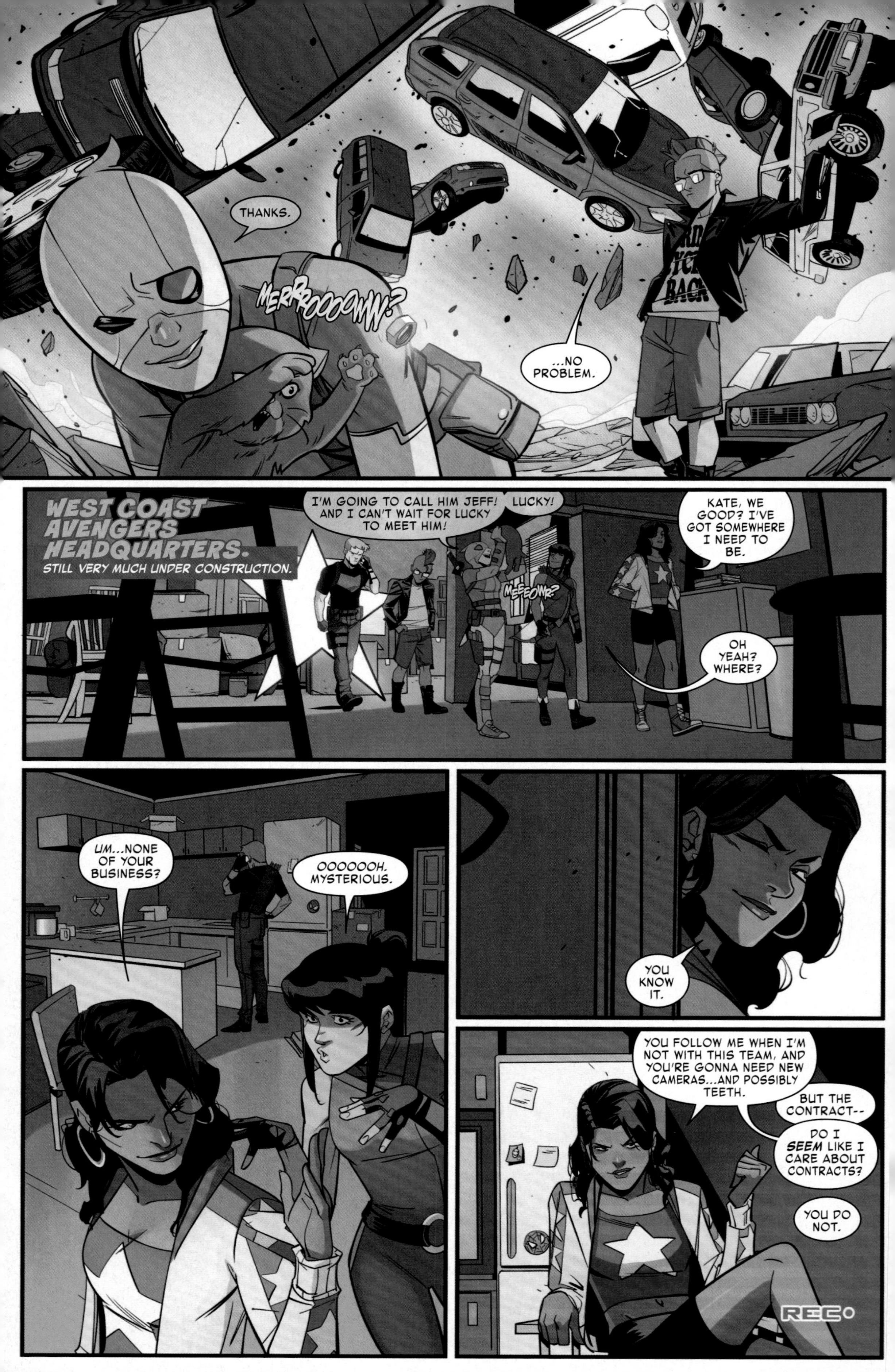

THANKS.
MERRROOOOWW?
...NO PROBLEM.
WEST COAST AVENGERS HEADQUARTERS.
STILL VERY MUCH UNDER CONSTRUCTION.
I'M GOING TO CALL HIM JEFF! AND I CAN'T WAIT FOR LUCKY TO MEET HIM!
LUCKY!
MEEEOWR?
KATE, WE GOOD? I'VE GOT SOMEWHERE I NEED TO BE.
OH YEAH? WHERE?
UM...NONE OF YOUR BUSINESS?
OOOOOOH. MYSTERIOUS.
YOU KNOW IT.
YOU FOLLOW ME WHEN I'M NOT WITH THIS TEAM, AND YOU'RE GONNA NEED NEW CAMERAS...AND POSSIBLY TEETH.
BUT THE CONTRACT--
DO I SEEM LIKE I CARE ABOUT CONTRACTS?
YOU DO NOT.
REC

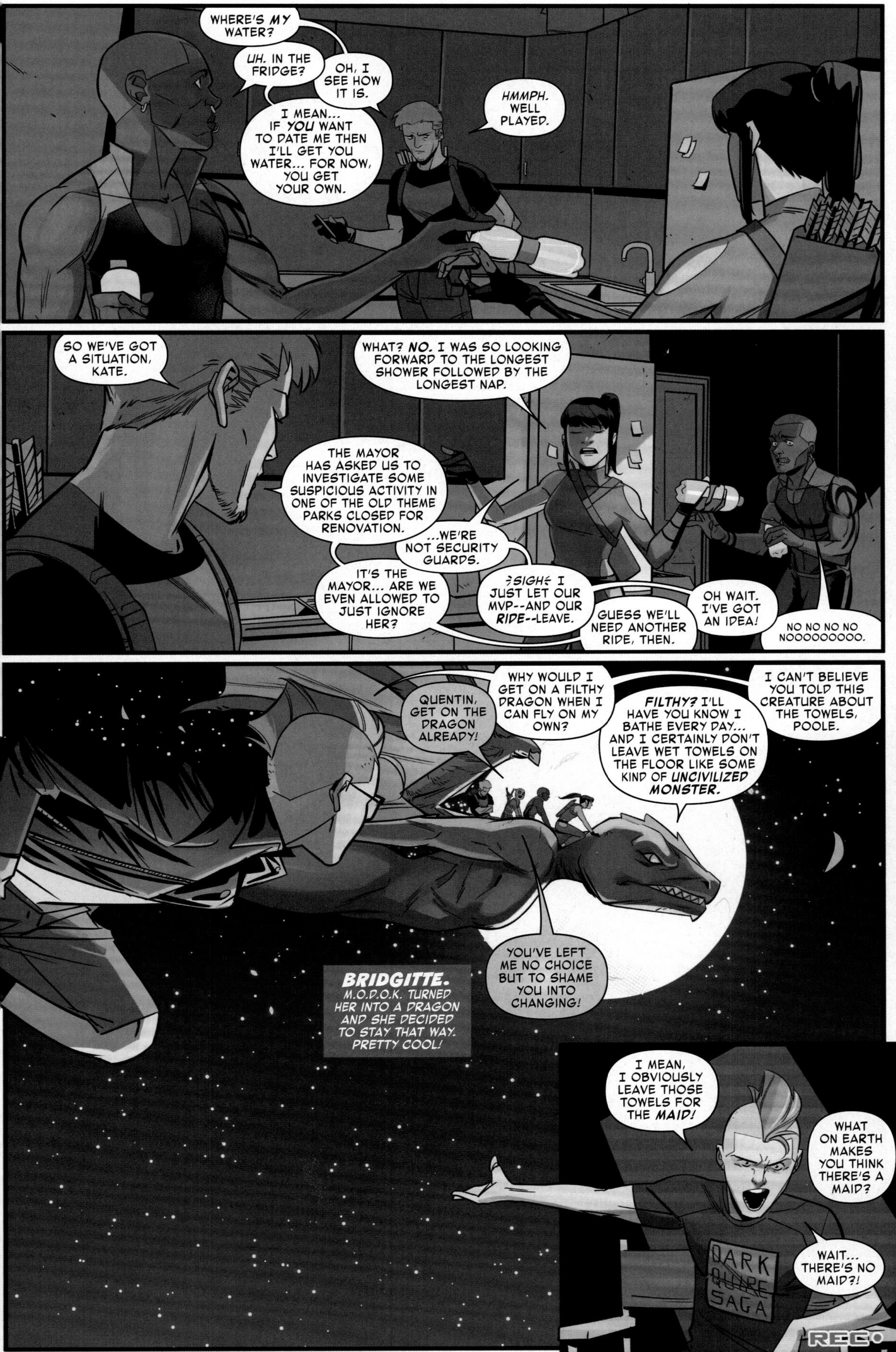

WHERE'S MY WATER?
UH. IN THE FRIDGE?
OH, I SEE HOW IT IS.
I MEAN... IF YOU WANT TO DATE ME THEN I'LL GET YOU WATER... FOR NOW, YOU GET YOUR OWN.
HMMPH. WELL PLAYED.
SO WE'VE GOT A SITUATION, KATE.
WHAT? NO. I WAS SO LOOKING FORWARD TO THE LONGEST SHOWER FOLLOWED BY THE LONGEST NAP.
THE MAYOR HAS ASKED US TO INVESTIGATE SOME SUSPICIOUS ACTIVITY IN ONE OF THE OLD THEME PARKS CLOSED FOR RENOVATION.
...WE'RE NOT SECURITY GUARDS.
IT'S THE MAYOR... ARE WE EVEN ALLOWED TO JUST IGNORE HER?
SIGH I JUST LET OUR MVP--AND OUR RIDE--LEAVE.
GUESS WE'LL NEED ANOTHER RIDE, THEN.
OH WAIT. I'VE GOT AN IDEA!
NO NO NO NO NOOOOOOOOO.
QUENTIN, GET ON THE DRAGON ALREADY!
WHY WOULD I GET ON A FILTHY DRAGON WHEN I CAN FLY ON MY OWN?
FILTHY? I'LL HAVE YOU KNOW I BATHE EVERY DAY... AND I CERTAINLY DON'T LEAVE WET TOWELS ON THE FLOOR LIKE SOME KIND OF UNCIVILIZED MONSTER.
I CAN'T BELIEVE YOU TOLD THIS CREATURE ABOUT THE TOWELS, POOLE.
YOU'VE LEFT ME NO CHOICE BUT TO SHAME YOU INTO CHANGING!
BRIDGITTE. M.O.D.O.K. TURNED HER INTO A DRAGON AND SHE DECIDED TO STAY THAT WAY. PRETTY COOL!
I MEAN, I OBVIOUSLY LEAVE THOSE TOWELS FOR THE MAID!
WHAT ON EARTH MAKES YOU THINK THERE'S A MAID?
WAIT... THERE'S NO MAID?!
DARK QUIRE SAGA

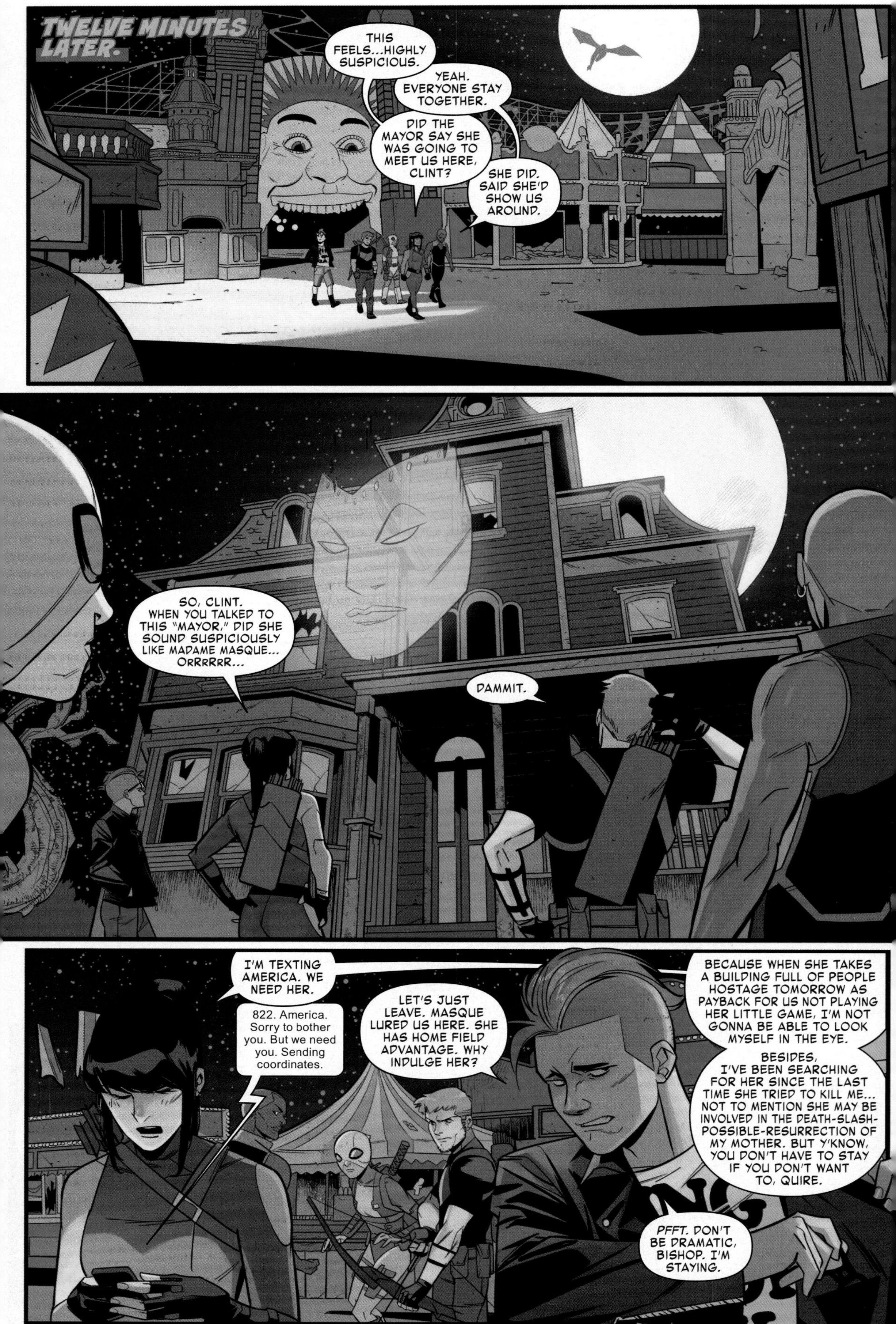

TWELVE MINUTES LATER.
THIS FEELS...HIGHLY SUSPICIOUS.
YEAH. EVERYONE STAY TOGETHER.
DID THE MAYOR SAY SHE WAS GOING TO MEET US HERE, CLINT?
SHE DID. SAID SHE'D SHOW US AROUND.
SO, CLINT. WHEN YOU TALKED TO THIS "MAYOR," DID SHE SOUND SUSPICIOUSLY LIKE MADAME MASQUE... ORRRRRR...
DAMMIT.
I'M TEXTING AMERICA. WE NEED HER.
822. America. Sorry to bother you. But we need you. Sending coordinates.
LET'S JUST LEAVE. MASQUE LURED US HERE. SHE HAS HOME FIELD ADVANTAGE. WHY INDULGE HER?
BECAUSE WHEN SHE TAKES A BUILDING FULL OF PEOPLE HOSTAGE TOMORROW AS PAYBACK FOR US NOT PLAYING HER LITTLE GAME, I'M NOT GONNA BE ABLE TO LOOK MYSELF IN THE EYE.
BESIDES, I'VE BEEN SEARCHING FOR HER SINCE THE LAST TIME SHE TRIED TO KILL ME... NOT TO MENTION SHE MAY BE INVOLVED IN THE DEATH-SLASH-POSSIBLE-RESURRECTION OF MY MOTHER. BUT Y'KNOW, YOU DON'T HAVE TO STAY IF YOU DON'T WANT TO, QUIRE.
PFFT. DON'T BE DRAMATIC, BISHOP. I'M STAYING.

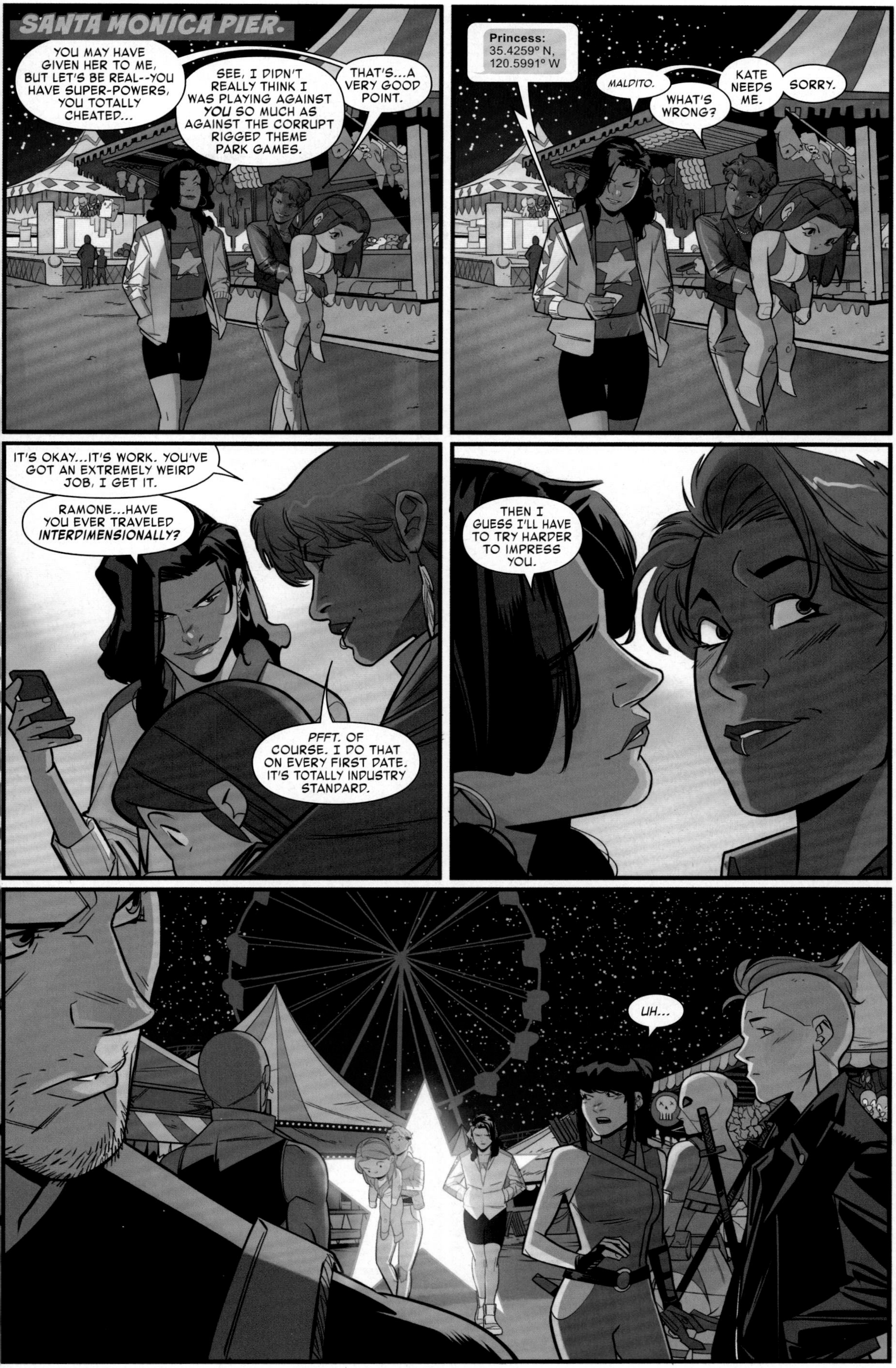
SANTA MONICA PIER.
YOU MAY HAVE GIVEN HER TO ME, BUT LET'S BE REAL--YOU HAVE SUPER-POWERS, YOU TOTALLY CHEATED...
SEE, I DIDN'T REALLY THINK I WAS PLAYING AGAINST *YOU* SO MUCH AS AGAINST THE CORRUPT RIGGED THEME PARK GAMES.
THAT'S...A VERY GOOD POINT.
Princess: 35.4259º N, 120.5991º W
MALDITO.
WHAT'S WRONG?
KATE NEEDS ME.
SORRY.
IT'S OKAY...IT'S WORK. YOU'VE GOT AN EXTREMELY WEIRD JOB, I GET IT.
RAMONE...HAVE YOU EVER TRAVELED *INTERDIMENSIONALLY?*
PFFT. OF COURSE. I DO THAT ON EVERY FIRST DATE. IT'S TOTALLY INDUSTRY STANDARD.
THEN I GUESS I'LL HAVE TO TRY HARDER TO IMPRESS YOU.
UH...

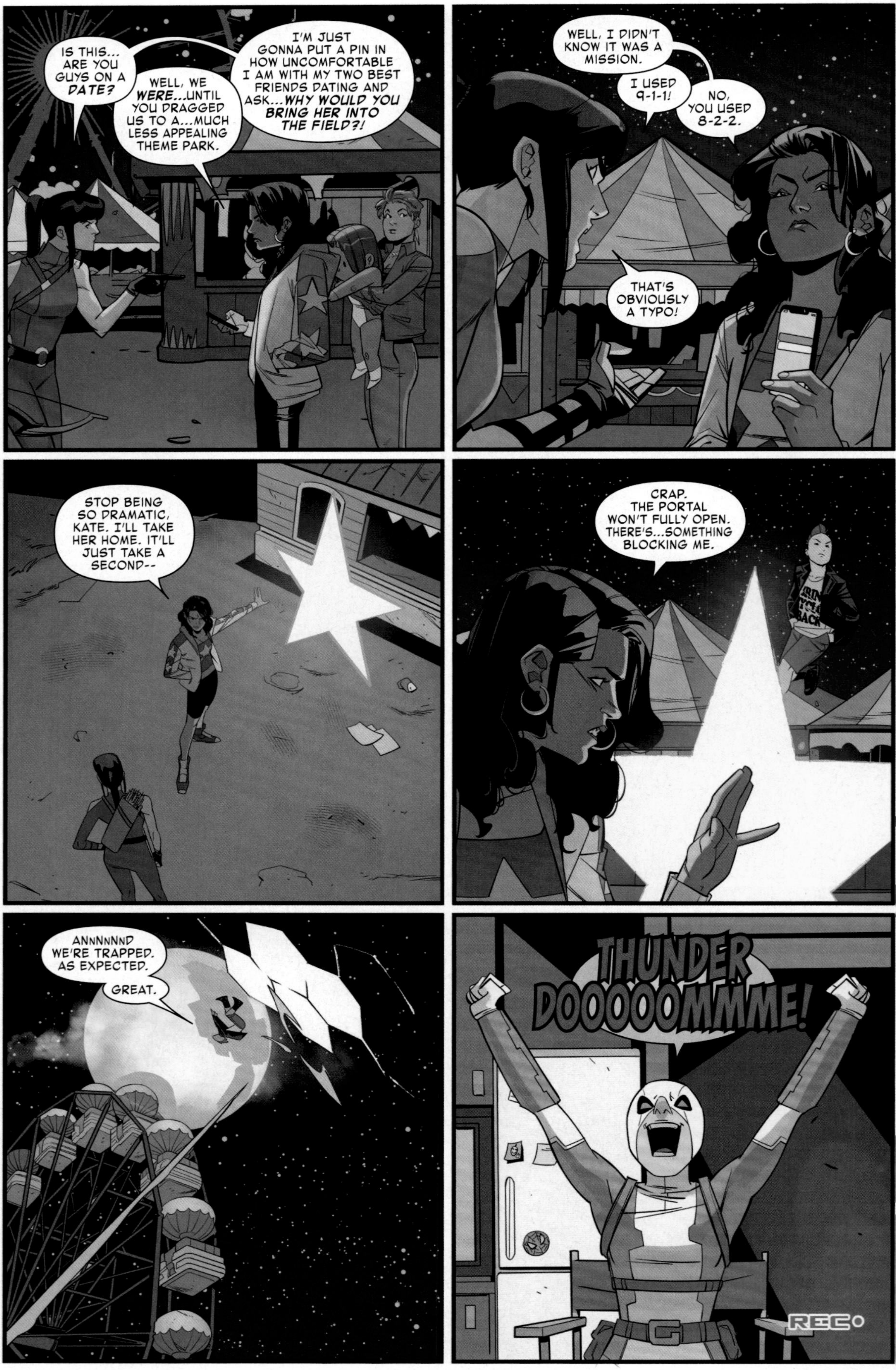
IS THIS... ARE YOU GUYS ON A DATE?
WELL, WE WERE...UNTIL YOU DRAGGED US TO A...MUCH LESS APPEALING THEME PARK.
I'M JUST GONNA PUT A PIN IN HOW UNCOMFORTABLE I AM WITH MY TWO BEST FRIENDS DATING AND ASK...WHY WOULD YOU BRING HER INTO THE FIELD?!
WELL, I DIDN'T KNOW IT WAS A MISSION.
I USED 9-1-1!
NO, YOU USED 8-2-2.
THAT'S OBVIOUSLY A TYPO!
STOP BEING SO DRAMATIC, KATE. I'LL TAKE HER HOME. IT'LL JUST TAKE A SECOND--
CRAP. THE PORTAL WON'T FULLY OPEN. THERE'S...SOMETHING BLOCKING ME.
ANNNNNND WE'RE TRAPPED. AS EXPECTED.
GREAT.
THUNDER DOOOOOMMME!
REC

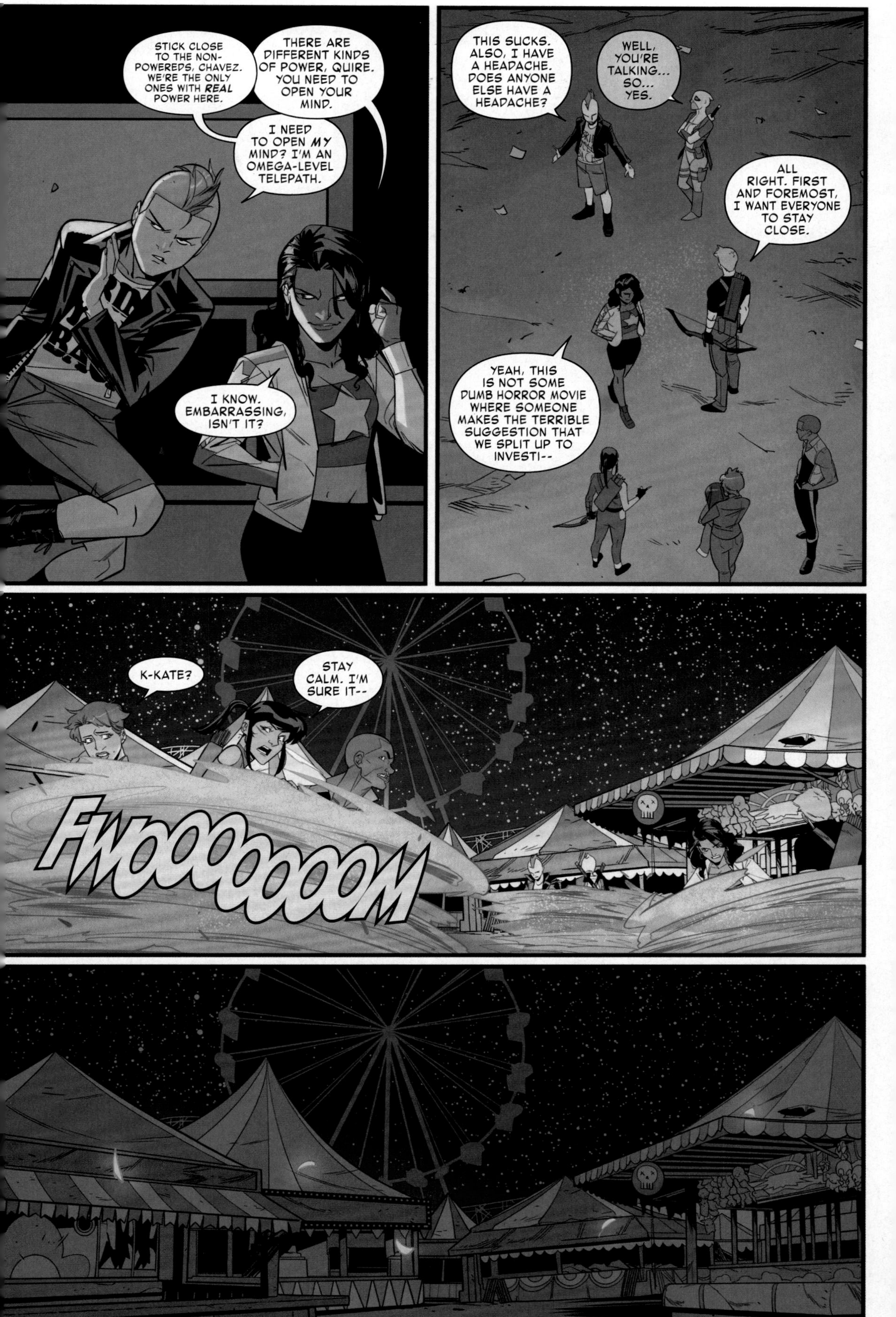

STICK CLOSE TO THE NON-POWEREDS, CHAVEZ. WE'RE THE ONLY ONES WITH REAL POWER HERE.
THERE ARE DIFFERENT KINDS OF POWER, QUIRE. YOU NEED TO OPEN YOUR MIND.
I NEED TO OPEN MY MIND? I'M AN OMEGA-LEVEL TELEPATH.
I KNOW. EMBARRASSING, ISN'T IT?
THIS SUCKS. ALSO, I HAVE A HEADACHE. DOES ANYONE ELSE HAVE A HEADACHE?
WELL, YOU'RE TALKING... SO... YES.
ALL RIGHT. FIRST AND FOREMOST, I WANT EVERYONE TO STAY CLOSE.
YEAH, THIS IS NOT SOME DUMB HORROR MOVIE WHERE SOMEONE MAKES THE TERRIBLE SUGGESTION THAT WE SPLIT UP TO INVESTI--
K-KATE?
STAY CALM. I'M SURE IT--
FWOOOOOOOM

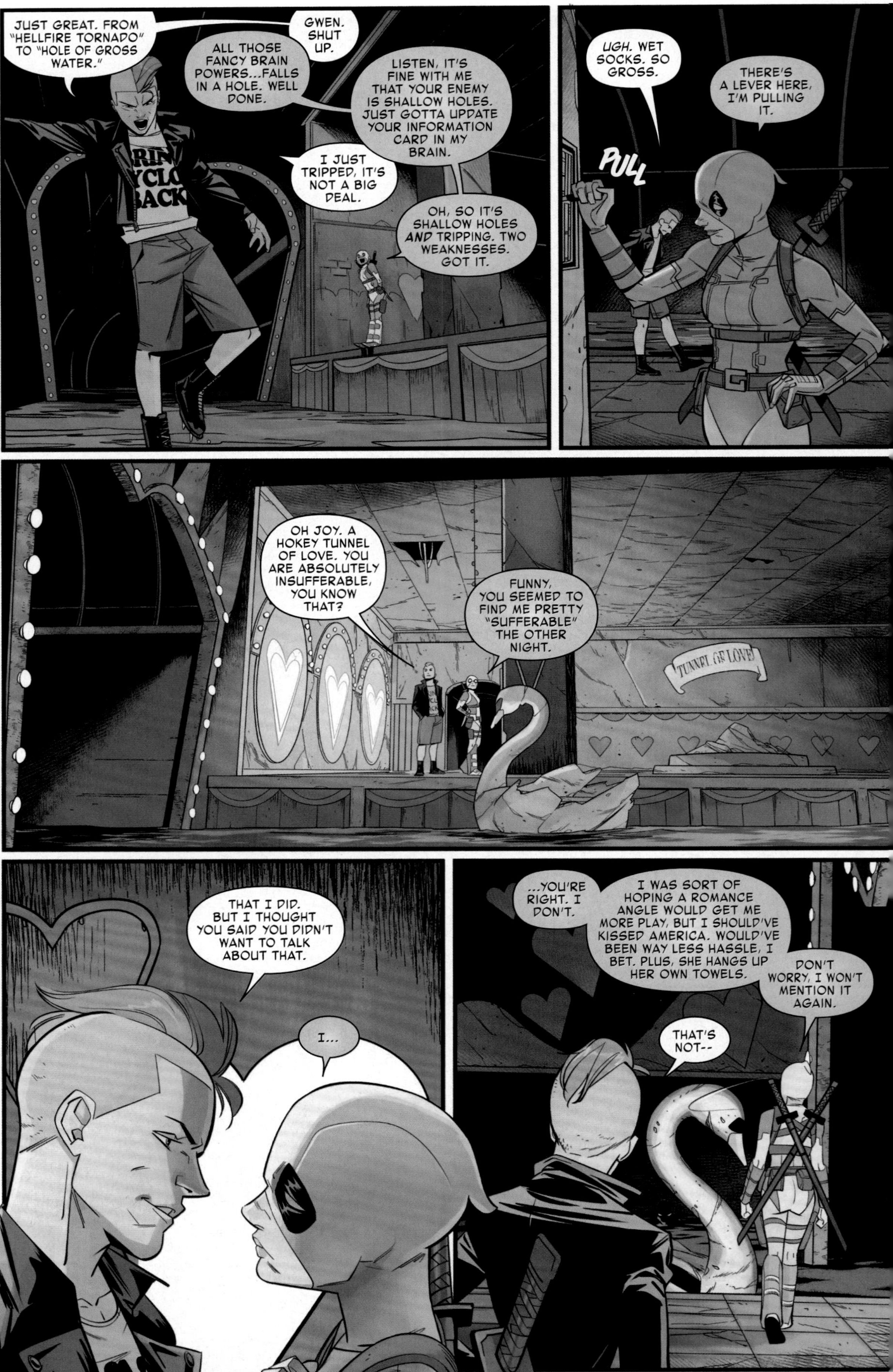

JUST GREAT. FROM "HELLFIRE TORNADO" TO "HOLE OF GROSS WATER."
GWEN. SHUT UP.
ALL THOSE FANCY BRAIN POWERS...FALLS IN A HOLE. WELL DONE.
LISTEN, IT'S FINE WITH ME THAT YOUR ENEMY IS SHALLOW HOLES. JUST GOTTA UPDATE YOUR INFORMATION CARD IN MY BRAIN.
I JUST TRIPPED, IT'S NOT A BIG DEAL.
OH, SO IT'S SHALLOW HOLES *AND* TRIPPING. TWO WEAKNESSES. GOT IT.
UGH. WET SOCKS. SO GROSS.
THERE'S A LEVER HERE, I'M PULLING IT.
PULL
OH JOY. A HOKEY TUNNEL OF LOVE. YOU ARE ABSOLUTELY INSUFFERABLE, YOU KNOW THAT?
FUNNY, YOU SEEMED TO FIND ME PRETTY "SUFFERABLE" THE OTHER NIGHT.
TUNNEL OF LOVE
THAT I DID. BUT I THOUGHT YOU SAID YOU DIDN'T WANT TO TALK ABOUT THAT.
I...
...YOU'RE RIGHT. I DON'T.
I WAS SORT OF HOPING A ROMANCE ANGLE WOULD GET ME MORE PLAY, BUT I SHOULD'VE KISSED AMERICA. WOULD'VE BEEN WAY LESS HASSLE, I BET. PLUS, SHE HANGS UP HER OWN TOWELS.
THAT'S NOT--
DON'T WORRY, I WON'T MENTION IT AGAIN.

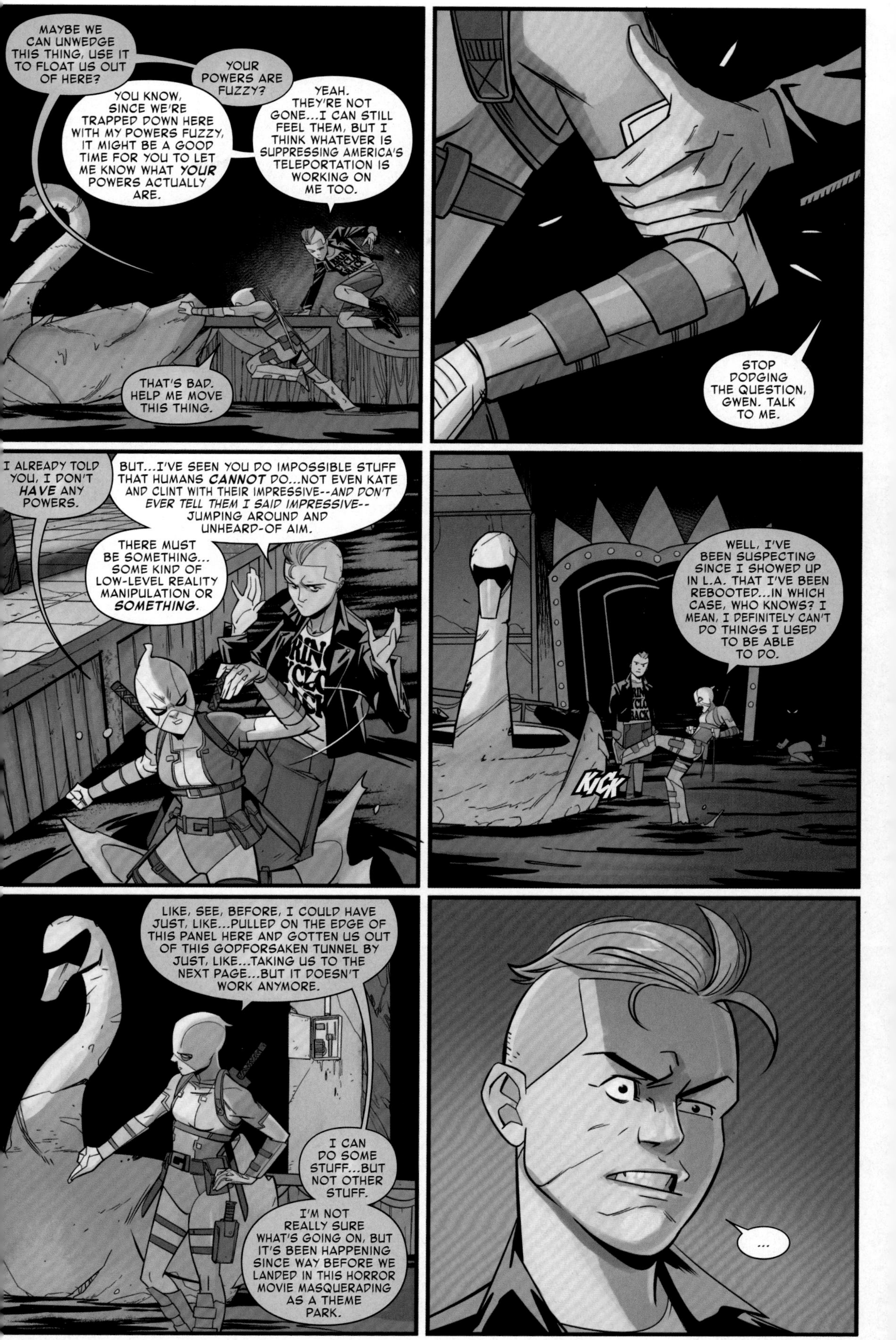
MAYBE WE CAN UNWEDGE THIS THING, USE IT TO FLOAT US OUT OF HERE?
YOUR POWERS ARE FUZZY?
YOU KNOW, SINCE WE'RE TRAPPED DOWN HERE WITH MY POWERS FUZZY, IT MIGHT BE A GOOD TIME FOR YOU TO LET ME KNOW WHAT *YOUR* POWERS ACTUALLY ARE.
YEAH. THEY'RE NOT GONE...I CAN STILL FEEL THEM, BUT I THINK WHATEVER IS SUPPRESSING AMERICA'S TELEPORTATION IS WORKING ON ME TOO.
THAT'S BAD. HELP ME MOVE THIS THING.
STOP DODGING THE QUESTION, GWEN. TALK TO ME.
I ALREADY TOLD YOU, I DON'T *HAVE* ANY POWERS.
BUT...I'VE SEEN YOU DO IMPOSSIBLE STUFF THAT HUMANS ***CANNOT*** DO...NOT EVEN KATE AND CLINT WITH THEIR IMPRESSIVE--*AND DON'T EVER TELL THEM I SAID IMPRESSIVE*--JUMPING AROUND AND UNHEARD-OF AIM.
THERE MUST BE SOMETHING... SOME KIND OF LOW-LEVEL REALITY MANIPULATION OR ***SOMETHING***.
WELL, I'VE BEEN SUSPECTING SINCE I SHOWED UP IN L.A. THAT I'VE BEEN REBOOTED...IN WHICH CASE, WHO KNOWS? I MEAN, I DEFINITELY CAN'T DO THINGS I USED TO BE ABLE TO DO.
KICK
LIKE, SEE, BEFORE, I COULD HAVE JUST, LIKE...PULLED ON THE EDGE OF THIS PANEL HERE AND GOTTEN US OUT OF THIS GODFORSAKEN TUNNEL BY JUST, LIKE...TAKING US TO THE NEXT PAGE...BUT IT DOESN'T WORK ANYMORE.
I CAN DO SOME STUFF...BUT NOT OTHER STUFF.
I'M NOT REALLY SURE WHAT'S GOING ON, BUT IT'S BEEN HAPPENING SINCE WAY BEFORE WE LANDED IN THIS HORROR MOVIE MASQUERADING AS A THEME PARK.
...

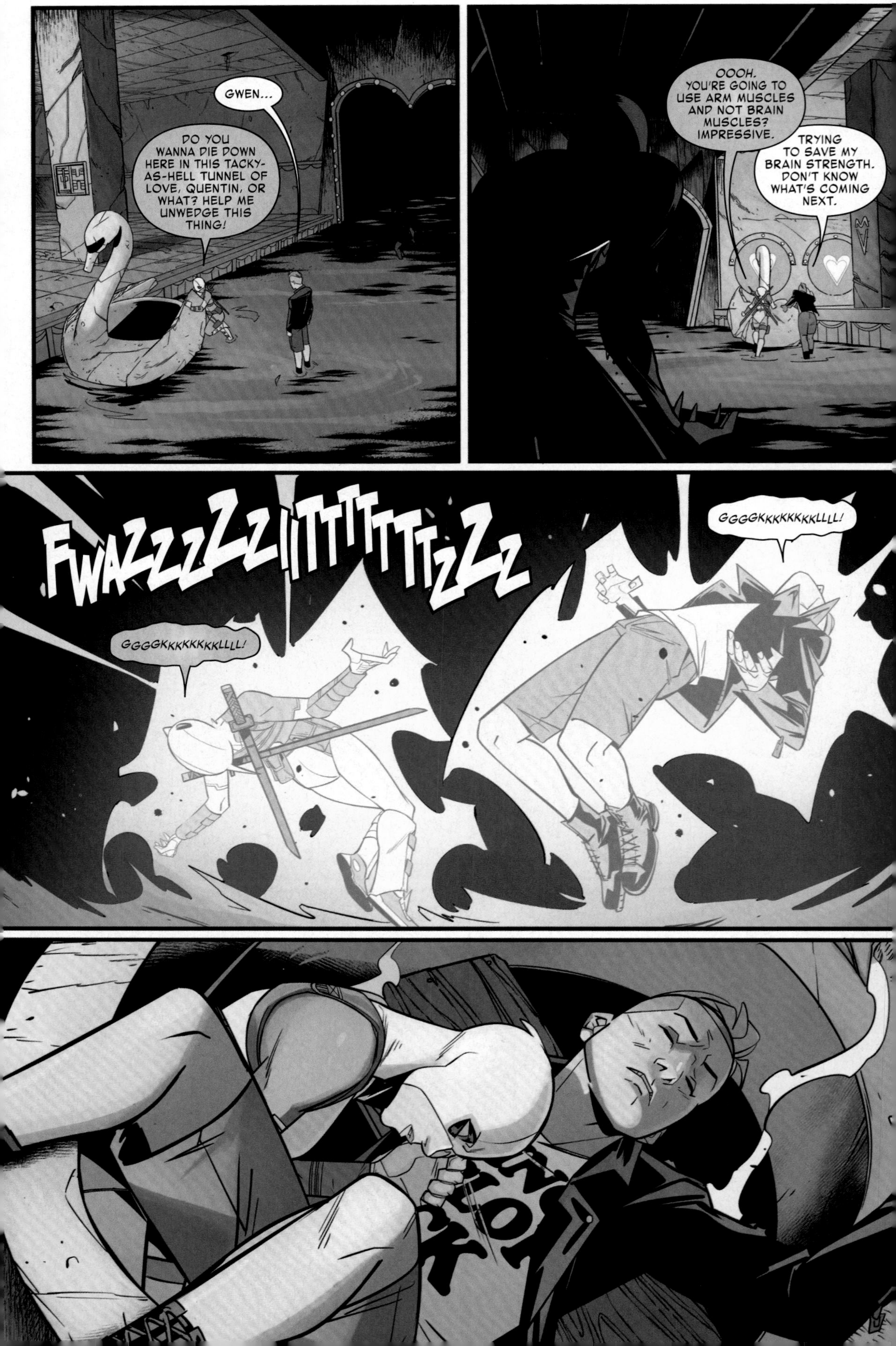
GWEN...
DO YOU WANNA DIE DOWN HERE IN THIS TACKY-AS-HELL TUNNEL OF LOVE, QUENTIN, OR WHAT? HELP ME UNWEDGE THIS THING!
OOOH. YOU'RE GOING TO USE ARM MUSCLES AND NOT BRAIN MUSCLES? IMPRESSIVE.
TRYING TO SAVE MY BRAIN STRENGTH. DON'T KNOW WHAT'S COMING NEXT.
FWAZZZZZZIIITTTTTTTZZZ
GGGGKKKKKKKKLLLL!
GGGGKKKKKKKKLLLL!

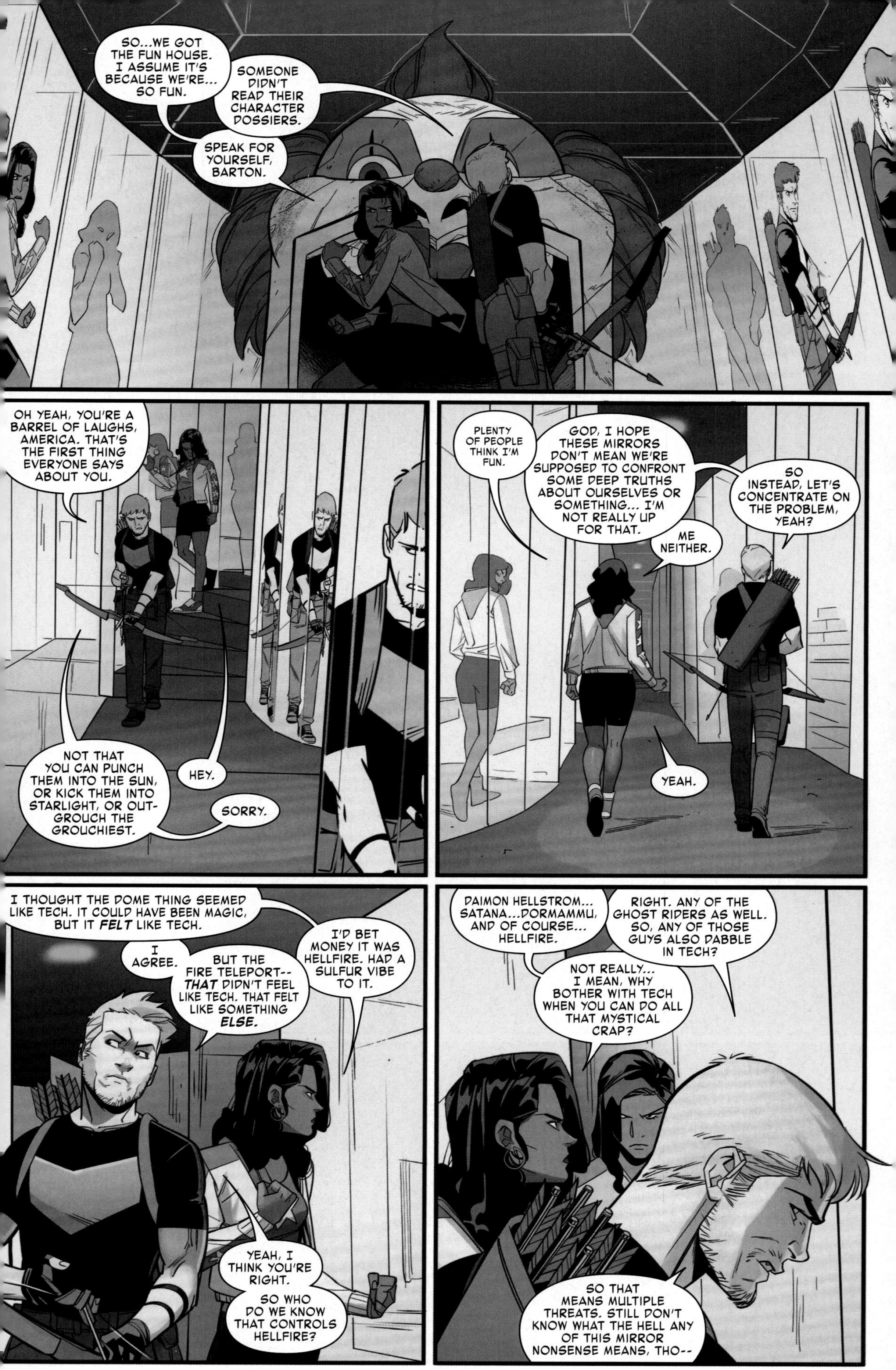
SO...WE GOT THE FUN HOUSE. I ASSUME IT'S BECAUSE WE'RE... SO FUN.
SOMEONE DIDN'T READ THEIR CHARACTER DOSSIERS.
SPEAK FOR YOURSELF, BARTON.
OH YEAH, YOU'RE A BARREL OF LAUGHS, AMERICA. THAT'S THE FIRST THING EVERYONE SAYS ABOUT YOU.
NOT THAT YOU CAN PUNCH THEM INTO THE SUN, OR KICK THEM INTO STARLIGHT, OR OUT-GROUCH THE GROUCHIEST.
HEY.
SORRY.
PLENTY OF PEOPLE THINK I'M FUN.
GOD, I HOPE THESE MIRRORS DON'T MEAN WE'RE SUPPOSED TO CONFRONT SOME DEEP TRUTHS ABOUT OURSELVES OR SOMETHING... I'M NOT REALLY UP FOR THAT.
ME NEITHER.
SO INSTEAD, LET'S CONCENTRATE ON THE PROBLEM, YEAH?
YEAH.
I THOUGHT THE DOME THING SEEMED LIKE TECH. IT COULD HAVE BEEN MAGIC, BUT IT *FELT* LIKE TECH.
I AGREE.
BUT THE FIRE TELEPORT-- *THAT* DIDN'T FEEL LIKE TECH. THAT FELT LIKE SOMETHING *ELSE.*
I'D BET MONEY IT WAS HELLFIRE. HAD A SULFUR VIBE TO IT.
YEAH, I THINK YOU'RE RIGHT.
SO WHO DO WE KNOW THAT CONTROLS HELLFIRE?
DAIMON HELLSTROM... SATANA...DORMAMMU, AND OF COURSE... HELLFIRE.
RIGHT. ANY OF THE GHOST RIDERS AS WELL. SO, ANY OF THOSE GUYS ALSO DABBLE IN TECH?
NOT REALLY... I MEAN, WHY BOTHER WITH TECH WHEN YOU CAN DO ALL THAT MYSTICAL CRAP?
SO THAT MEANS MULTIPLE THREATS. STILL DON'T KNOW WHAT THE HELL ANY OF THIS MIRROR NONSENSE MEANS, THO--

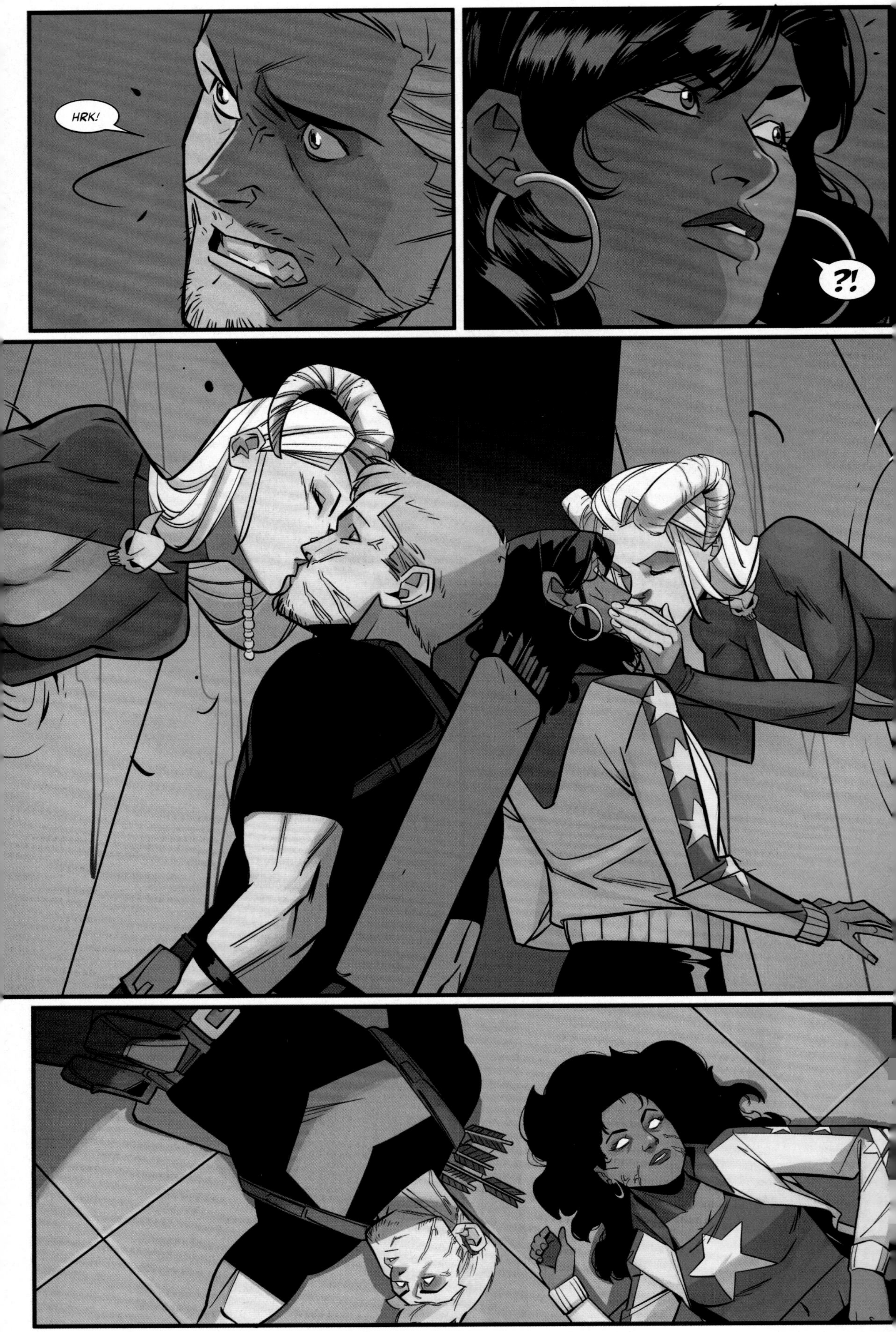
HRK!
?!

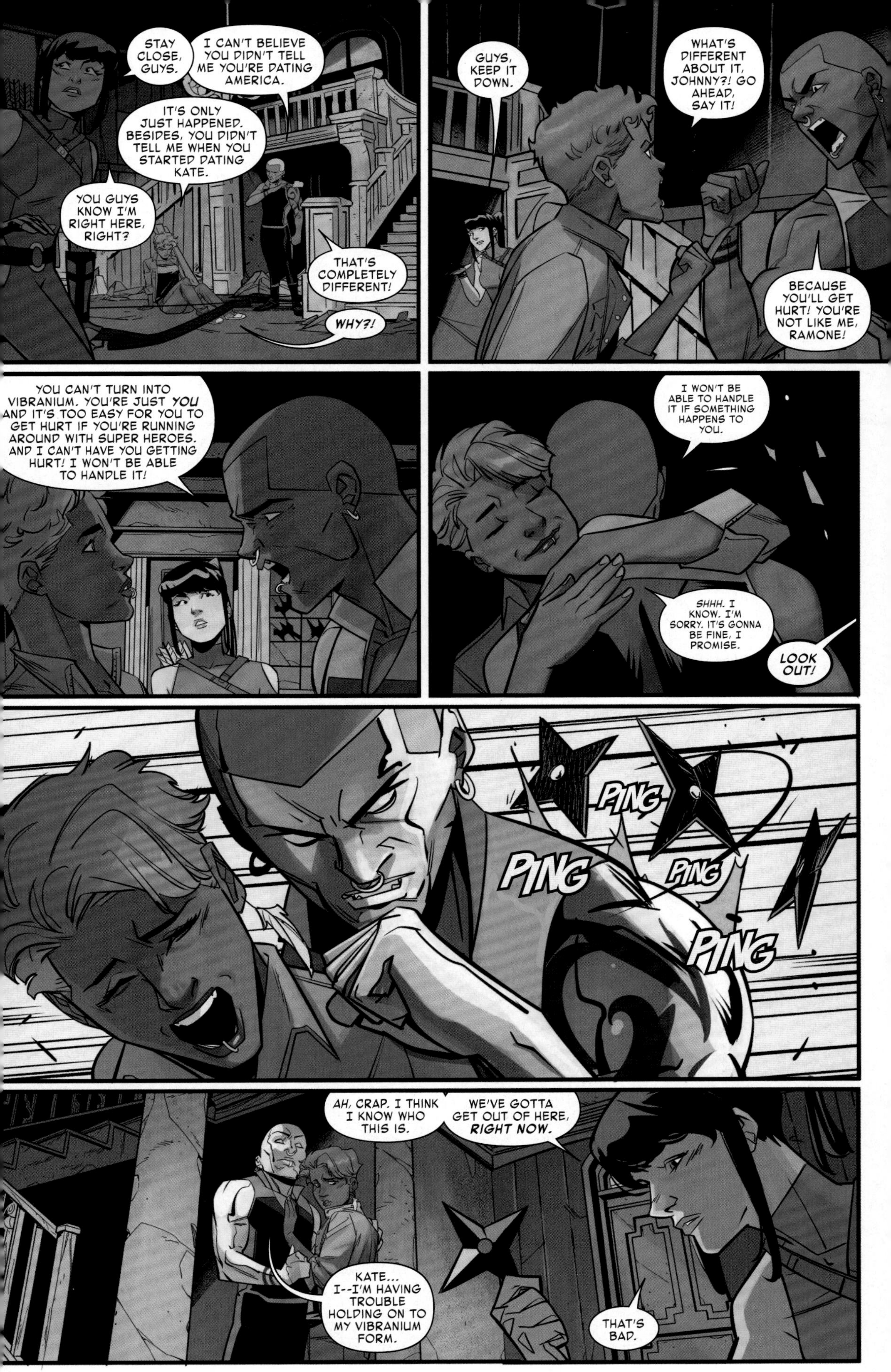
STAY CLOSE, GUYS.
I CAN'T BELIEVE YOU DIDN'T TELL ME YOU'RE DATING AMERICA.
IT'S ONLY JUST HAPPENED. BESIDES, YOU DIDN'T TELL ME WHEN YOU STARTED DATING KATE.
YOU GUYS KNOW I'M RIGHT HERE, RIGHT?
THAT'S COMPLETELY DIFFERENT!
WHY?!
GUYS, KEEP IT DOWN.
WHAT'S DIFFERENT ABOUT IT, JOHNNY?! GO AHEAD, SAY IT!
BECAUSE YOU'LL GET HURT! YOU'RE NOT LIKE ME, RAMONE!
YOU CAN'T TURN INTO VIBRANIUM. YOU'RE JUST YOU AND IT'S TOO EASY FOR YOU TO GET HURT IF YOU'RE RUNNING AROUND WITH SUPER HEROES. AND I CAN'T HAVE YOU GETTING HURT! I WON'T BE ABLE TO HANDLE IT!
I WON'T BE ABLE TO HANDLE IT IF SOMETHING HAPPENS TO YOU.
SHHH. I KNOW. I'M SORRY. IT'S GONNA BE FINE, I PROMISE.
LOOK OUT!
PING
PING
PING
PING
AH, CRAP. I THINK I KNOW WHO THIS IS.
WE'VE GOTTA GET OUT OF HERE, RIGHT NOW.
KATE... I--I'M HAVING TROUBLE HOLDING ON TO MY VIBRANIUM FORM.
THAT'S BAD.

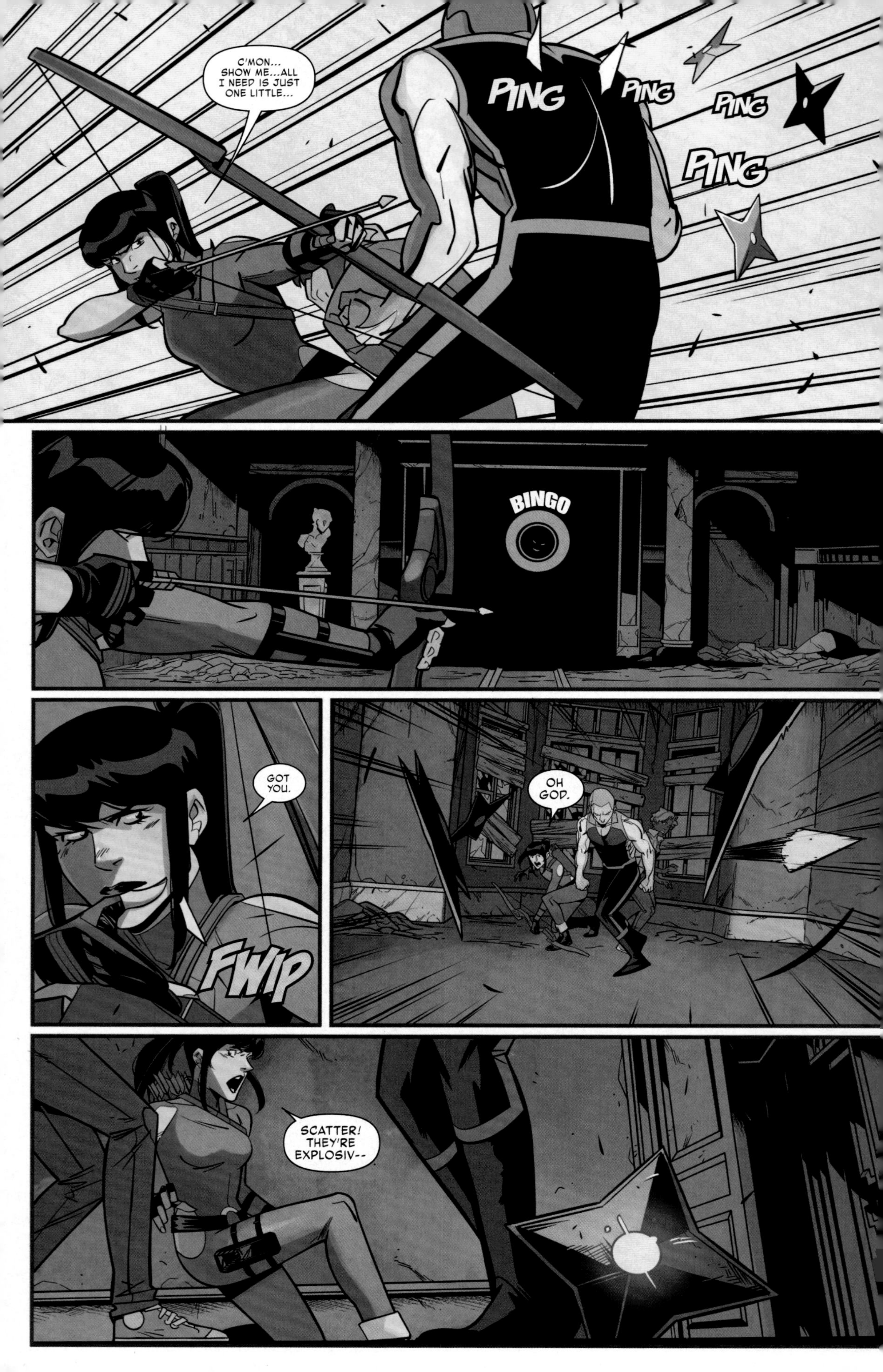
C'MON... SHOW ME...ALL I NEED IS JUST ONE LITTLE...
PING
PING
PING
PING
BINGO
GOT YOU.
FWIP
OH GOD.
SCATTER! THEY'RE EXPLOSIV--

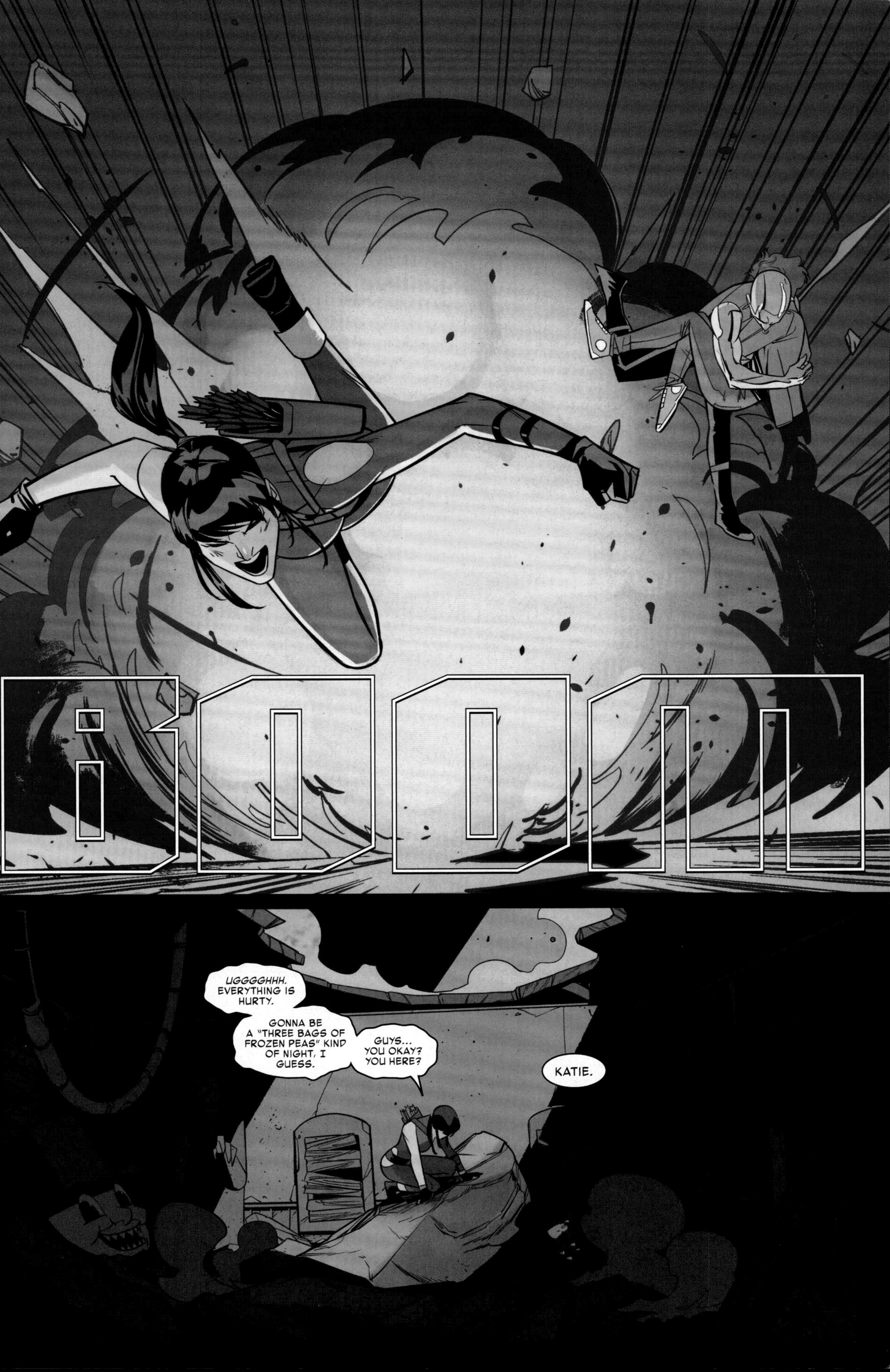
BOOM
UGGGGHHH. EVERYTHING IS HURTY.
GONNA BE A "THREE BAGS OF FROZEN PEAS" KIND OF NIGHT, I GUESS.
GUYS... YOU OKAY? YOU HERE?
KATIE.

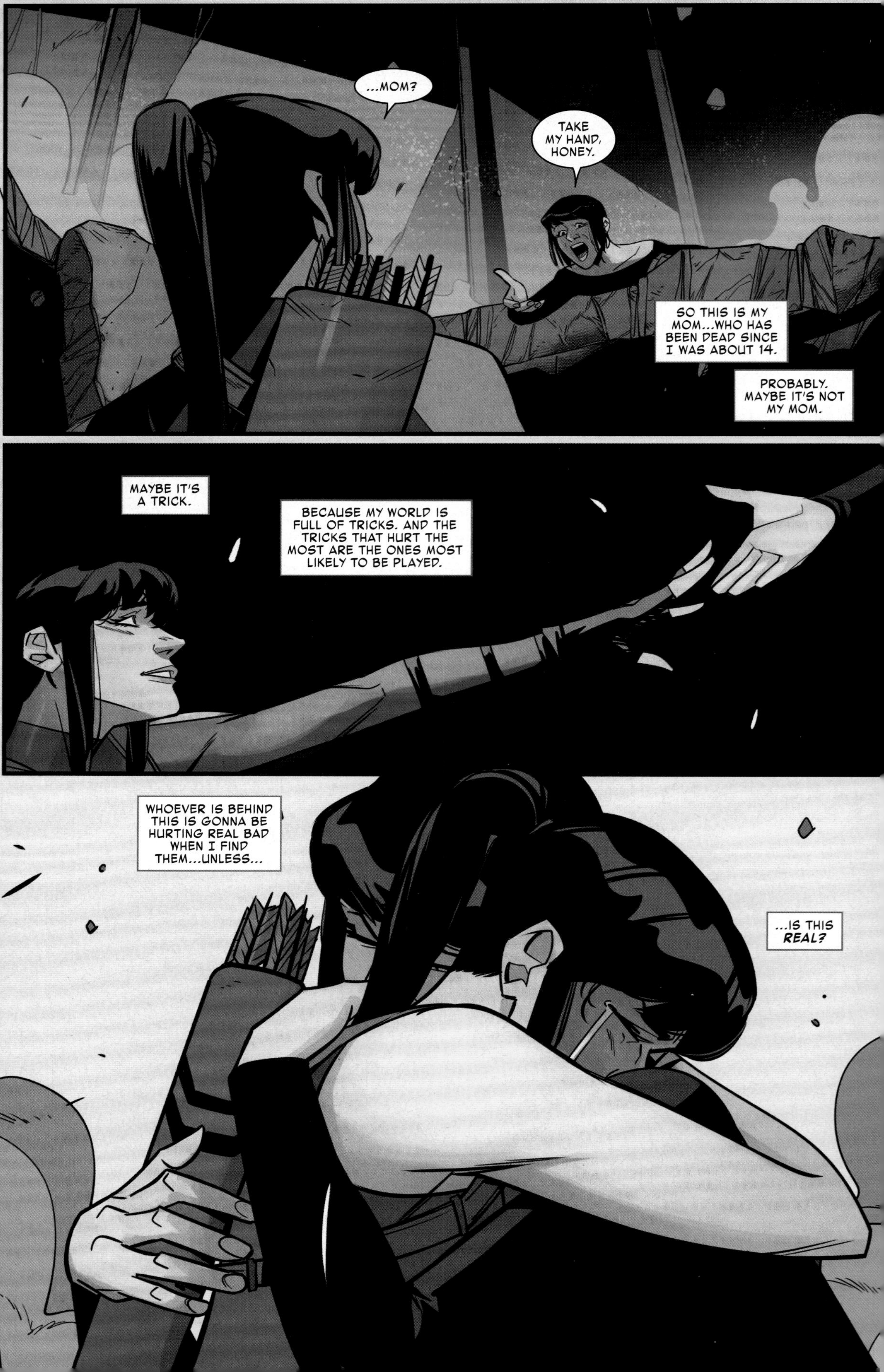
...MOM?
TAKE MY HAND, HONEY.
SO THIS IS MY MOM...WHO HAS BEEN DEAD SINCE I WAS ABOUT 14.
PROBABLY. MAYBE IT'S NOT MY MOM.
MAYBE IT'S A TRICK.
BECAUSE MY WORLD IS FULL OF TRICKS. AND THE TRICKS THAT HURT THE MOST ARE THE ONES MOST LIKELY TO BE PLAYED.
WHOEVER IS BEHIND THIS IS GONNA BE HURTING REAL BAD WHEN I FIND THEM...UNLESS...
...IS THIS *REAL?*

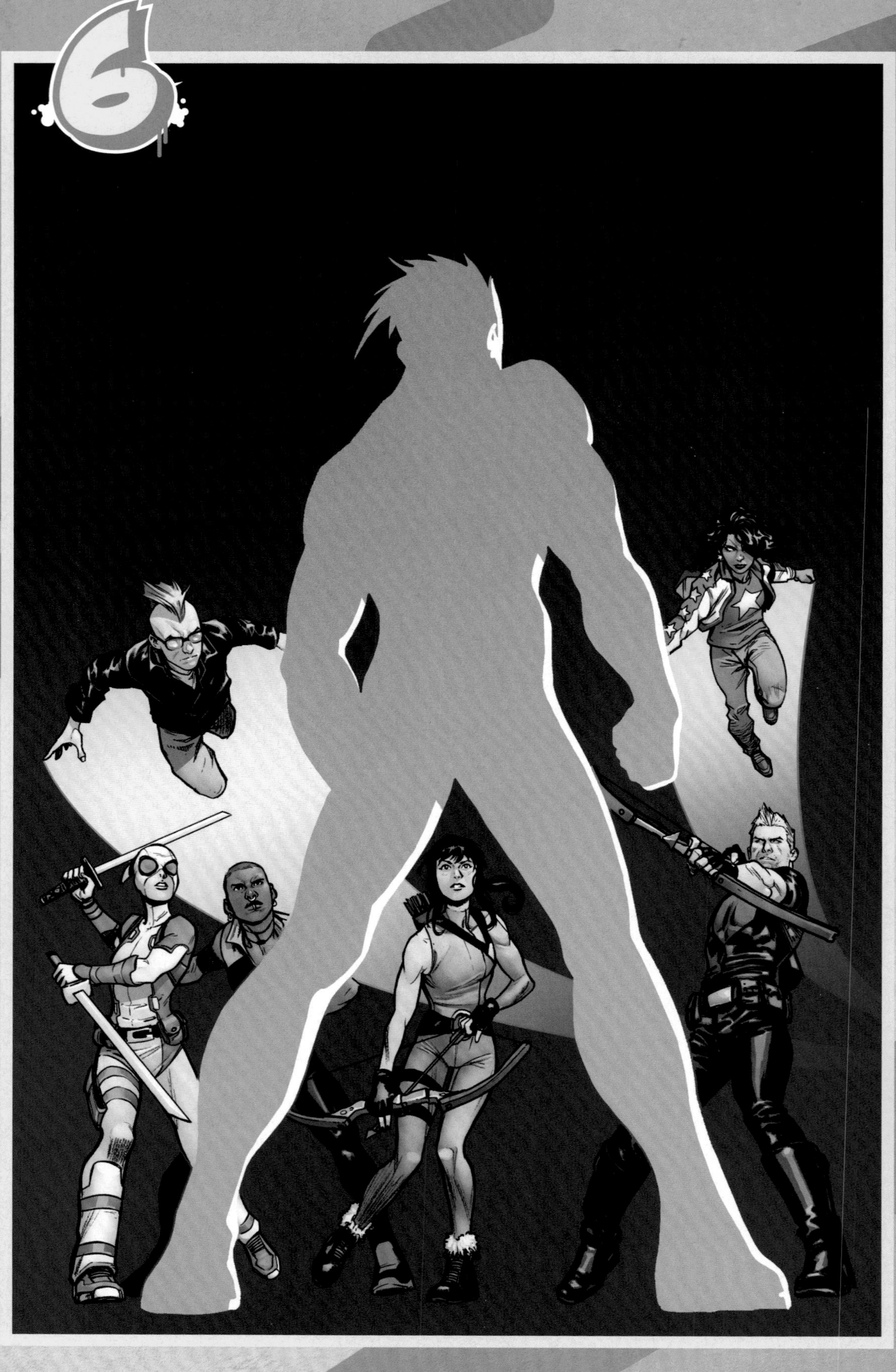
6

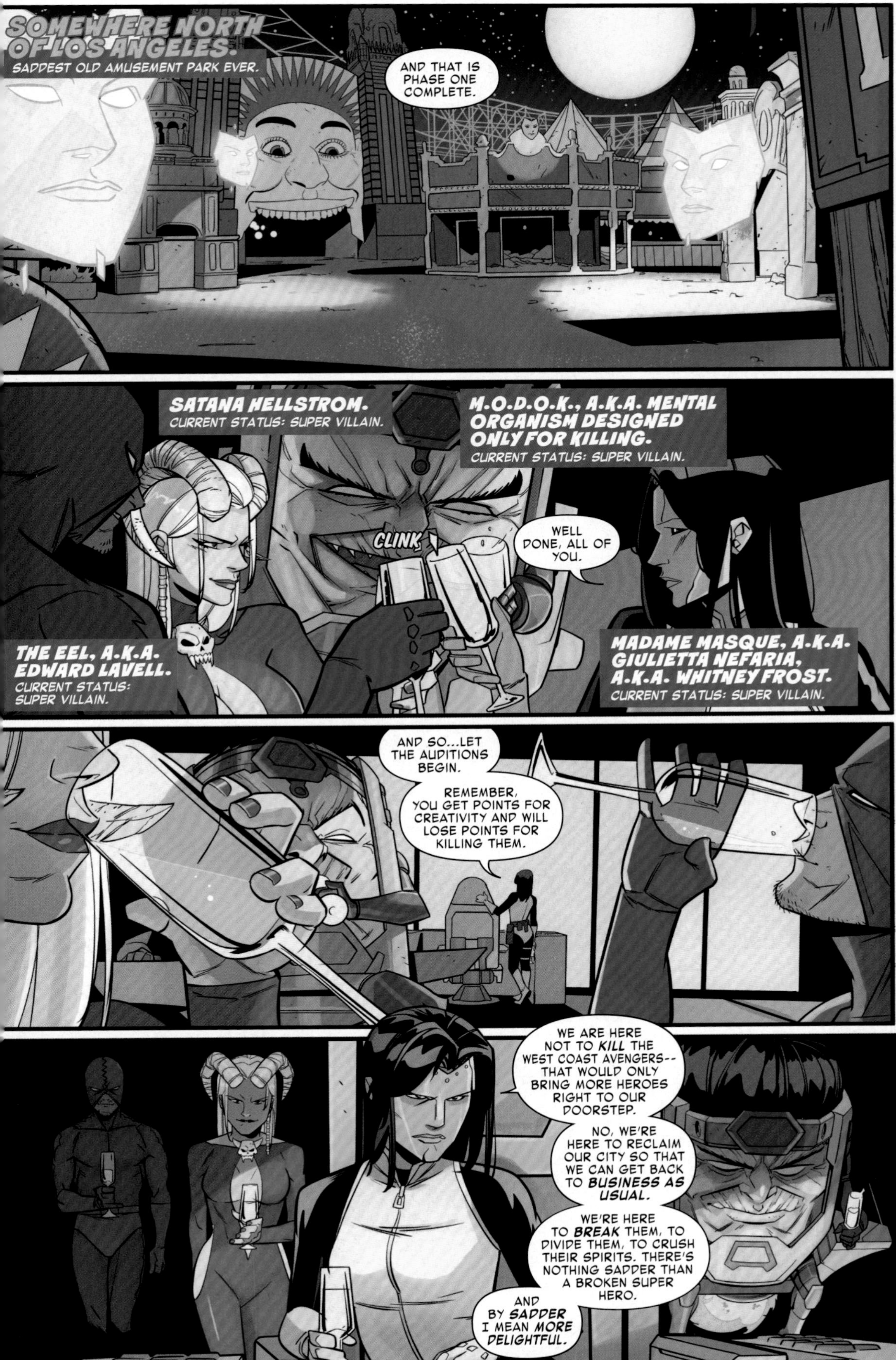
SOMEWHERE NORTH OF LOS ANGELES.
SADDEST OLD AMUSEMENT PARK EVER.
AND THAT IS PHASE ONE COMPLETE.
SATANA HELLSTROM. CURRENT STATUS: SUPER VILLAIN.
M.O.D.O.K., A.K.A. MENTAL ORGANISM DESIGNED ONLY FOR KILLING. CURRENT STATUS: SUPER VILLAIN.
CLINK
WELL DONE, ALL OF YOU.
THE EEL, A.K.A. EDWARD LAVELL. CURRENT STATUS: SUPER VILLAIN.
MADAME MASQUE, A.K.A. GIULIETTA NEFARIA, A.K.A. WHITNEY FROST. CURRENT STATUS: SUPER VILLAIN.
AND SO...LET THE AUDITIONS BEGIN.
REMEMBER, YOU GET POINTS FOR CREATIVITY AND WILL LOSE POINTS FOR KILLING THEM.
WE ARE HERE NOT TO KILL THE WEST COAST AVENGERS--THAT WOULD ONLY BRING MORE HEROES RIGHT TO OUR DOORSTEP.
NO, WE'RE HERE TO RECLAIM OUR CITY SO THAT WE CAN GET BACK TO BUSINESS AS USUAL.
WE'RE HERE TO BREAK THEM, TO DIVIDE THEM, TO CRUSH THEIR SPIRITS. THERE'S NOTHING SADDER THAN A BROKEN SUPER HERO.
AND BY SADDER I MEAN MORE DELIGHTFUL.

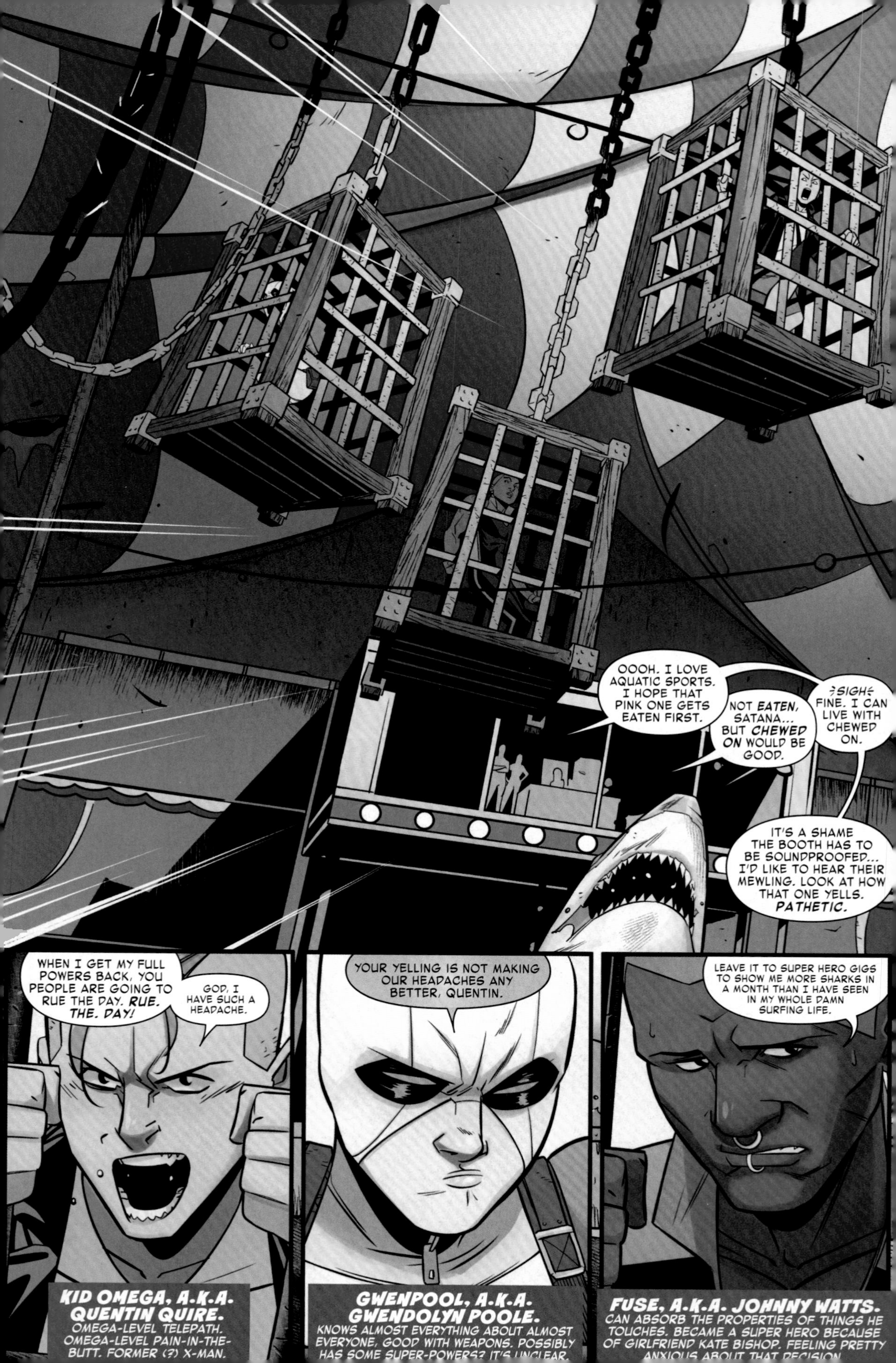
OOOH. I LOVE AQUATIC SPORTS. I HOPE THAT PINK ONE GETS EATEN FIRST.
NOT EATEN, SATANA... BUT CHEWED ON WOULD BE GOOD.
SIGH FINE. I CAN LIVE WITH CHEWED ON.
IT'S A SHAME THE BOOTH HAS TO BE SOUNDPROOFED... I'D LIKE TO HEAR THEIR MEWLING. LOOK AT HOW THAT ONE YELLS. PATHETIC.
WHEN I GET MY FULL POWERS BACK, YOU PEOPLE ARE GOING TO RUE THE DAY. RUE. THE. DAY!
GOD, I HAVE SUCH A HEADACHE.
KID OMEGA, A.K.A. QUENTIN QUIRE.
OMEGA-LEVEL TELEPATH. OMEGA-LEVEL PAIN-IN-THE-BUTT. FORMER (?) X-MAN.
YOUR YELLING IS NOT MAKING OUR HEADACHES ANY BETTER, QUENTIN.
GWENPOOL, A.K.A. GWENDOLYN POOLE.
KNOWS ALMOST EVERYTHING ABOUT ALMOST EVERYONE, GOOD WITH WEAPONS. POSSIBLY HAS SOME SUPER-POWERS? IT'S UNCLEAR.
LEAVE IT TO SUPER HERO GIGS TO SHOW ME MORE SHARKS IN A MONTH THAN I HAVE SEEN IN MY WHOLE DAMN SURFING LIFE.
FUSE, A.K.A. JOHNNY WATTS.
CAN ABSORB THE PROPERTIES OF THINGS HE TOUCHES. BECAME A SUPER HERO BECAUSE OF GIRLFRIEND KATE BISHOP. FEELING PRETTY ANXIOUS ABOUT THAT DECISION.

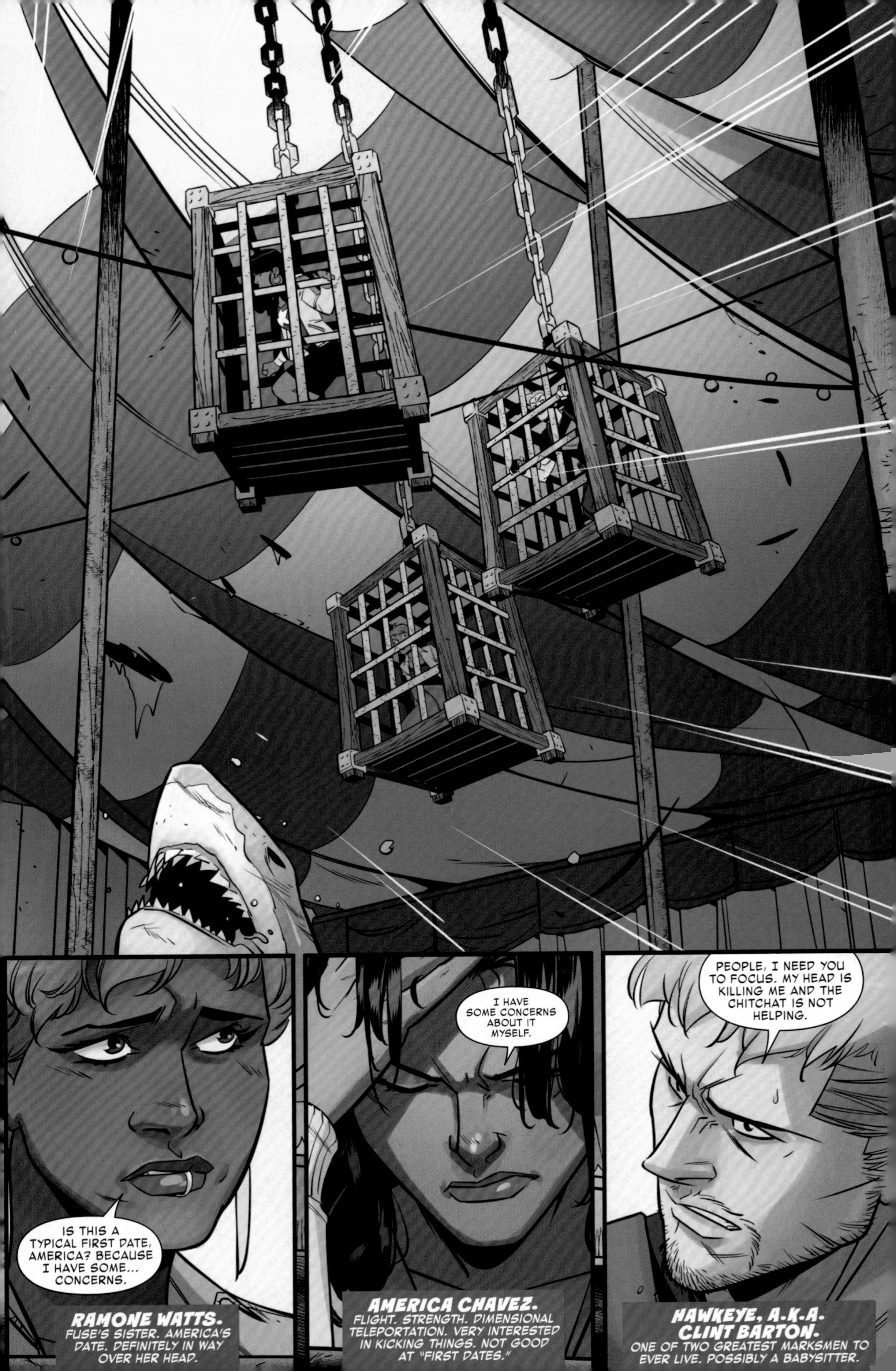
IS THIS A TYPICAL FIRST DATE, AMERICA? BECAUSE I HAVE SOME... CONCERNS.
RAMONE WATTS.
FUSE'S SISTER. AMERICA'S DATE. DEFINITELY IN WAY OVER HER HEAD.
I HAVE SOME CONCERNS ABOUT IT MYSELF.
AMERICA CHAVEZ.
FLIGHT. STRENGTH. DIMENSIONAL TELEPORTATION. VERY INTERESTED IN KICKING THINGS. NOT GOOD AT "FIRST DATES."
PEOPLE, I NEED YOU TO FOCUS. MY HEAD IS KILLING ME AND THE CHITCHAT IS NOT HELPING.
HAWKEYE, A.K.A. CLINT BARTON.
ONE OF TWO GREATEST MARKSMEN TO EVER LIVE. POSSIBLY A BABYSITTER.

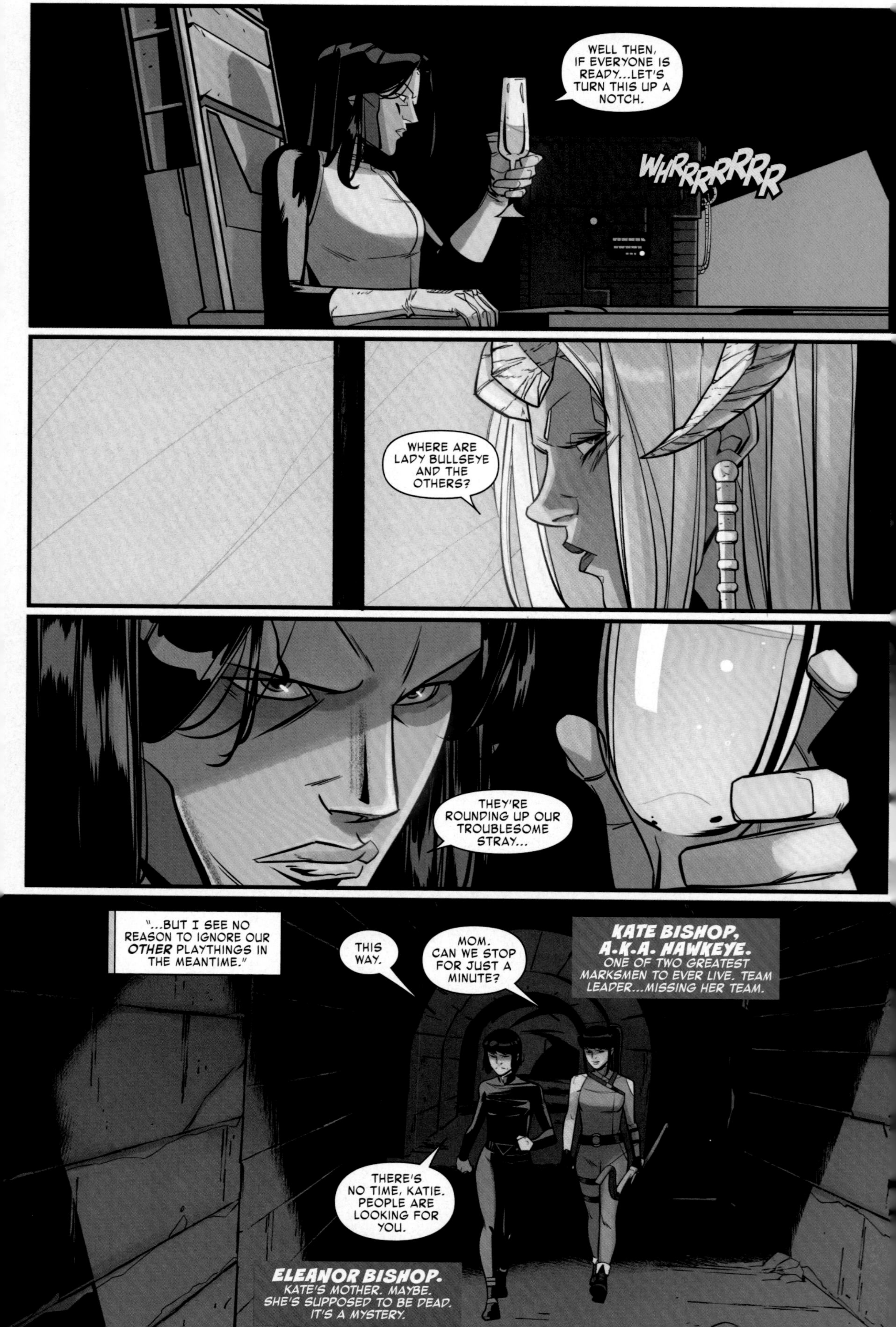
WELL THEN, IF EVERYONE IS READY...LET'S TURN THIS UP A NOTCH.
WHRRRRRRR
WHERE ARE LADY BULLSEYE AND THE OTHERS?
THEY'RE ROUNDING UP OUR TROUBLESOME STRAY...
"...BUT I SEE NO REASON TO IGNORE OUR OTHER PLAYTHINGS IN THE MEANTIME."
THIS WAY.
MOM. CAN WE STOP FOR JUST A MINUTE?
KATE BISHOP, A.K.A. HAWKEYE. ONE OF TWO GREATEST MARKSMEN TO EVER LIVE. TEAM LEADER...MISSING HER TEAM.
THERE'S NO TIME, KATIE. PEOPLE ARE LOOKING FOR YOU.
ELEANOR BISHOP. KATE'S MOTHER. MAYBE. SHE'S SUPPOSED TO BE DEAD. IT'S A MYSTERY.

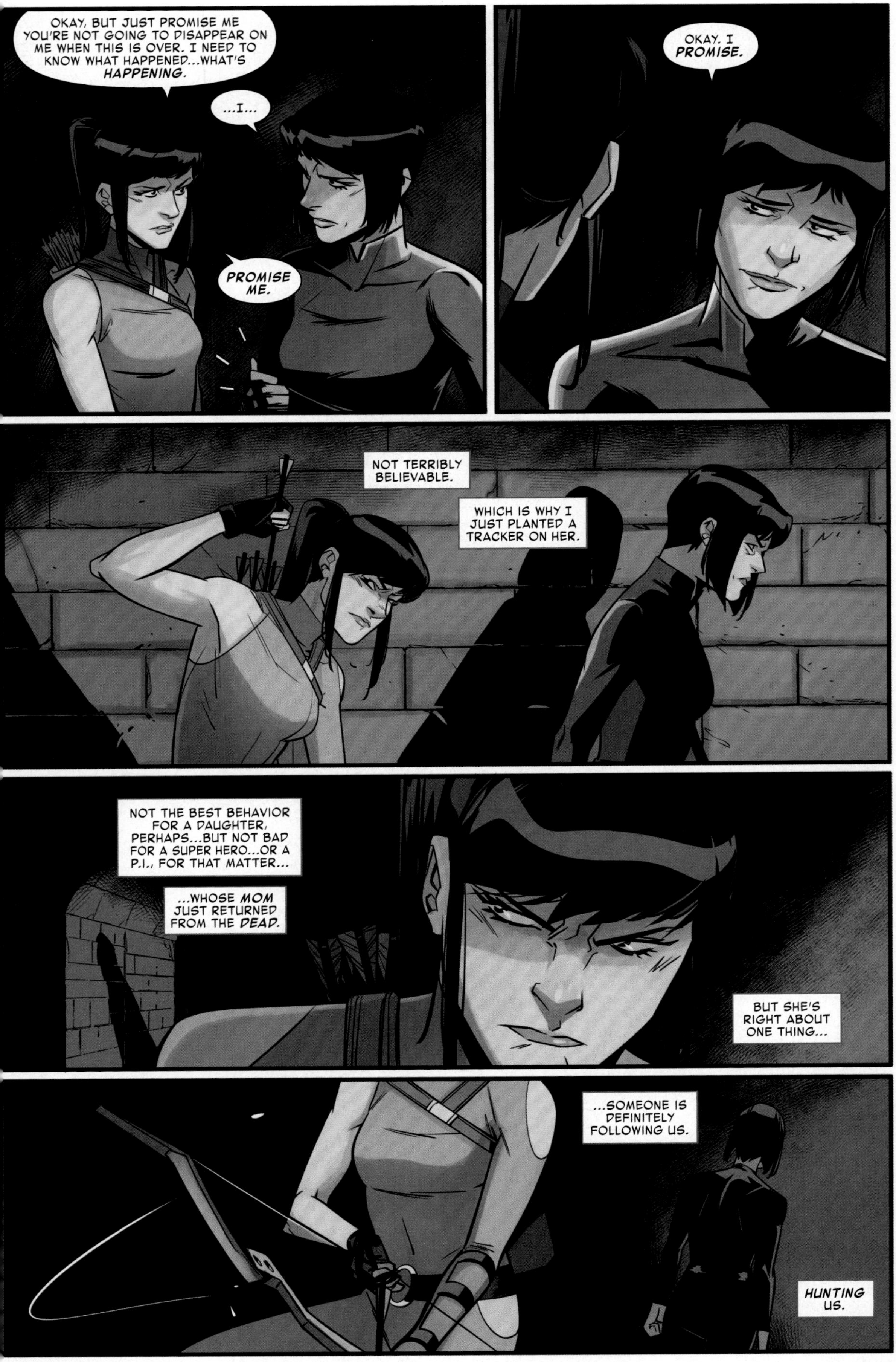
OKAY, BUT JUST PROMISE ME YOU'RE NOT GOING TO DISAPPEAR ON ME WHEN THIS IS OVER. I NEED TO KNOW WHAT HAPPENED...WHAT'S *HAPPENING.*
...I...
PROMISE ME.
OKAY. I *PROMISE.*
NOT TERRIBLY BELIEVABLE.
WHICH IS WHY I JUST PLANTED A TRACKER ON HER.
NOT THE BEST BEHAVIOR FOR A DAUGHTER, PERHAPS...BUT NOT BAD FOR A SUPER HERO...OR A P.I., FOR THAT MATTER...
...WHOSE *MOM* JUST RETURNED FROM THE *DEAD.*
BUT SHE'S RIGHT ABOUT ONE THING...
...SOMEONE IS DEFINITELY FOLLOWING US.
HUNTING US.

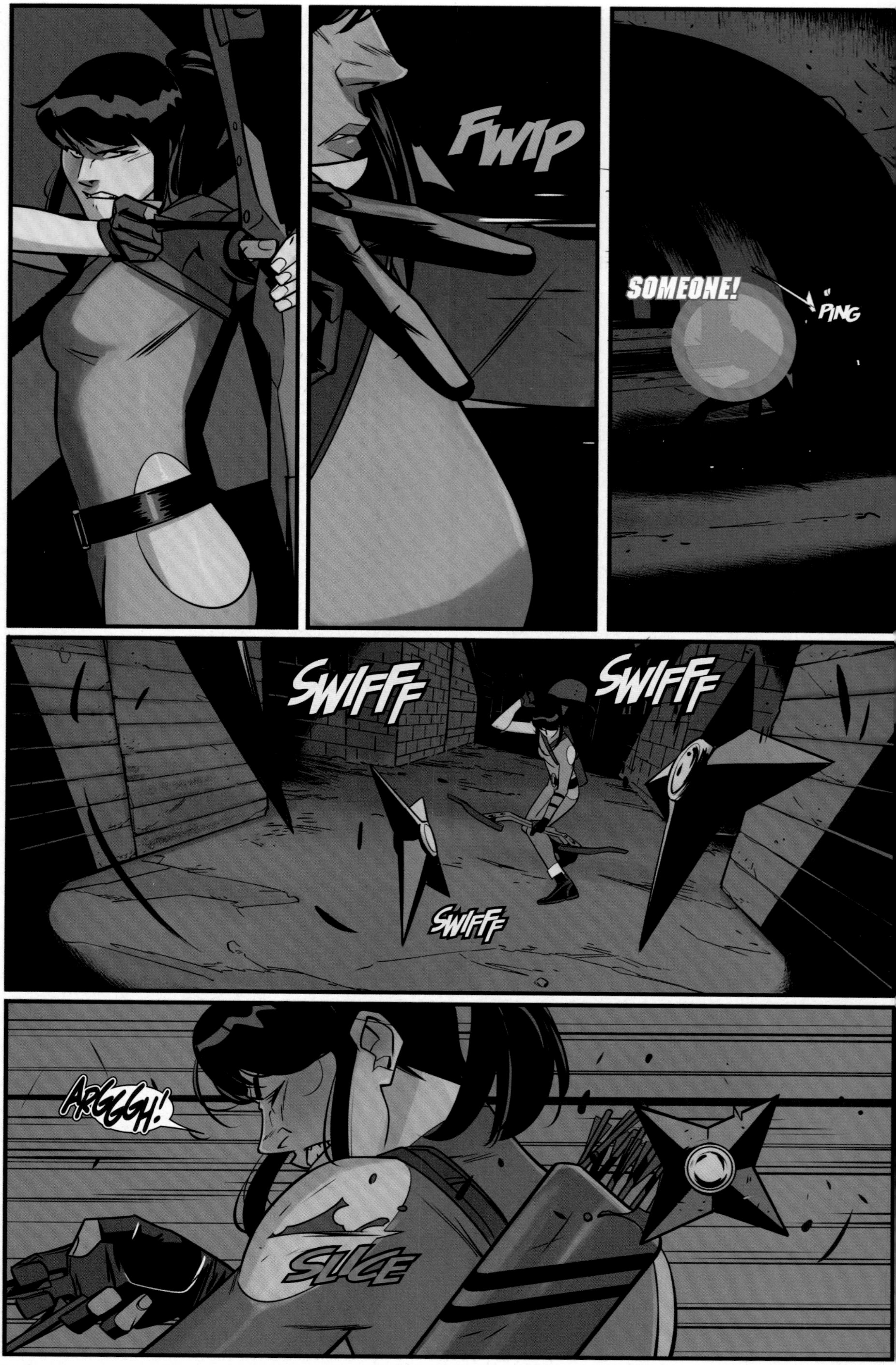
FWIP
SOMEONE!
PING
SWIFFF
SWIFFF
SWIFFF
ARGGGH!
SLICE

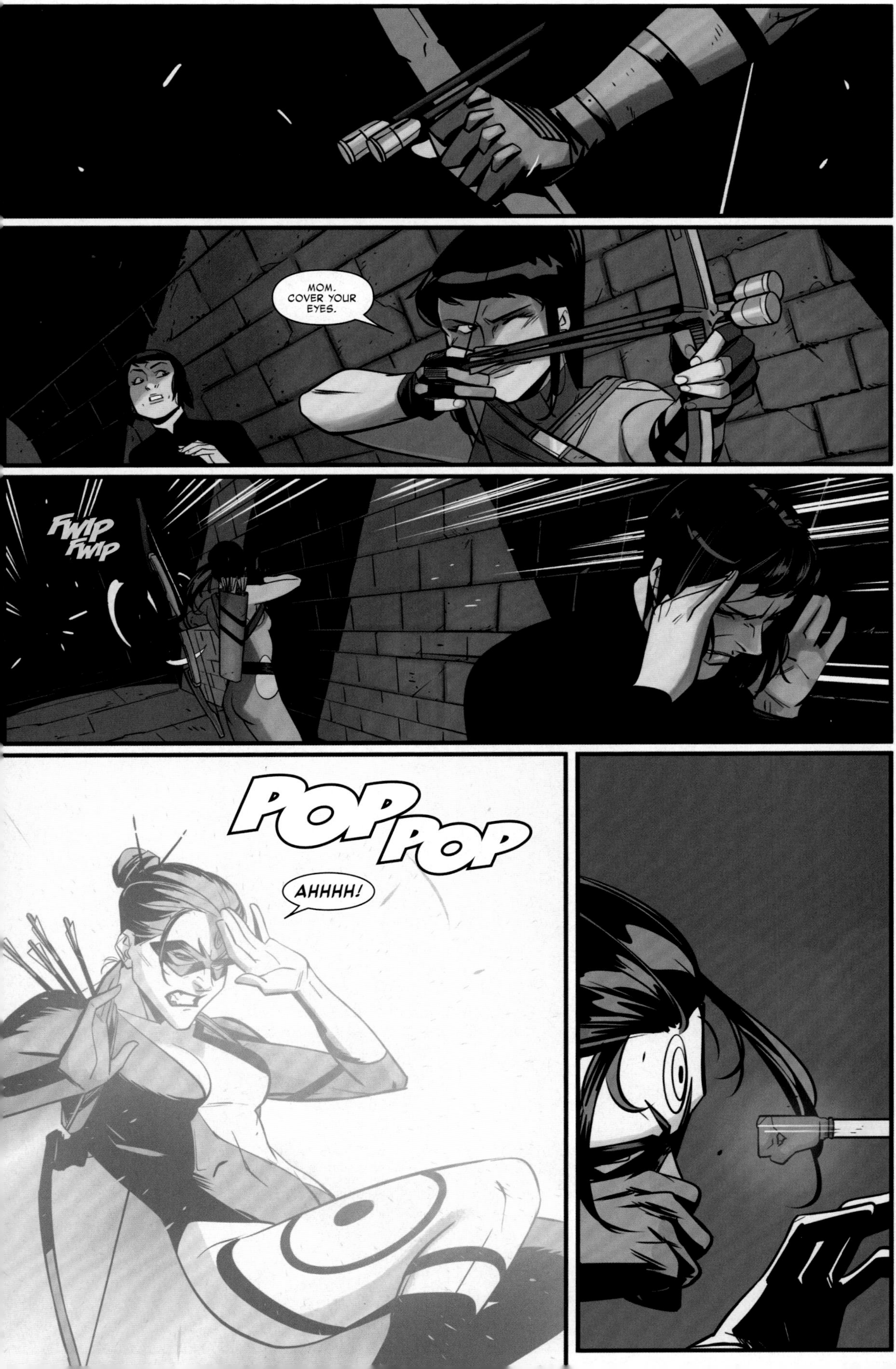
MOM. COVER YOUR EYES.
FWIP FWIP
POP POP
AHHHH!

BOOM

UNGGG!

SMACK

KATE, WE HAVE TO HURRY. SHE WON'T BE ALONE.

OKAY, JUST GIVE ME A MINUTE.

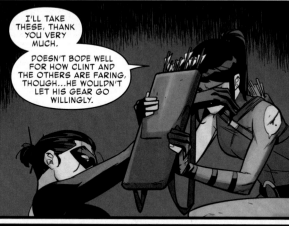

I'LL TAKE THESE, THANK YOU VERY MUCH.

DOESN'T BODE WELL FOR HOW CLINT AND THE OTHERS ARE FARING, THOUGH...HE WOULDN'T LET HIS GEAR GO WILLINGLY.

WHAT'S THIS? EARPLUGS?

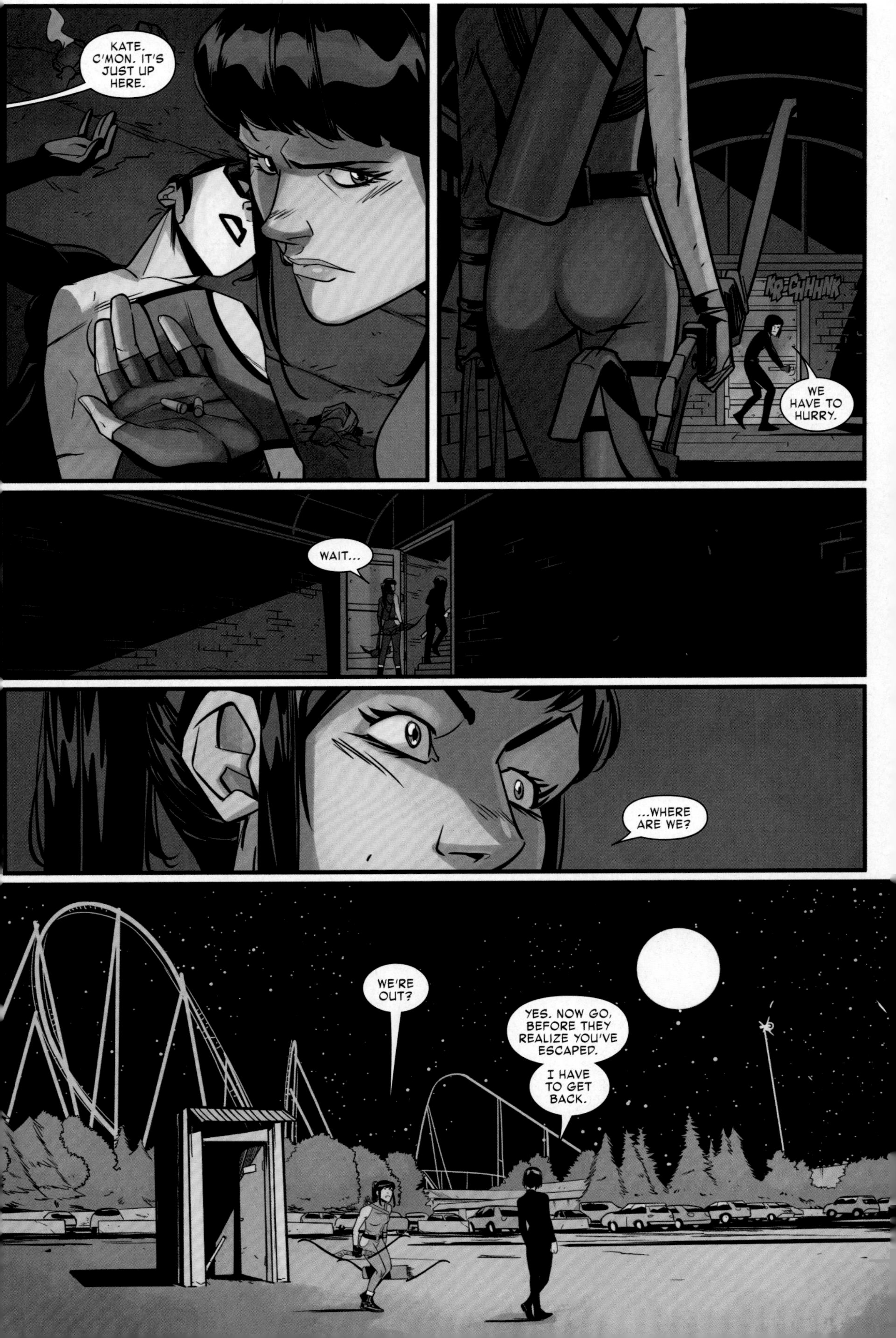
KATE. C'MON. IT'S JUST UP HERE.
KR-CHHHNK
WE HAVE TO HURRY.
WAIT...
...WHERE ARE WE?
WE'RE OUT?
YES. NOW GO, BEFORE THEY REALIZE YOU'VE ESCAPED.
I HAVE TO GET BACK.

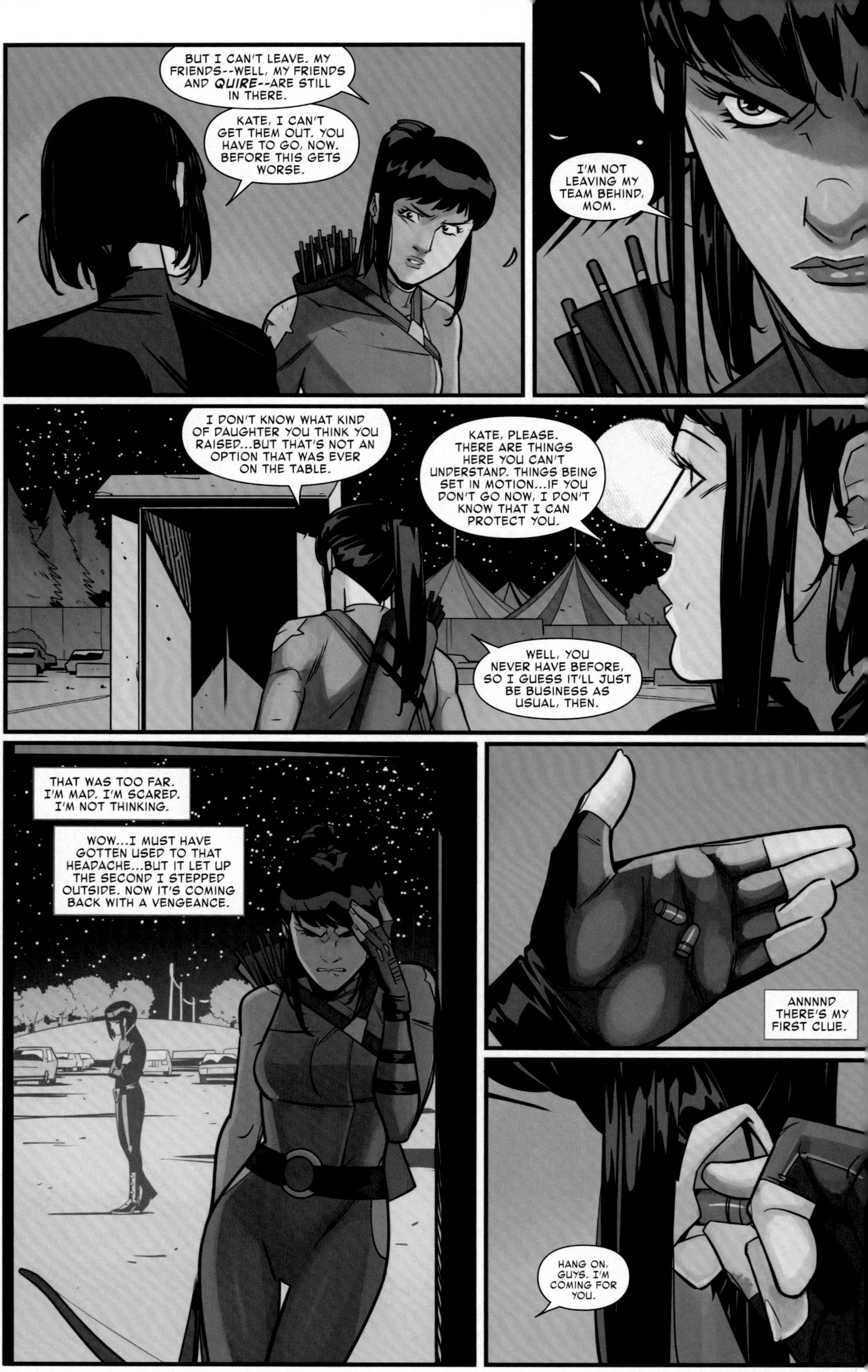

BUT I CAN'T LEAVE. MY FRIENDS--WELL, MY FRIENDS AND QUIRE--ARE STILL IN THERE.
KATE, I CAN'T GET THEM OUT. YOU HAVE TO GO, NOW. BEFORE THIS GETS WORSE.
I'M NOT LEAVING MY TEAM BEHIND, MOM.
I DON'T KNOW WHAT KIND OF DAUGHTER YOU THINK YOU RAISED...BUT THAT'S NOT AN OPTION THAT WAS EVER ON THE TABLE.
KATE, PLEASE. THERE ARE THINGS HERE YOU CAN'T UNDERSTAND. THINGS BEING SET IN MOTION...IF YOU DON'T GO NOW, I DON'T KNOW THAT I CAN PROTECT YOU.
WELL, YOU NEVER HAVE BEFORE, SO I GUESS IT'LL JUST BE BUSINESS AS USUAL, THEN.
THAT WAS TOO FAR. I'M MAD. I'M SCARED. I'M NOT THINKING.
WOW...I MUST HAVE GOTTEN USED TO THAT HEADACHE...BUT IT LET UP THE SECOND I STEPPED OUTSIDE. NOW IT'S COMING BACK WITH A VENGEANCE.
ANNNND THERE'S MY FIRST CLUE.
HANG ON, GUYS. I'M COMING FOR YOU.

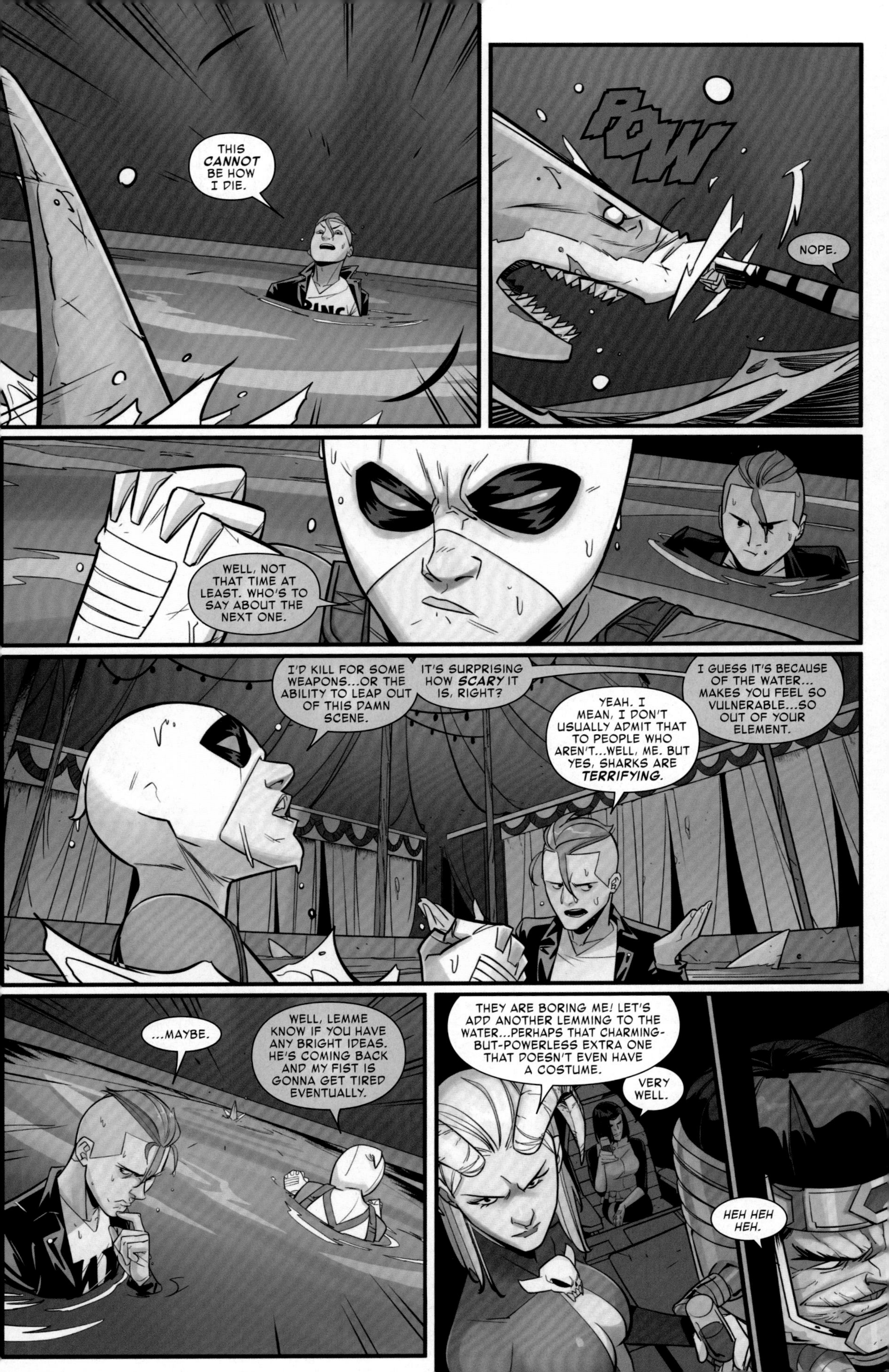
THIS *CANNOT* BE HOW I DIE.
POW
NOPE.
WELL, NOT THAT TIME AT LEAST. WHO'S TO SAY ABOUT THE NEXT ONE.
I'D KILL FOR SOME WEAPONS...OR THE ABILITY TO LEAP OUT OF THIS DAMN SCENE.
IT'S SURPRISING HOW *SCARY* IT IS, RIGHT?
I GUESS IT'S BECAUSE OF THE WATER... MAKES YOU FEEL SO VULNERABLE...SO OUT OF YOUR ELEMENT.
YEAH. I MEAN, I DON'T USUALLY ADMIT THAT TO PEOPLE WHO AREN'T...WELL, ME. BUT YES, SHARKS ARE *TERRIFYING.*
...MAYBE.
WELL, LEMME KNOW IF YOU HAVE ANY BRIGHT IDEAS. HE'S COMING BACK AND MY FIST IS GONNA GET TIRED EVENTUALLY.
THEY ARE BORING ME! LET'S ADD ANOTHER LEMMING TO THE WATER...PERHAPS THAT CHARMING-BUT-POWERLESS EXTRA ONE THAT DOESN'T EVEN HAVE A COSTUME.
VERY WELL.
HEH HEH HEH.

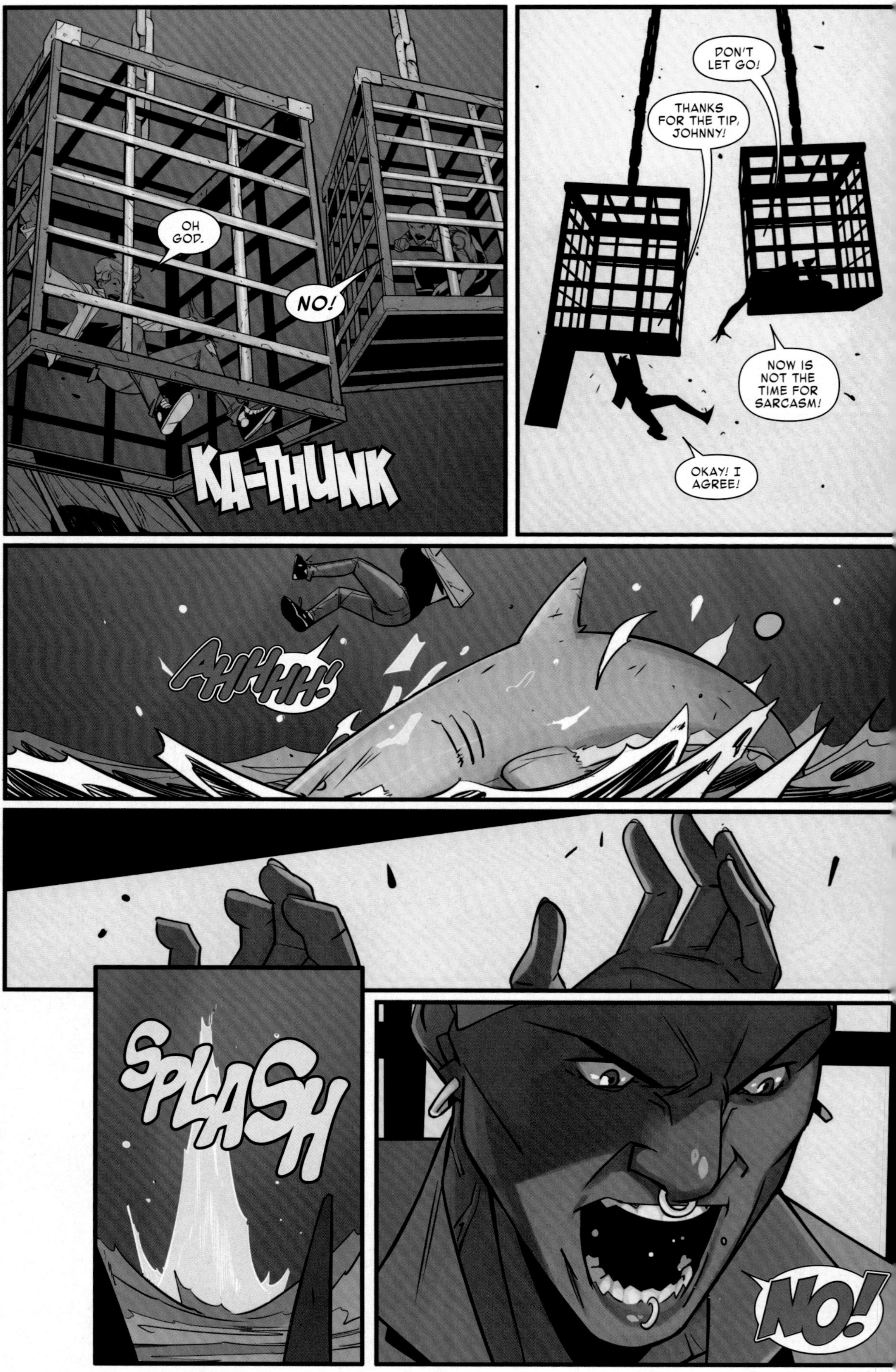
OH GOD.
NO!
KA-THUNK
DON'T LET GO!
THANKS FOR THE TIP, JOHNNY!
NOW IS NOT THE TIME FOR SARCASM!
OKAY! I AGREE!
AHHHH!
SPLASH
NO!

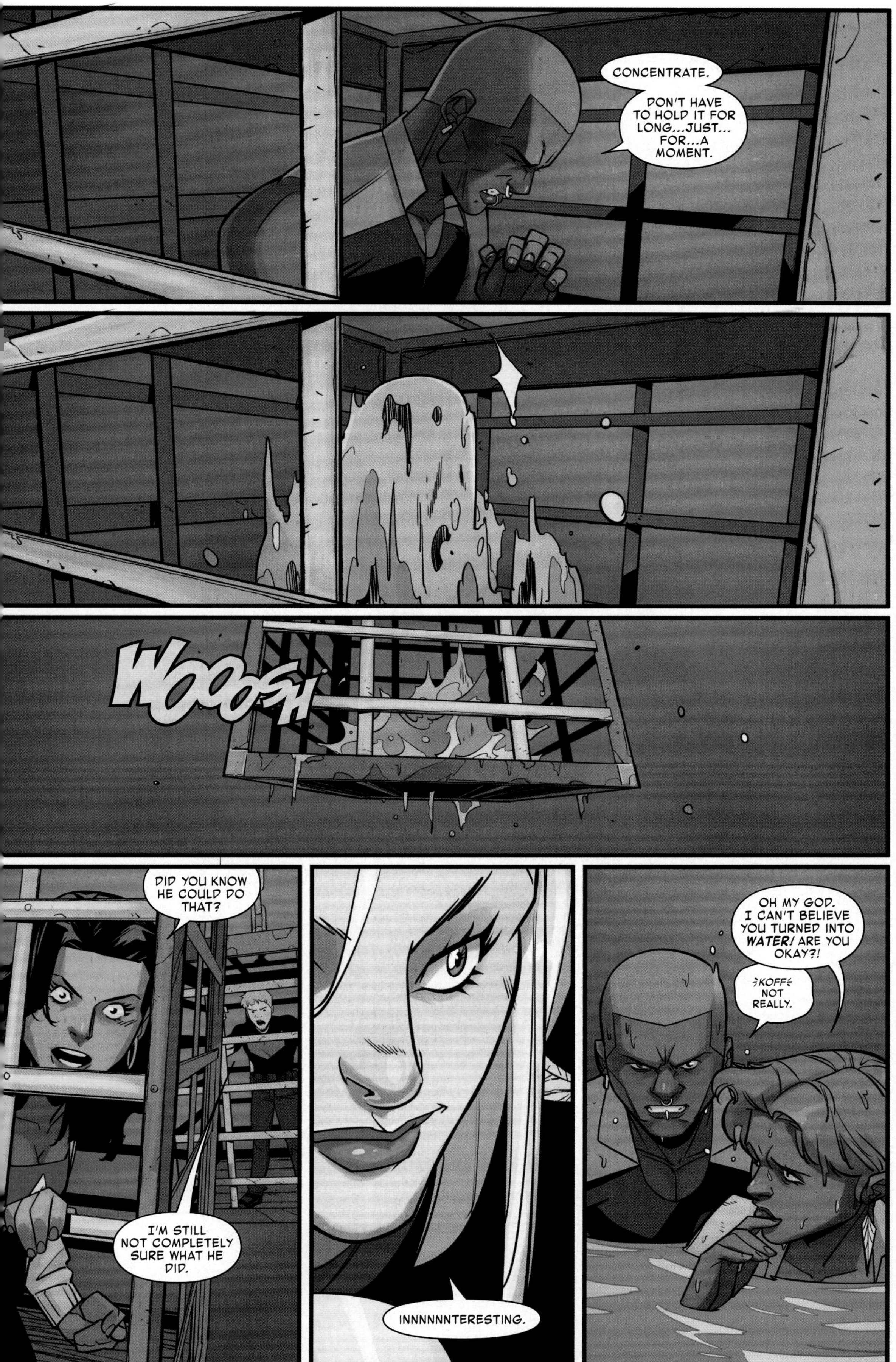
CONCENTRATE.
DON'T HAVE TO HOLD IT FOR LONG...JUST... FOR...A MOMENT.
WOOOSH
DID YOU KNOW HE COULD DO THAT?
I'M STILL NOT COMPLETELY SURE WHAT HE DID.
INNNNNNTERESTING.
OH MY GOD. I CAN'T BELIEVE YOU TURNED INTO WATER! ARE YOU OKAY?!
KOFF NOT REALLY.

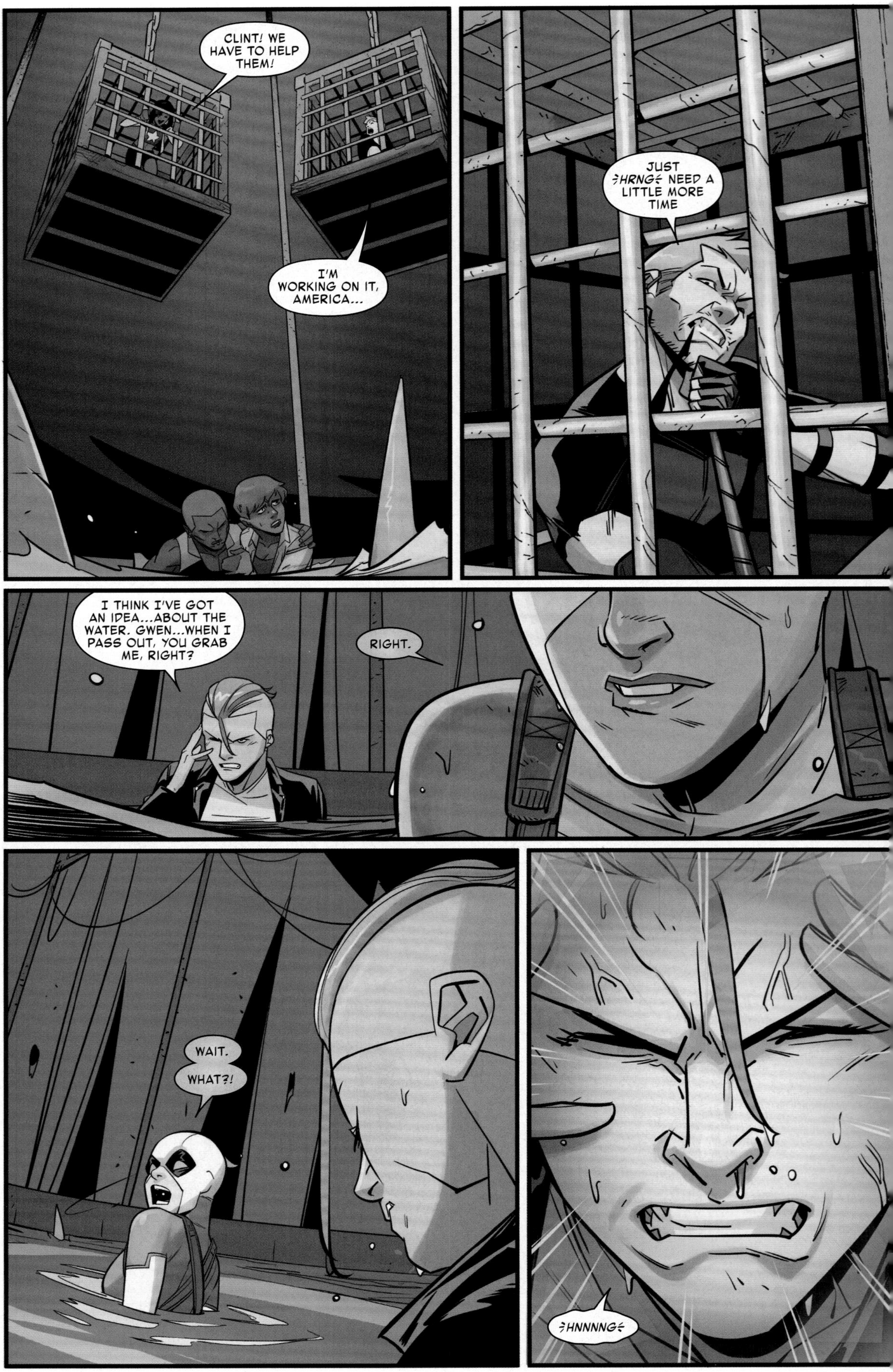
CLINT! WE HAVE TO HELP THEM!
I'M WORKING ON IT, AMERICA...
JUST ⫘HRNG⫘ NEED A LITTLE MORE TIME
I THINK I'VE GOT AN IDEA...ABOUT THE WATER. GWEN...WHEN I PASS OUT, YOU GRAB ME, RIGHT?
RIGHT.
WAIT.
WHAT?!
⫘HNNNNG⫘

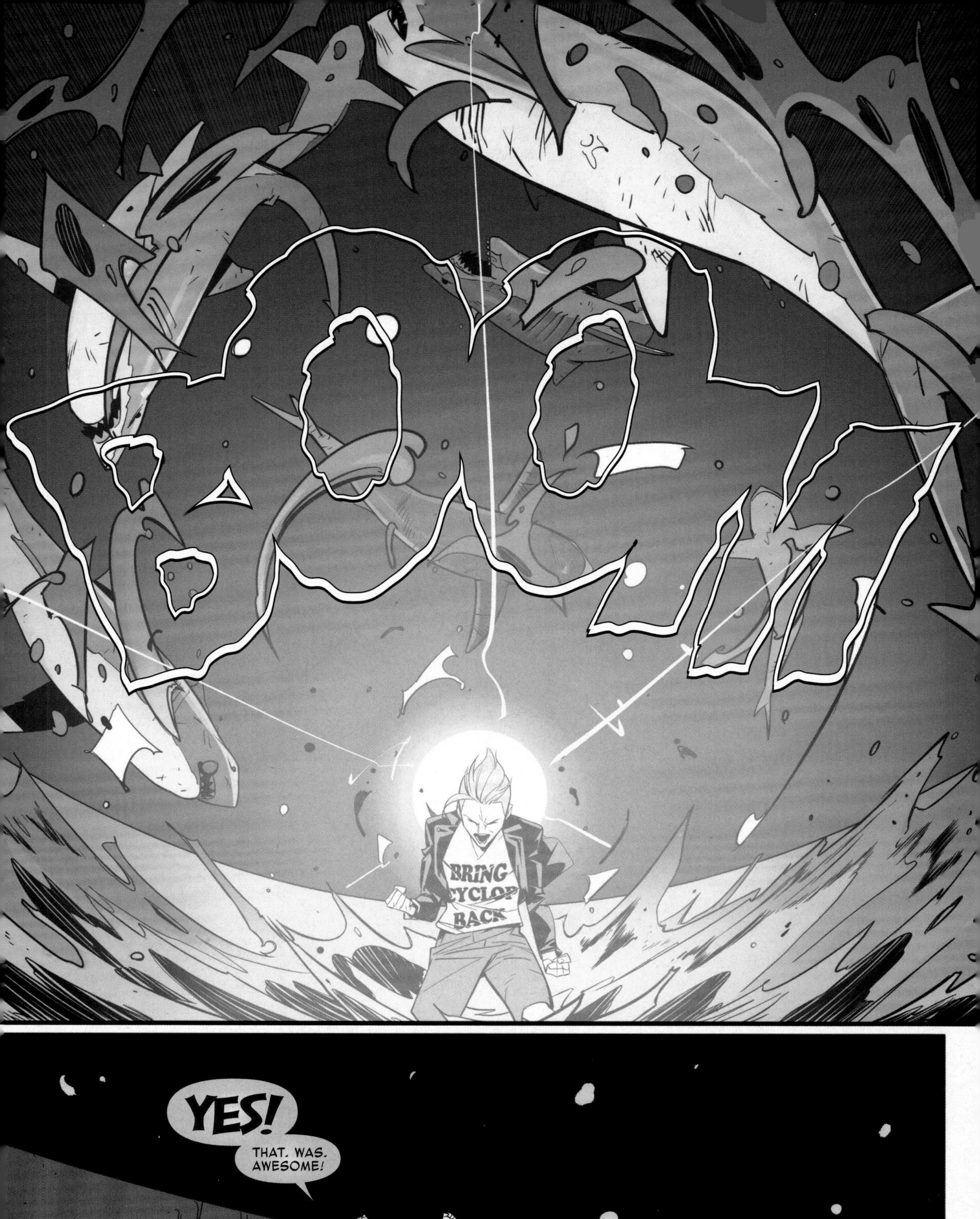
BOOM
BRING CYCLOP BACK

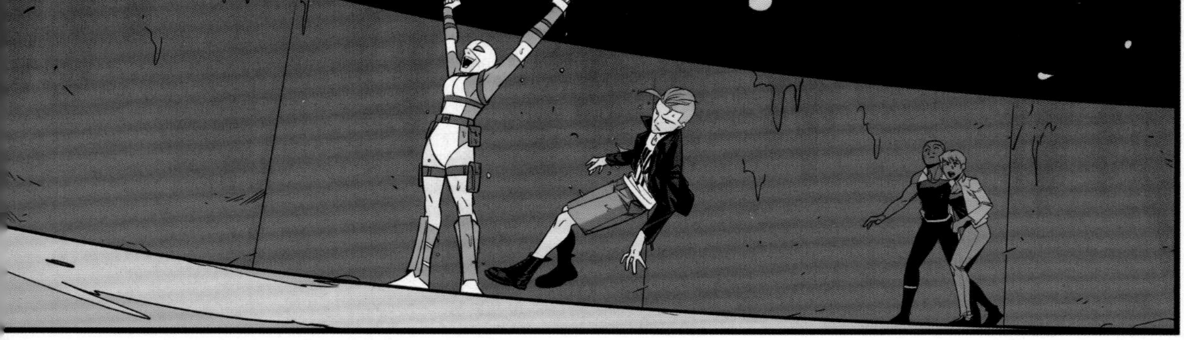
YES!
THAT. WAS. AWESOME!

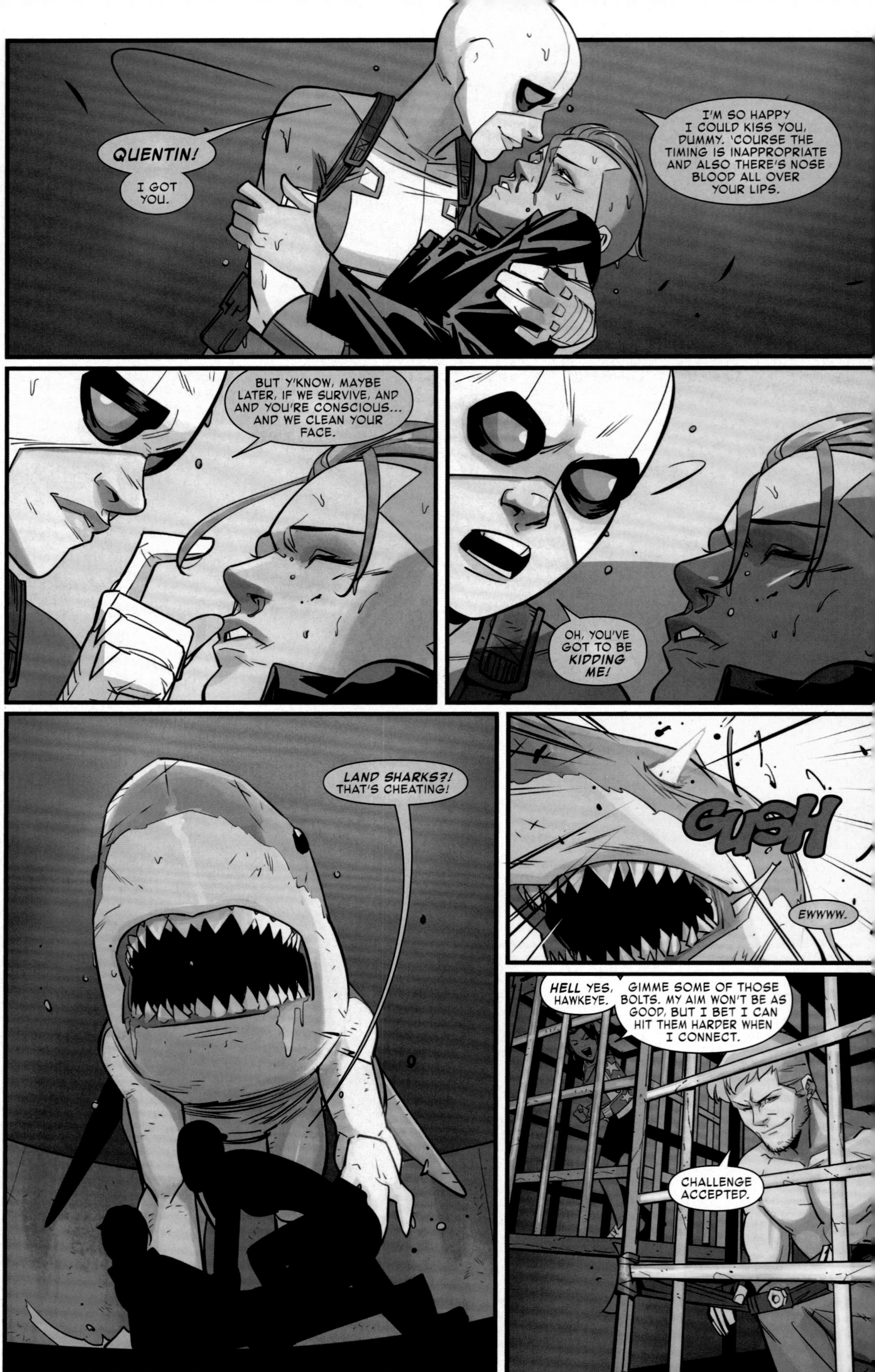
QUENTIN!
I GOT YOU.
I'M SO HAPPY I COULD KISS YOU, DUMMY. 'COURSE THE TIMING IS INAPPROPRIATE AND ALSO THERE'S NOSE BLOOD ALL OVER YOUR LIPS.
BUT Y'KNOW, MAYBE LATER, IF WE SURVIVE, AND AND YOU'RE CONSCIOUS... AND WE CLEAN YOUR FACE.
OH, YOU'VE GOT TO BE KIDDING ME!
LAND SHARKS?! THAT'S CHEATING!
GUSH
EWWWW.
HELL YES, HAWKEYE.
GIMME SOME OF THOSE BOLTS. MY AIM WON'T BE AS GOOD, BUT I BET I CAN HIT THEM HARDER WHEN I CONNECT.
CHALLENGE ACCEPTED.

?!

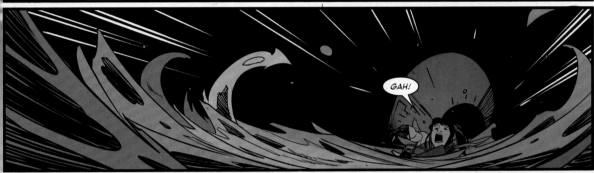

GAH!

≶GASP≶ WELL, THAT ≶CHOKE≶ WAS... BRISK.

WHOZZAT?

KICK

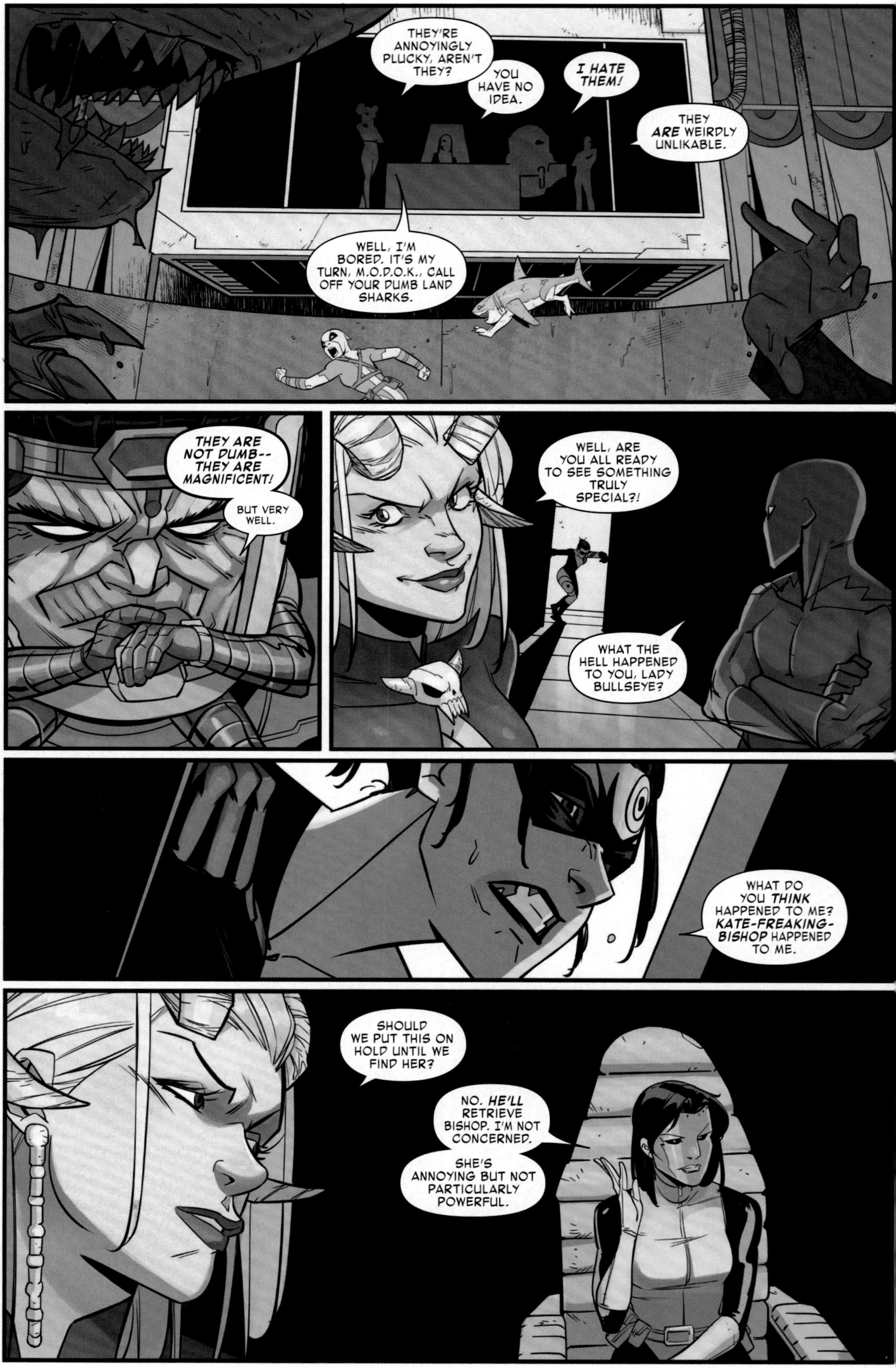
THEY'RE ANNOYINGLY PLUCKY, AREN'T THEY?
YOU HAVE NO IDEA.
I HATE THEM!
THEY ARE WEIRDLY UNLIKABLE.
WELL, I'M BORED. IT'S MY TURN, M.O.D.O.K., CALL OFF YOUR DUMB LAND SHARKS.
THEY ARE NOT DUMB-- THEY ARE MAGNIFICENT!
BUT VERY WELL.
WELL, ARE YOU ALL READY TO SEE SOMETHING TRULY SPECIAL?!
WHAT THE HELL HAPPENED TO YOU, LADY BULLSEYE?
WHAT DO YOU THINK HAPPENED TO ME? KATE-FREAKING-BISHOP HAPPENED TO ME.
SHOULD WE PUT THIS ON HOLD UNTIL WE FIND HER?
NO. HE'LL RETRIEVE BISHOP. I'M NOT CONCERNED.
SHE'S ANNOYING BUT NOT PARTICULARLY POWERFUL.

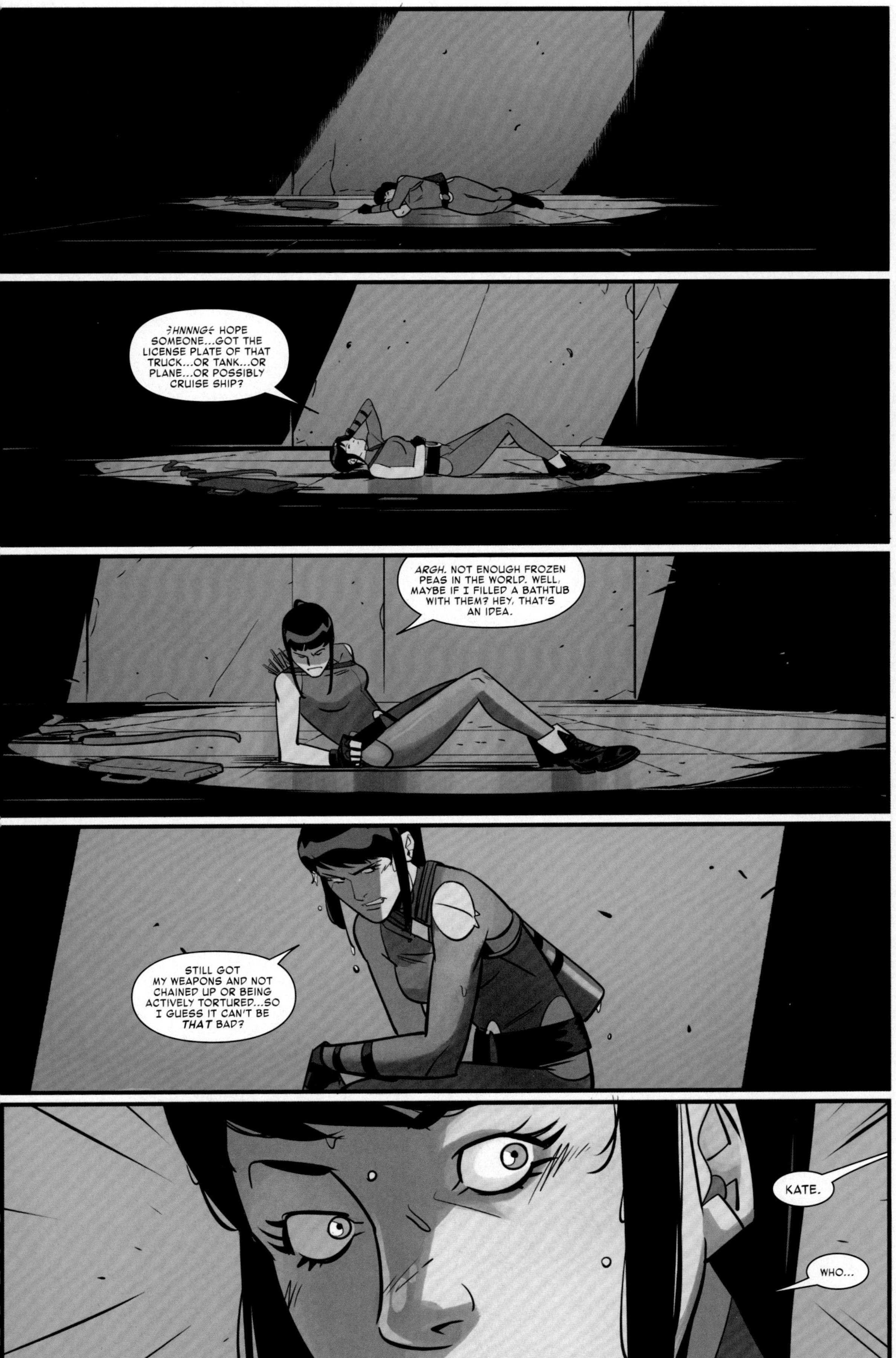

=HNNNG= HOPE SOMEONE...GOT THE LICENSE PLATE OF THAT TRUCK...OR TANK...OR PLANE...OR POSSIBLY CRUISE SHIP?
ARGH. NOT ENOUGH FROZEN PEAS IN THE WORLD. WELL, MAYBE IF I FILLED A BATHTUB WITH THEM? HEY, THAT'S AN IDEA.
STILL GOT MY WEAPONS AND NOT CHAINED UP OR BEING ACTIVELY TORTURED...SO I GUESS IT CAN'T BE THAT BAD?
KATE.
WHO...

SPOKE TOO SOON. IT *IS* THAT BAD.
...NOH-VARR?
HI. SORRY ABOUT BEFORE, BUT I CAN EXPLAIN EVERYTHING.
NOH-VARR, A.K.A. MARVEL BOY, A.K.A....
...KATE'S EX-BOYFRIEND.

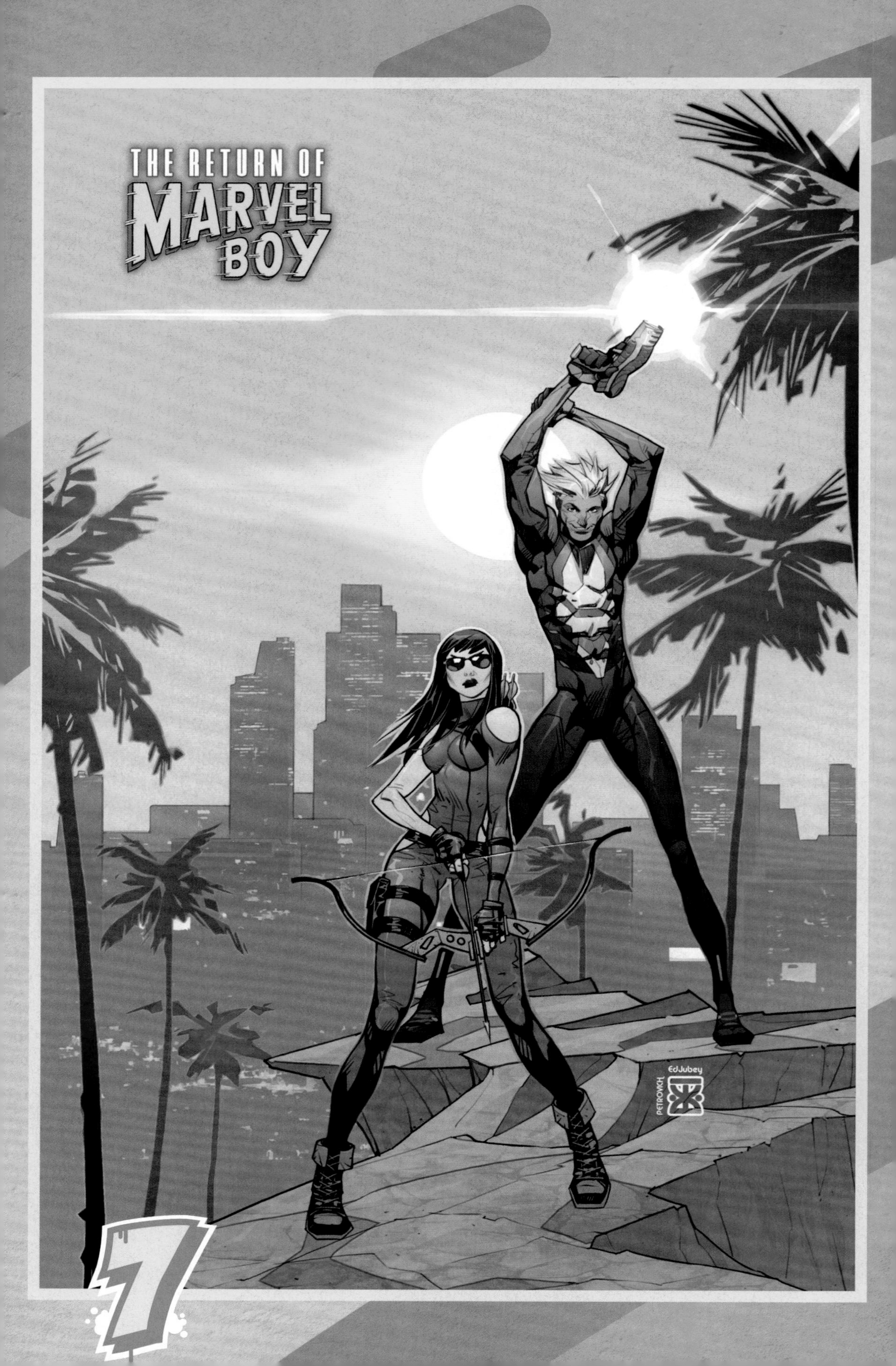
THE RETURN OF
MARVEL BOY
7
PETROVICH
EdJubey

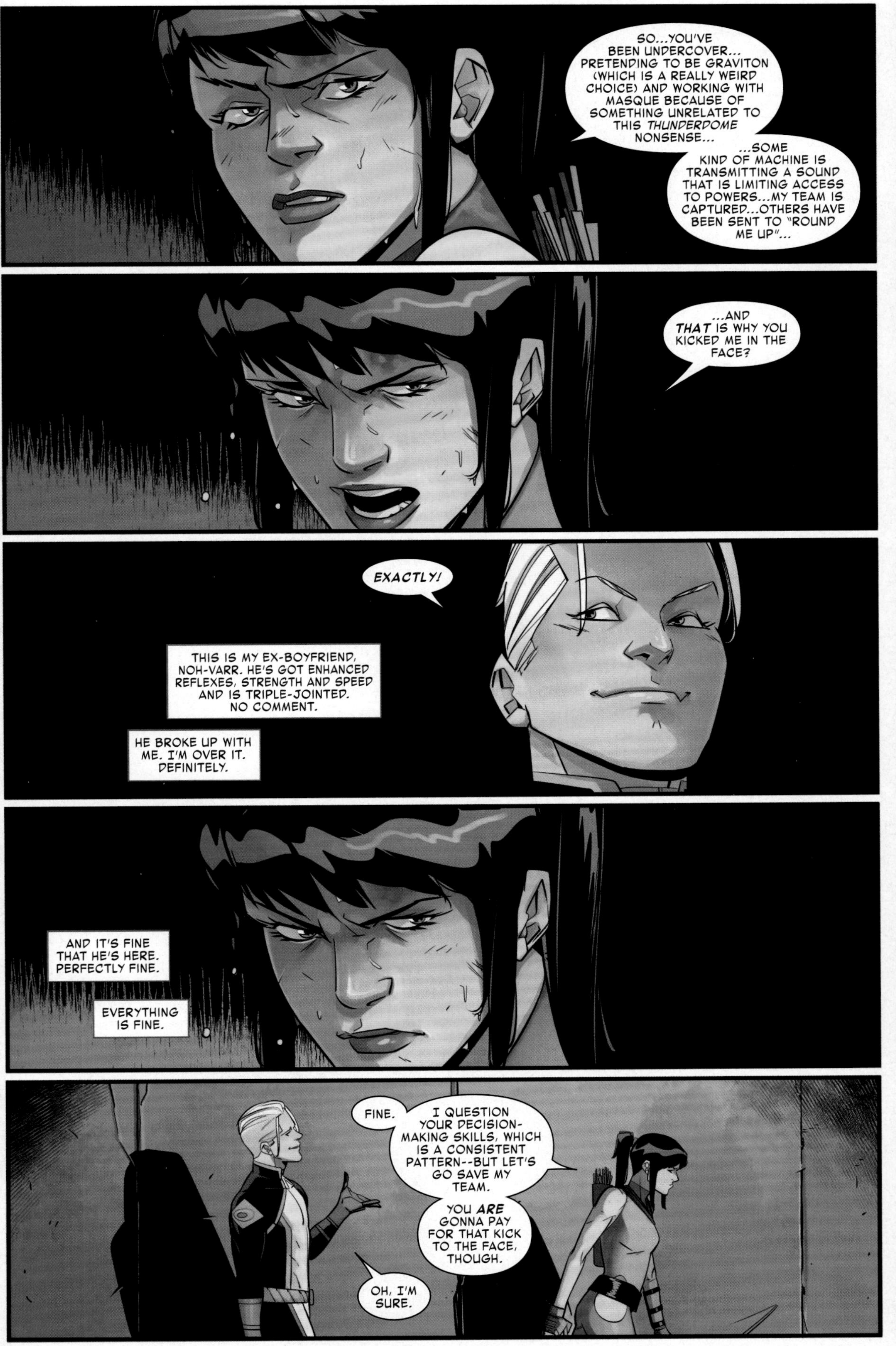
SO...YOU'VE BEEN UNDERCOVER... PRETENDING TO BE GRAVITON (WHICH IS A REALLY WEIRD CHOICE) AND WORKING WITH MASQUE BECAUSE OF SOMETHING UNRELATED TO THIS *THUNDERDOME* NONSENSE...
...SOME KIND OF MACHINE IS TRANSMITTING A SOUND THAT IS LIMITING ACCESS TO POWERS...MY TEAM IS CAPTURED...OTHERS HAVE BEEN SENT TO "ROUND ME UP"...
...AND ***THAT*** IS WHY YOU KICKED ME IN THE FACE?
EXACTLY!
THIS IS MY EX-BOYFRIEND, NOH-VARR. HE'S GOT ENHANCED REFLEXES, STRENGTH AND SPEED AND IS TRIPLE-JOINTED. NO COMMENT.
HE BROKE UP WITH ME. I'M OVER IT. DEFINITELY.
AND IT'S FINE THAT HE'S HERE. PERFECTLY FINE.
EVERYTHING IS FINE.
FINE.
I QUESTION YOUR DECISION-MAKING SKILLS, WHICH IS A CONSISTENT PATTERN--BUT LET'S GO SAVE MY TEAM.
YOU ***ARE*** GONNA PAY FOR THAT KICK TO THE FACE, THOUGH.
OH, I'M SURE.

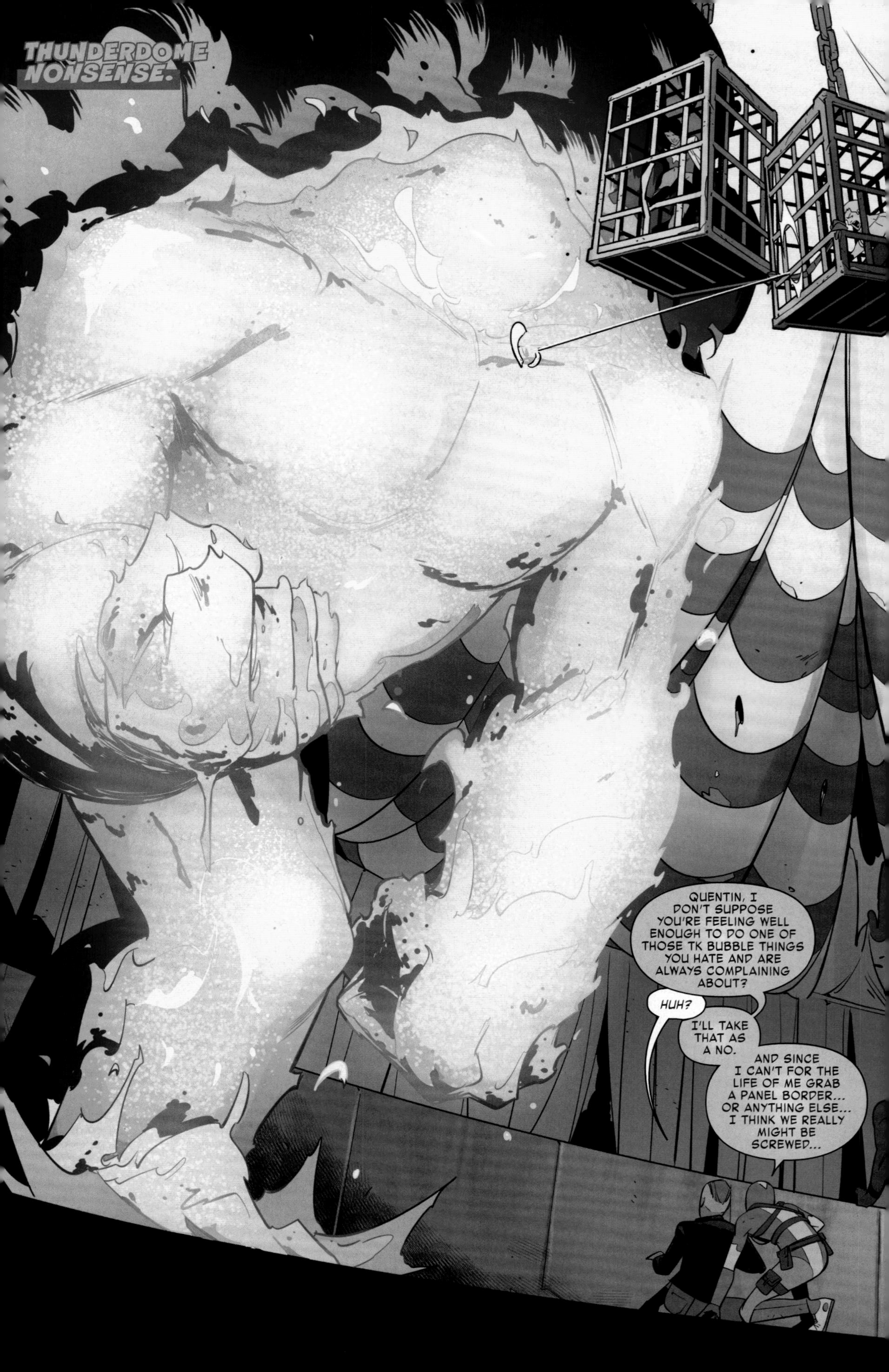
THUNDERDOME NONSENSE.
QUENTIN, I DON'T SUPPOSE YOU'RE FEELING WELL ENOUGH TO DO ONE OF THOSE TK BUBBLE THINGS YOU HATE AND ARE ALWAYS COMPLAINING ABOUT?
HUH?
I'LL TAKE THAT AS A NO.
AND SINCE I CAN'T FOR THE LIFE OF ME GRAB A PANEL BORDER... OR ANYTHING ELSE... I THINK WE REALLY MIGHT BE SCREWED...

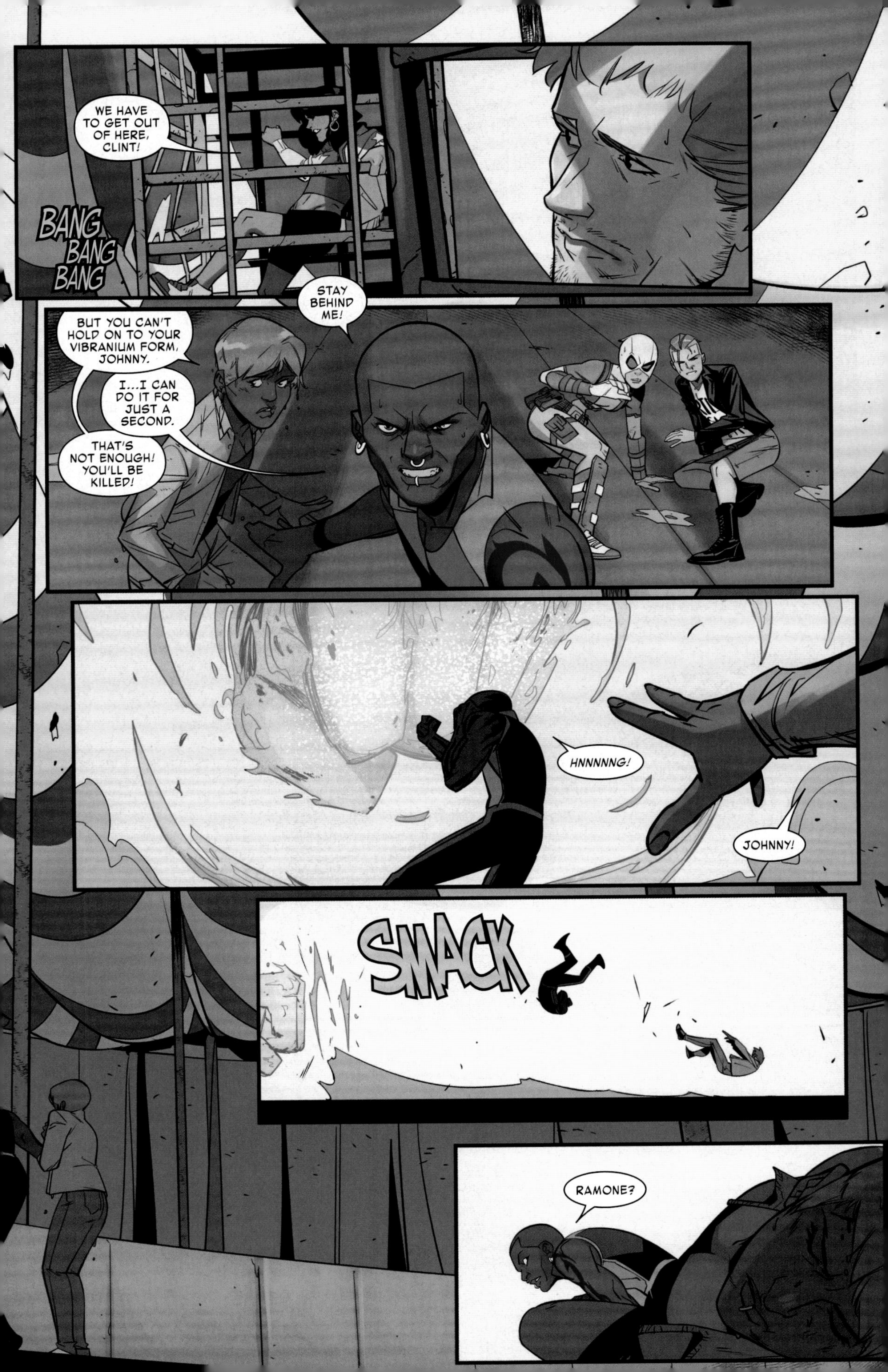
WE HAVE TO GET OUT OF HERE, CLINT!
BANG BANG BANG
STAY BEHIND ME!
BUT YOU CAN'T HOLD ON TO YOUR VIBRANIUM FORM, JOHNNY.
I...I CAN DO IT FOR JUST A SECOND.
THAT'S NOT ENOUGH! YOU'LL BE KILLED!
HNNNNNG!
JOHNNY!
SMACK
RAMONE?

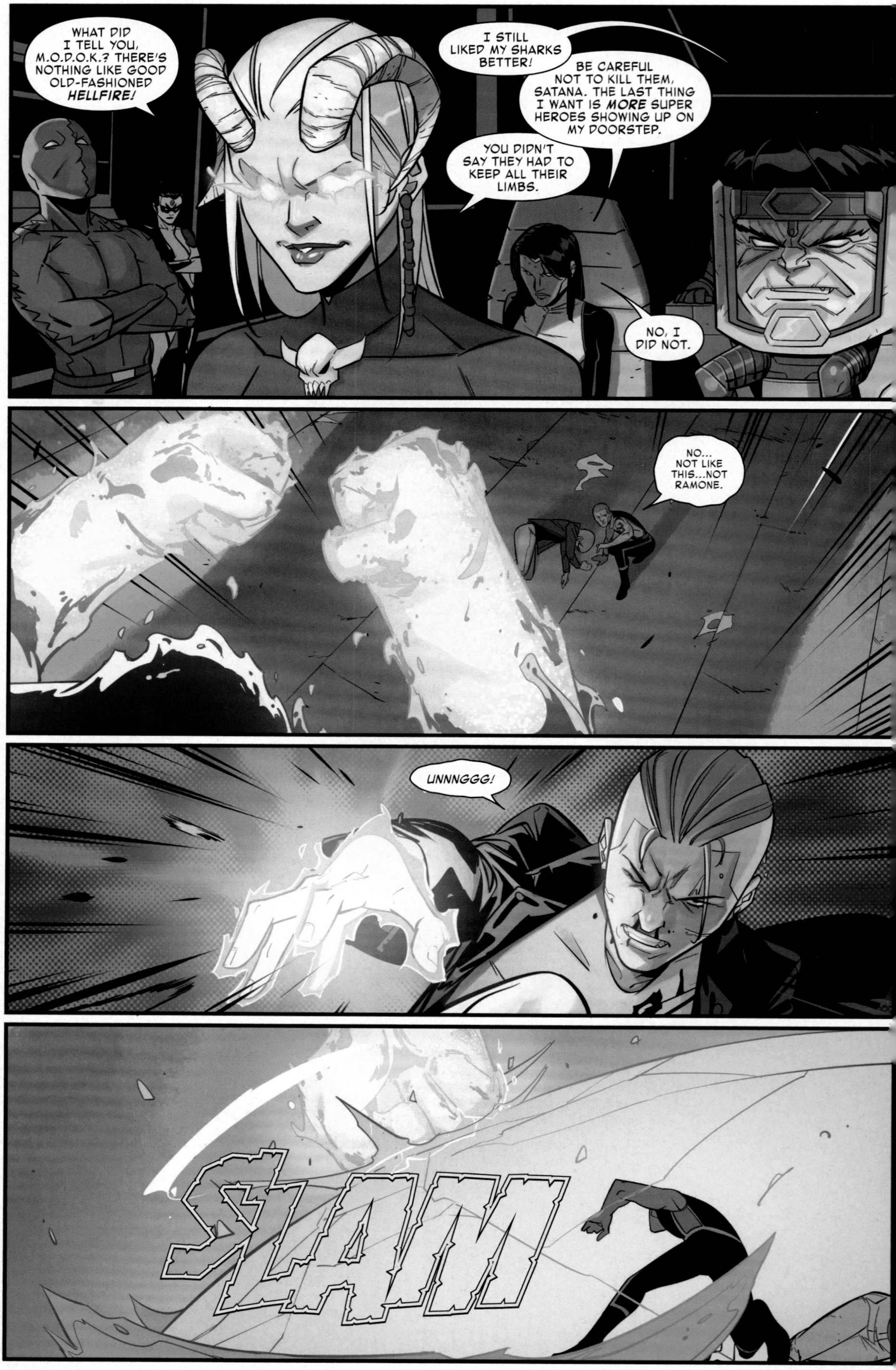
WHAT DID I TELL YOU, M.O.D.O.K.? THERE'S NOTHING LIKE GOOD OLD-FASHIONED HELLFIRE!
I STILL LIKED MY SHARKS BETTER!
BE CAREFUL NOT TO KILL THEM, SATANA. THE LAST THING I WANT IS MORE SUPER HEROES SHOWING UP ON MY DOORSTEP.
YOU DIDN'T SAY THEY HAD TO KEEP ALL THEIR LIMBS.
NO, I DID NOT.
NO... NOT LIKE THIS...NOT RAMONE.
UNNNGGG!
SLAM

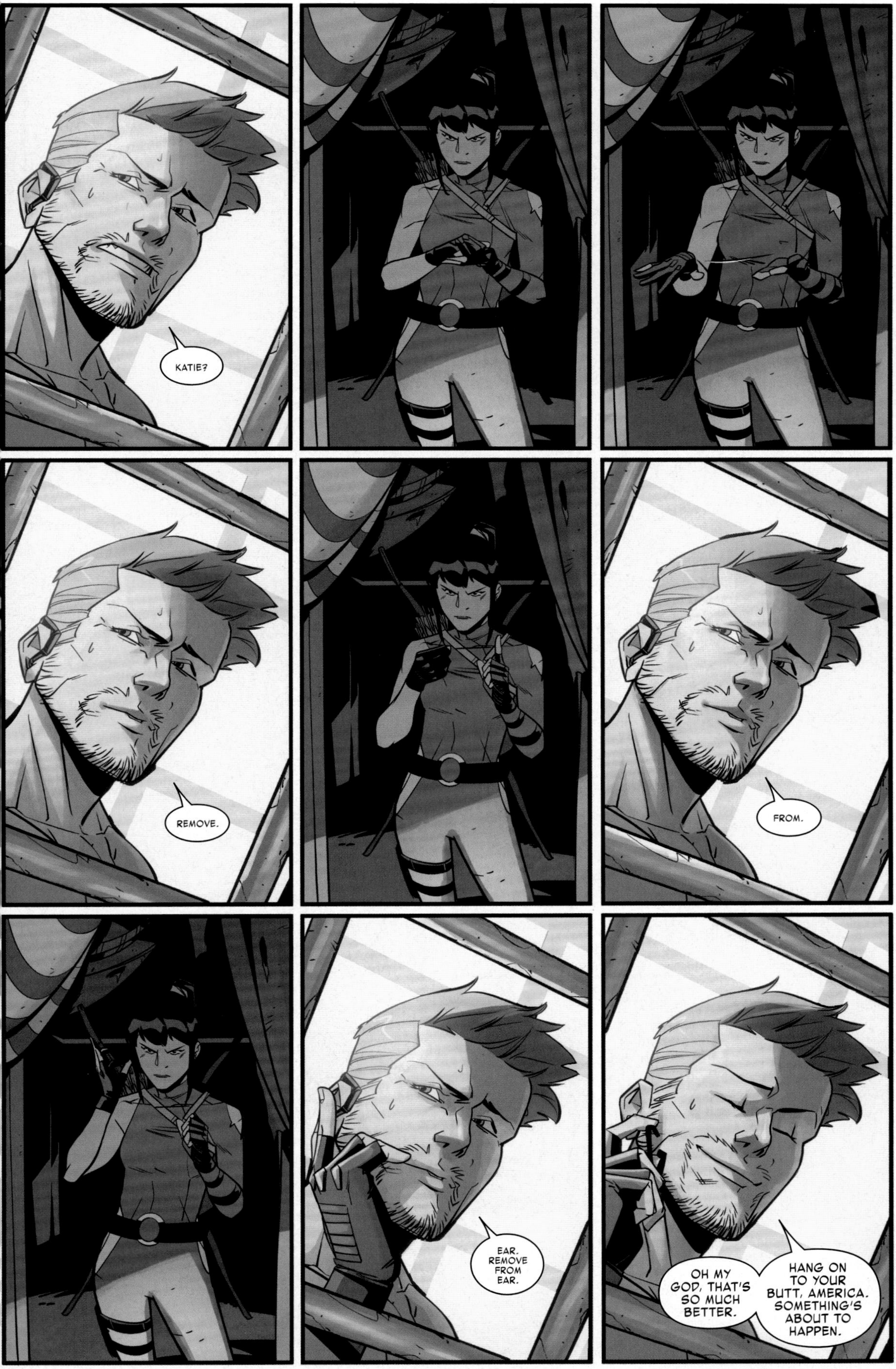
KATIE?
REMOVE.
FROM.
EAR. REMOVE FROM EAR.
OH MY GOD, THAT'S SO MUCH BETTER.
HANG ON TO YOUR BUTT, AMERICA. SOMETHING'S ABOUT TO HAPPEN.

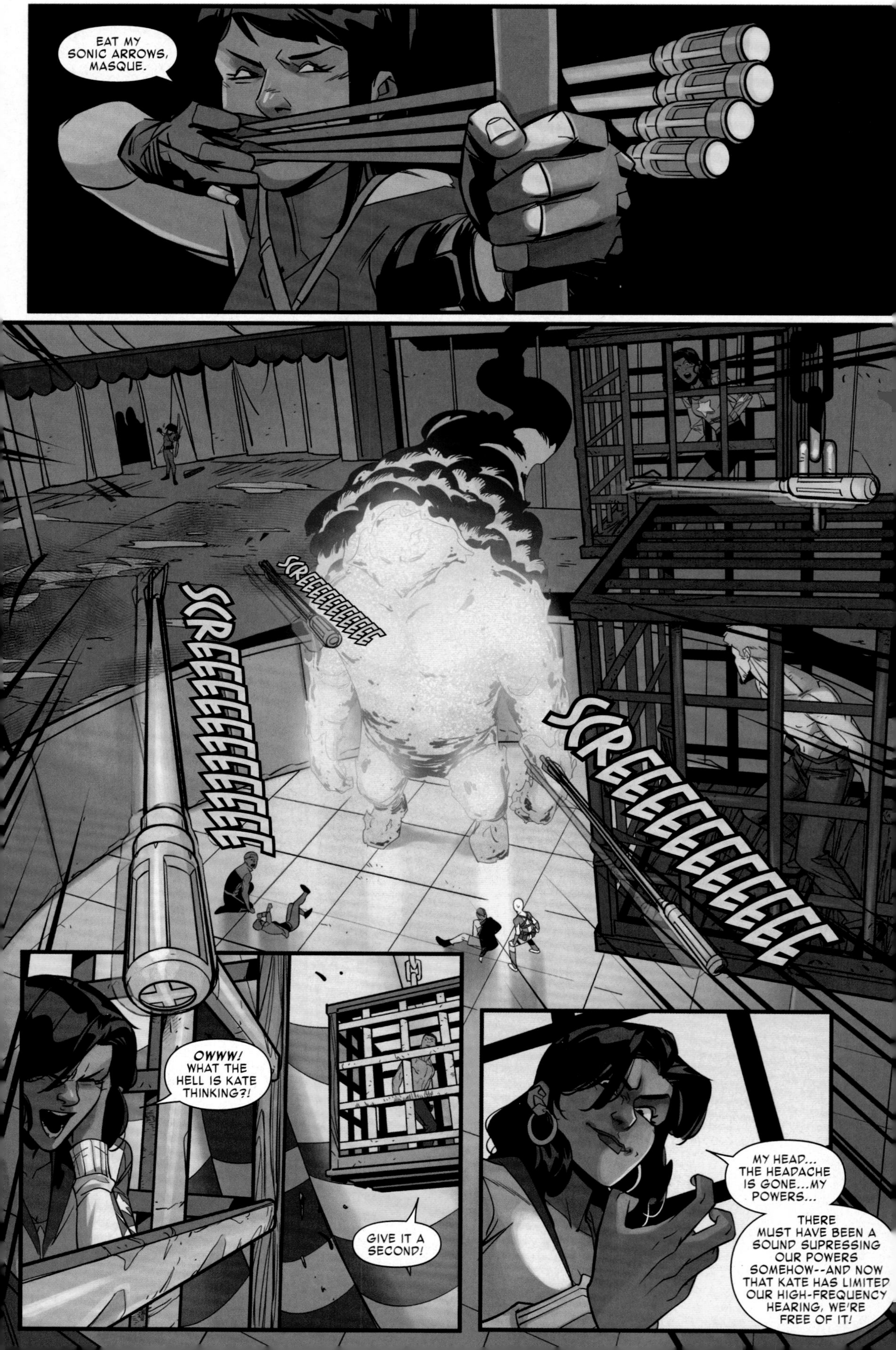
EAT MY SONIC ARROWS, MASQUE.
SCREEEEEEEEEEE
SCREEEEEEEEEEEE
SCREEEEEEEEEEEE
OWWW! WHAT THE HELL IS KATE THINKING?!
GIVE IT A SECOND!
MY HEAD... THE HEADACHE IS GONE...MY POWERS...
THERE MUST HAVE BEEN A SOUND SUPRESSING OUR POWERS SOMEHOW--AND NOW THAT KATE HAS LIMITED OUR HIGH-FREQUENCY HEARING, WE'RE FREE OF IT!

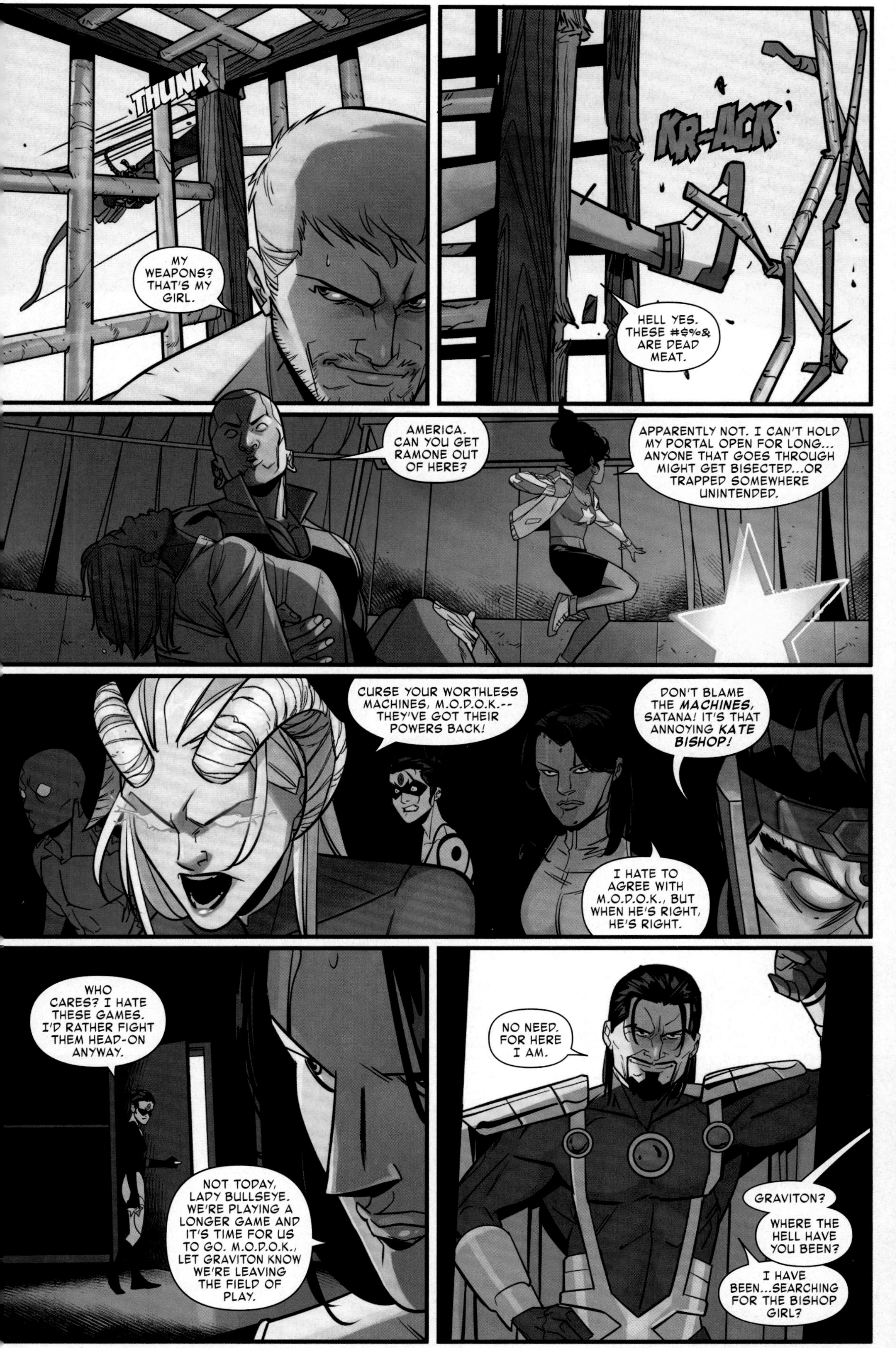
THUNK
MY WEAPONS? THAT'S MY GIRL.
KR-ACK
HELL YES. THESE #$%& ARE DEAD MEAT.
AMERICA. CAN YOU GET RAMONE OUT OF HERE?
APPARENTLY NOT. I CAN'T HOLD MY PORTAL OPEN FOR LONG... ANYONE THAT GOES THROUGH MIGHT GET BISECTED...OR TRAPPED SOMEWHERE UNINTENDED.
CURSE YOUR WORTHLESS MACHINES, M.O.D.O.K.-- THEY'VE GOT THEIR POWERS BACK!
DON'T BLAME THE MACHINES, SATANA! IT'S THAT ANNOYING KATE BISHOP!
I HATE TO AGREE WITH M.O.D.O.K., BUT WHEN HE'S RIGHT, HE'S RIGHT.
WHO CARES? I HATE THESE GAMES. I'D RATHER FIGHT THEM HEAD-ON ANYWAY.
NOT TODAY, LADY BULLSEYE. WE'RE PLAYING A LONGER GAME AND IT'S TIME FOR US TO GO. M.O.D.O.K., LET GRAVITON KNOW WE'RE LEAVING THE FIELD OF PLAY.
NO NEED. FOR HERE I AM.
GRAVITON?
WHERE THE HELL HAVE YOU BEEN?
I HAVE BEEN...SEARCHING FOR THE BISHOP GIRL?

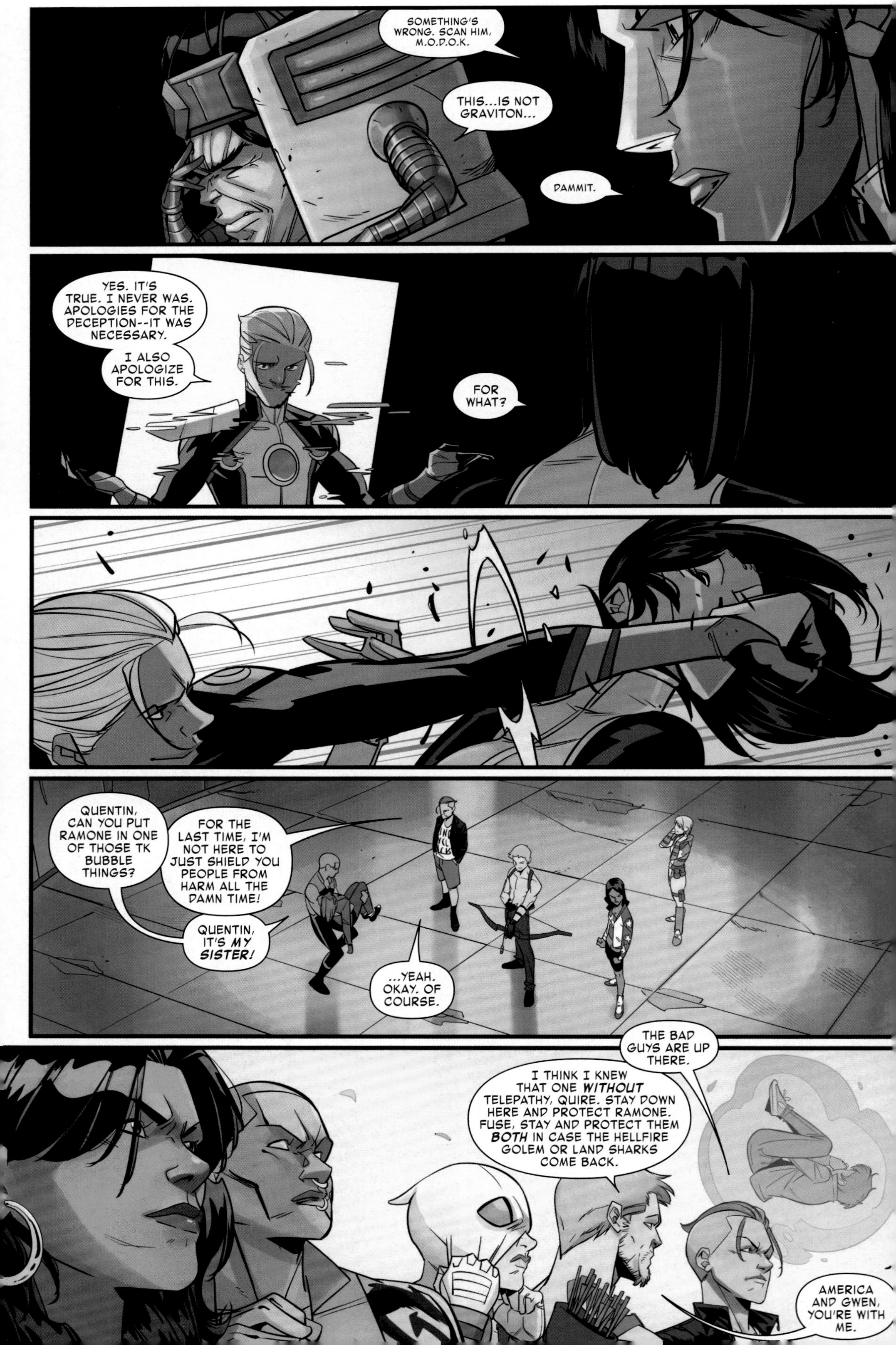
SOMETHING'S WRONG. SCAN HIM, M.O.D.O.K.
THIS...IS NOT GRAVITON...
DAMMIT.
YES. IT'S TRUE. I NEVER WAS. APOLOGIES FOR THE DECEPTION--IT WAS NECESSARY.
I ALSO APOLOGIZE FOR THIS.
FOR WHAT?
QUENTIN, CAN YOU PUT RAMONE IN ONE OF THOSE TK BUBBLE THINGS?
FOR THE LAST TIME, I'M NOT HERE TO JUST SHIELD YOU PEOPLE FROM HARM ALL THE DAMN TIME!
QUENTIN, IT'S MY SISTER!
...YEAH. OKAY. OF COURSE.
THE BAD GUYS ARE UP THERE.
I THINK I KNEW THAT ONE WITHOUT TELEPATHY, QUIRE. STAY DOWN HERE AND PROTECT RAMONE. FUSE, STAY AND PROTECT THEM BOTH IN CASE THE HELLFIRE GOLEM OR LAND SHARKS COME BACK.
AMERICA AND GWEN, YOU'RE WITH ME.

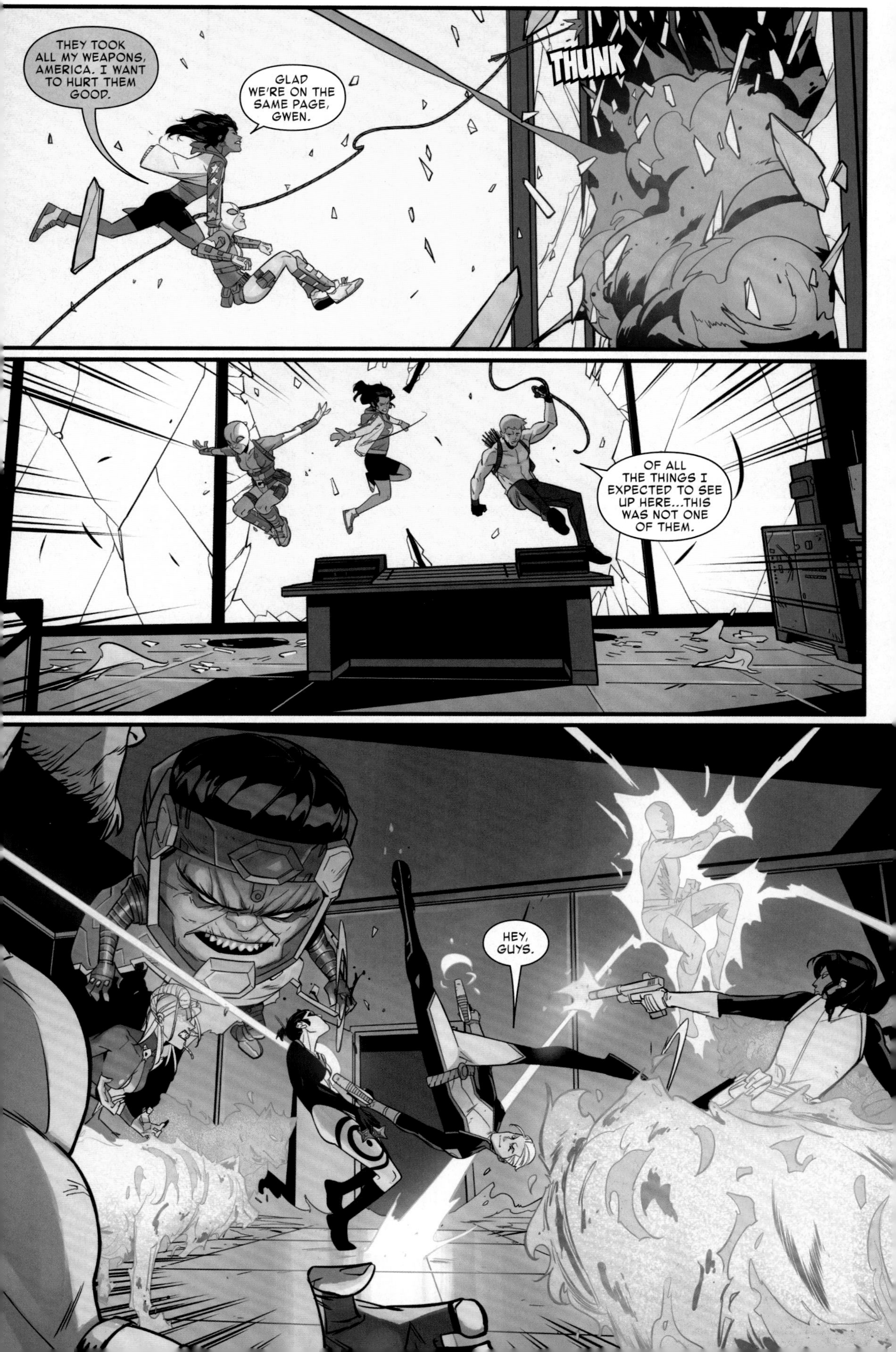
THEY TOOK ALL MY WEAPONS, AMERICA. I WANT TO HURT THEM GOOD.
GLAD WE'RE ON THE SAME PAGE, GWEN.
THUNK
OF ALL THE THINGS I EXPECTED TO SEE UP HERE...THIS WAS NOT ONE OF THEM.
HEY, GUYS.

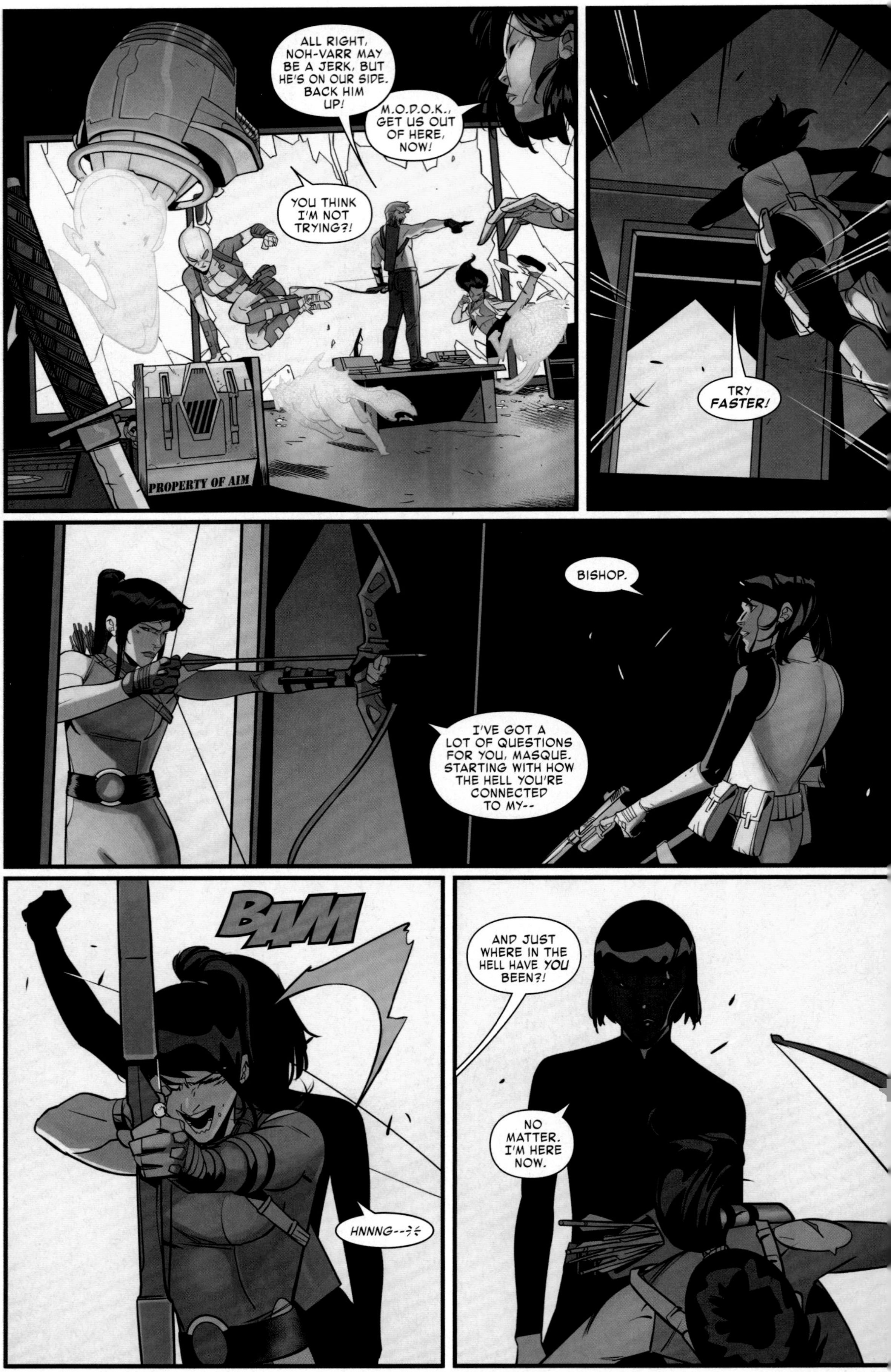
ALL RIGHT, NOH-VARR MAY BE A JERK, BUT HE'S ON OUR SIDE. BACK HIM UP!
M.O.D.O.K., GET US OUT OF HERE, NOW!
YOU THINK I'M NOT TRYING?!
PROPERTY OF AIM
TRY FASTER!
BISHOP.
I'VE GOT A LOT OF QUESTIONS FOR YOU, MASQUE. STARTING WITH HOW THE HELL YOU'RE CONNECTED TO MY--
BAM
HNNNG--
AND JUST WHERE IN THE HELL HAVE YOU BEEN?!
NO MATTER. I'M HERE NOW.

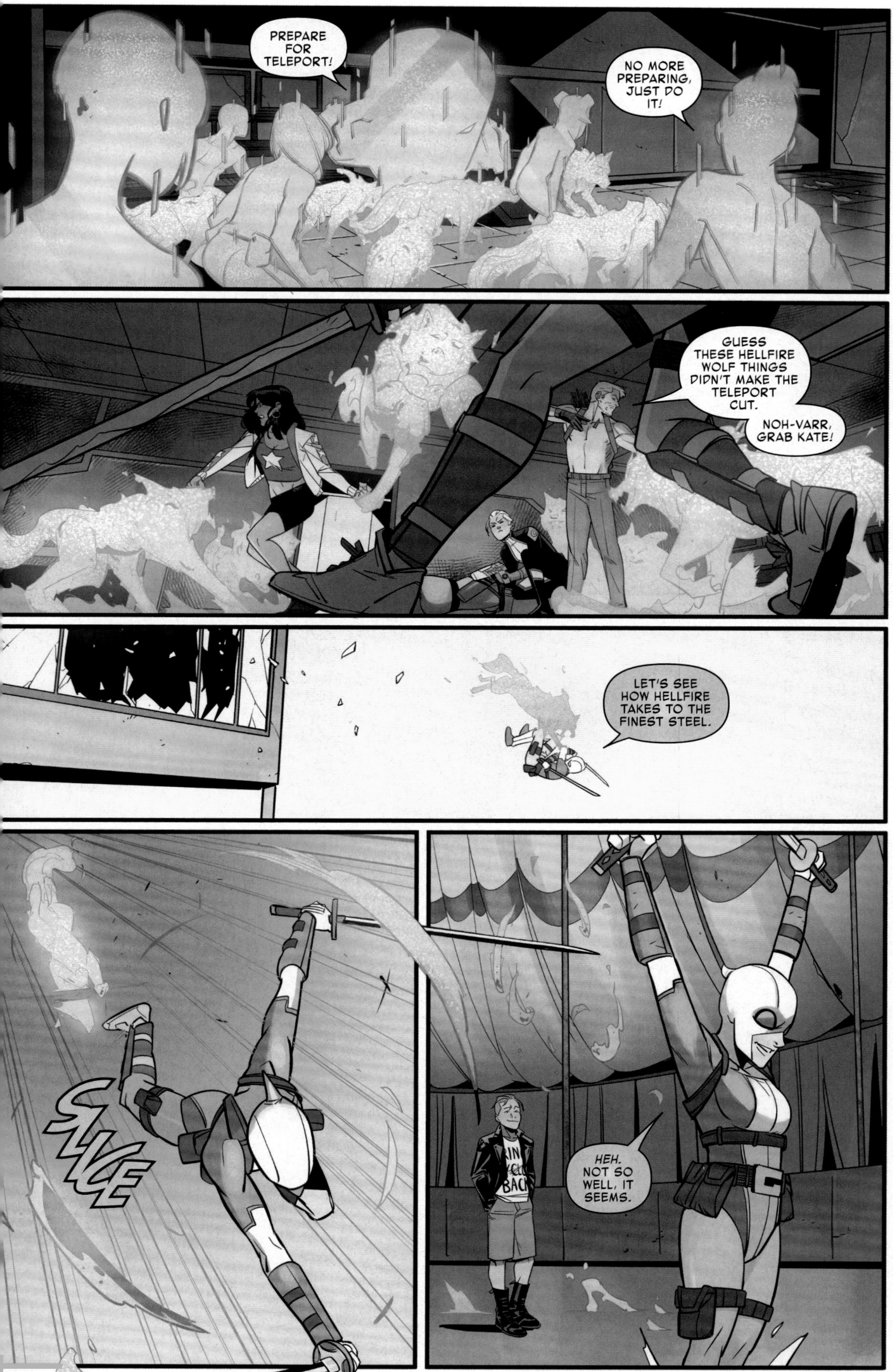
PREPARE FOR TELEPORT!
NO MORE PREPARING, JUST DO IT!
GUESS THESE HELLFIRE WOLF THINGS DIDN'T MAKE THE TELEPORT CUT.
NOH-VARR, GRAB KATE!
LET'S SEE HOW HELLFIRE TAKES TO THE FINEST STEEL.
SLICE
HEH. NOT SO WELL, IT SEEMS.

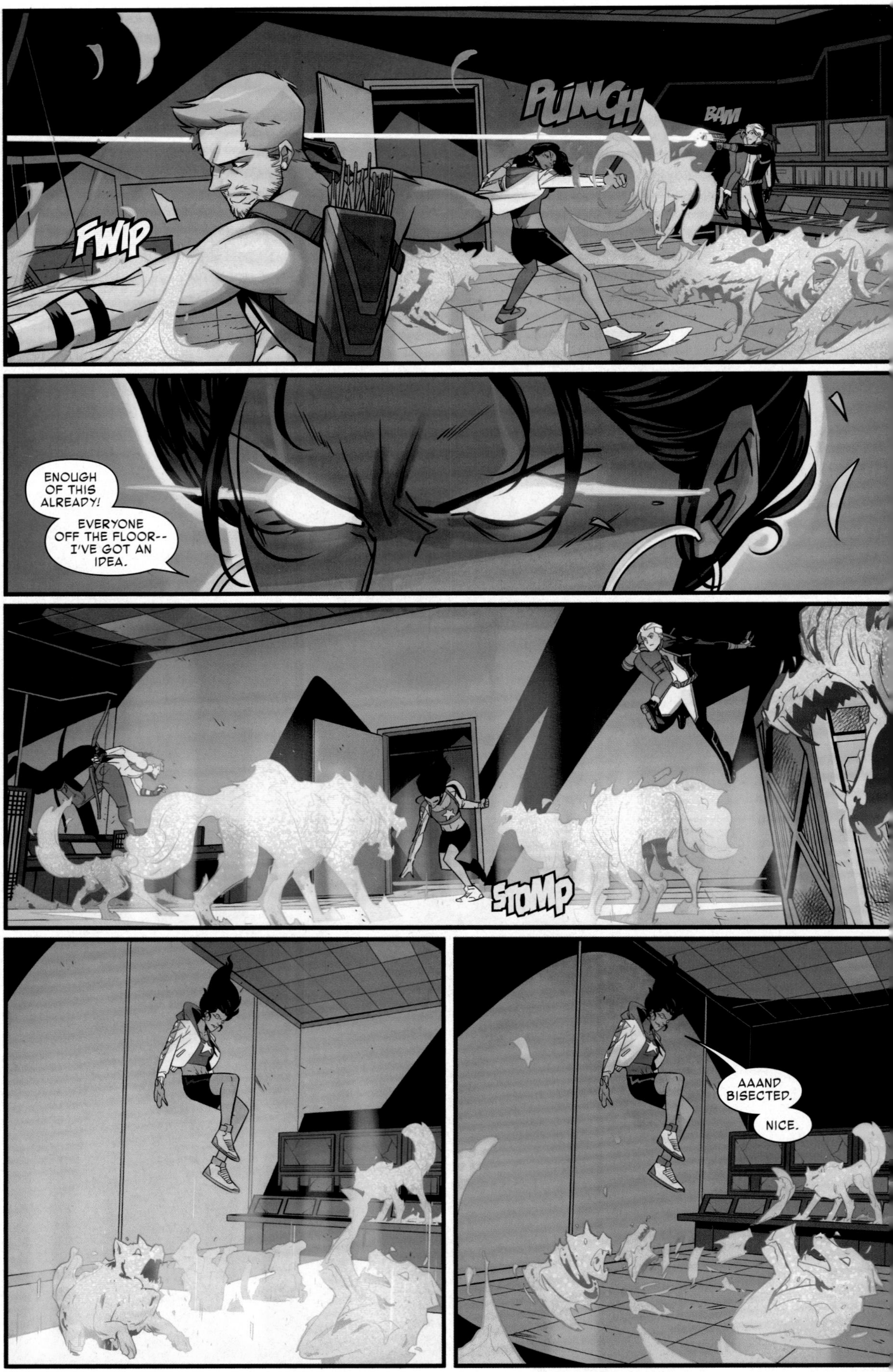
PUNCH
BAM
FWIP
ENOUGH OF THIS ALREADY!
EVERYONE OFF THE FLOOR-- I'VE GOT AN IDEA.
STOMP
AAAND BISECTED.
NICE.

WHAT DO YOU WANT TO BET THAT GIANT BOX IS WHAT'S POWERING THIS WHOLE DAMN PLACE?

NO BET. THROW THE WOLF.

PROPERTY OF AIM

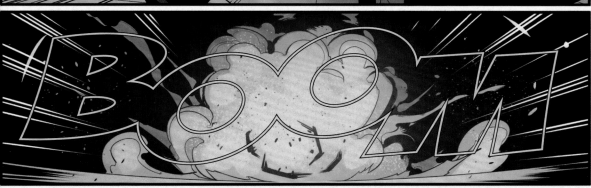

TOSS

FWIP

OH, YEAH. THAT DID IT. I'M BACK. NOH-VARR?

YES. SAME. ALTHOUGH...I HAD THE EARPLUGS ALL ALONG, SO I WAS FINE.

OF COURSE YOU DID.

YES!

FROM THE SOUND OF IT, QUIRE IS BACK TOO. WHICH IS, OF COURSE, BOTH BLESSING AND CURSE.

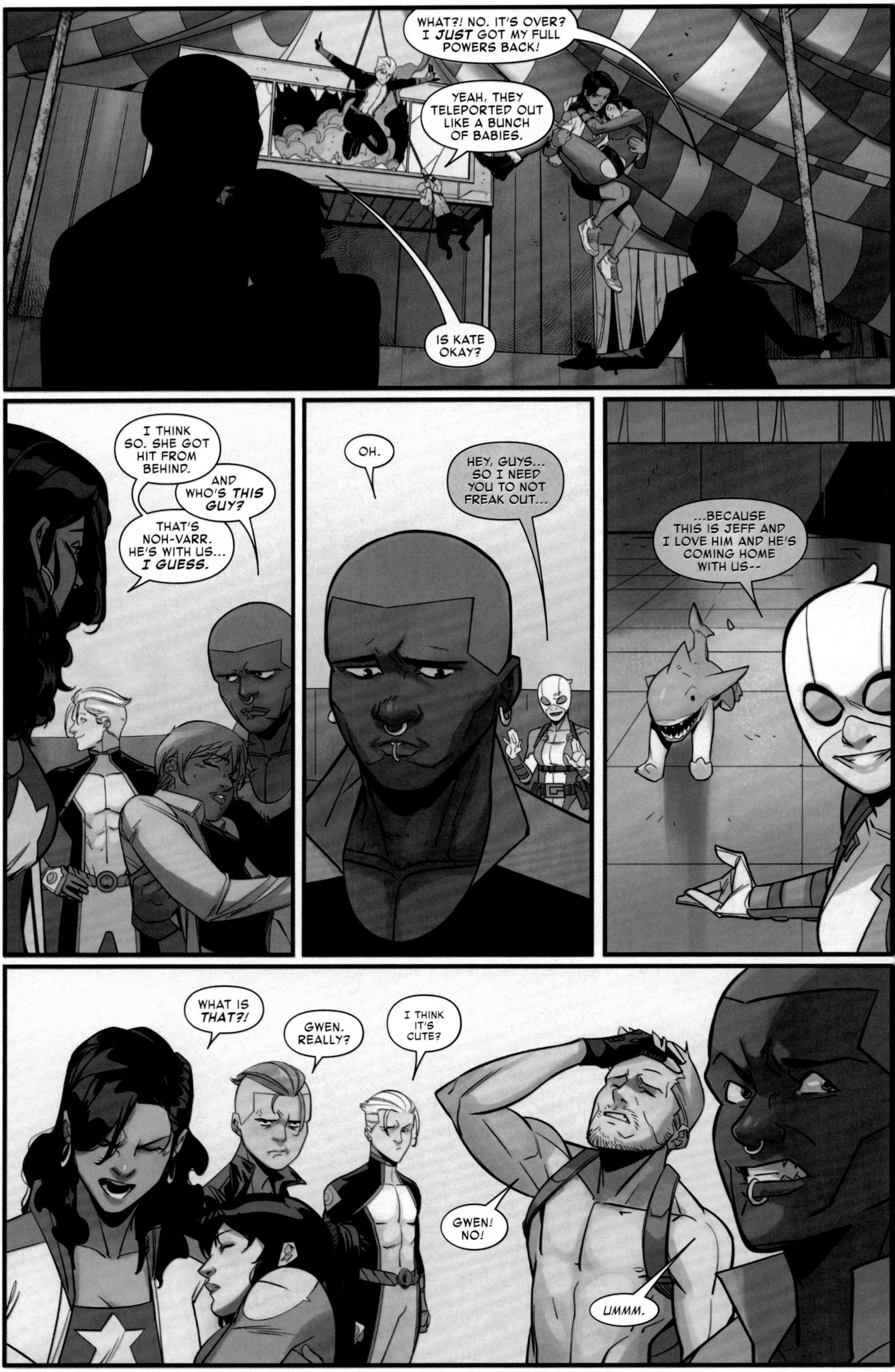
WHAT?! NO. IT'S OVER? I JUST GOT MY FULL POWERS BACK!
YEAH, THEY TELEPORTED OUT LIKE A BUNCH OF BABIES.
IS KATE OKAY?
I THINK SO. SHE GOT HIT FROM BEHIND.
AND WHO'S THIS GUY?
THAT'S NOH-VARR. HE'S WITH US... I GUESS.
OH.
HEY, GUYS... SO I NEED YOU TO NOT FREAK OUT...
...BECAUSE THIS IS JEFF AND I LOVE HIM AND HE'S COMING HOME WITH US--
WHAT IS THAT?!
GWEN. REALLY?
I THINK IT'S CUTE?
GWEN! NO!
UMMM.

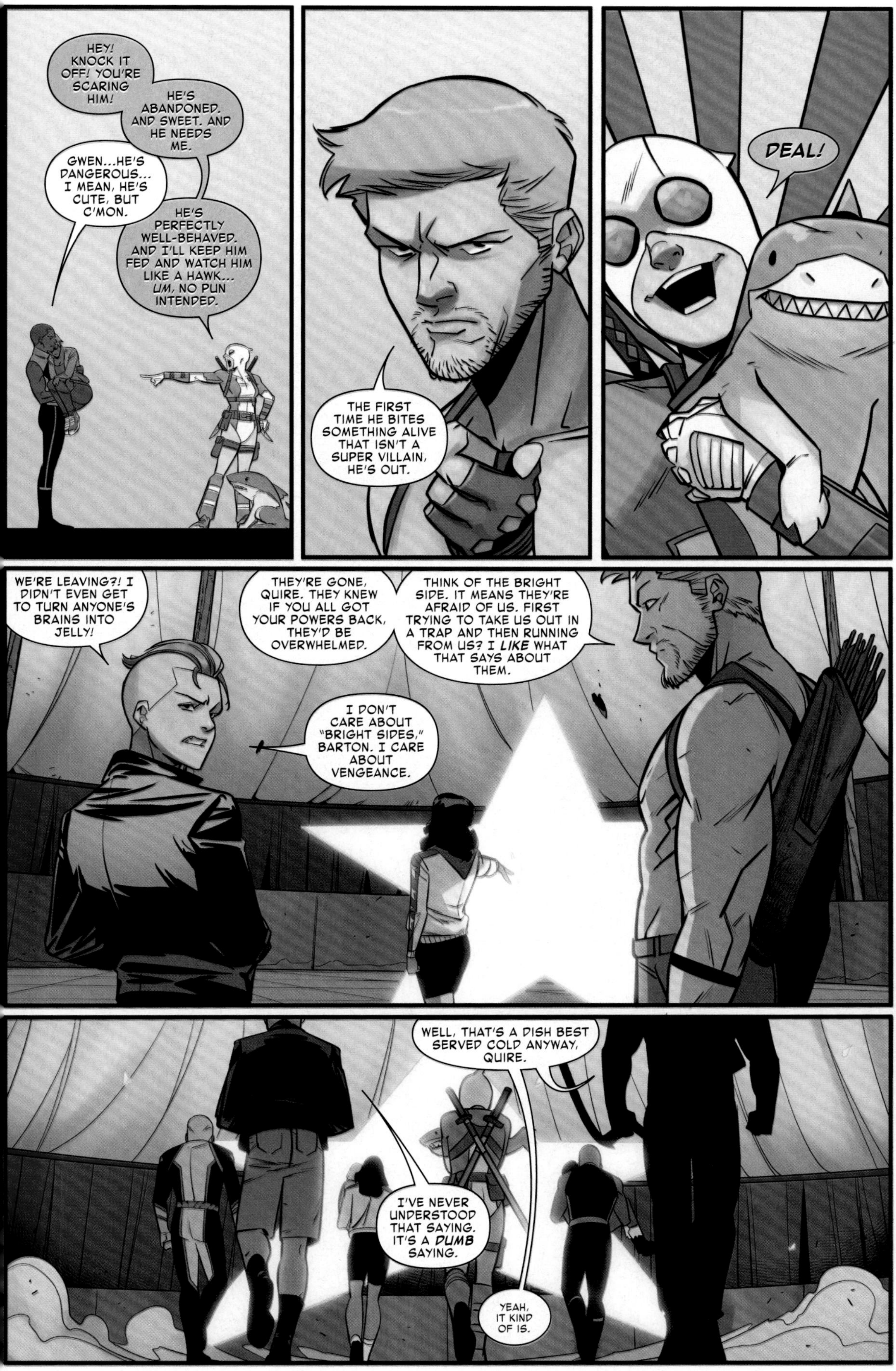

HEY! KNOCK IT OFF! YOU'RE SCARING HIM!
HE'S ABANDONED. AND SWEET. AND HE NEEDS ME.
GWEN...HE'S DANGEROUS... I MEAN, HE'S CUTE, BUT C'MON.
HE'S PERFECTLY WELL-BEHAVED. AND I'LL KEEP HIM FED AND WATCH HIM LIKE A HAWK... *UM,* NO PUN INTENDED.
THE FIRST TIME HE BITES SOMETHING ALIVE THAT ISN'T A SUPER VILLAIN, HE'S OUT.
DEAL!
WE'RE LEAVING?! I DIDN'T EVEN GET TO TURN ANYONE'S BRAINS INTO JELLY!
THEY'RE GONE, QUIRE. THEY KNEW IF YOU ALL GOT YOUR POWERS BACK, THEY'D BE OVERWHELMED.
THINK OF THE BRIGHT SIDE. IT MEANS THEY'RE AFRAID OF US. FIRST TRYING TO TAKE US OUT IN A TRAP AND THEN RUNNING FROM US? I *LIKE* WHAT THAT SAYS ABOUT THEM.
I DON'T CARE ABOUT "BRIGHT SIDES," BARTON. I CARE ABOUT VENGEANCE.
WELL, THAT'S A DISH BEST SERVED COLD ANYWAY, QUIRE.
I'VE NEVER UNDERSTOOD THAT SAYING. IT'S A *DUMB* SAYING.
YEAH, IT KIND OF IS.

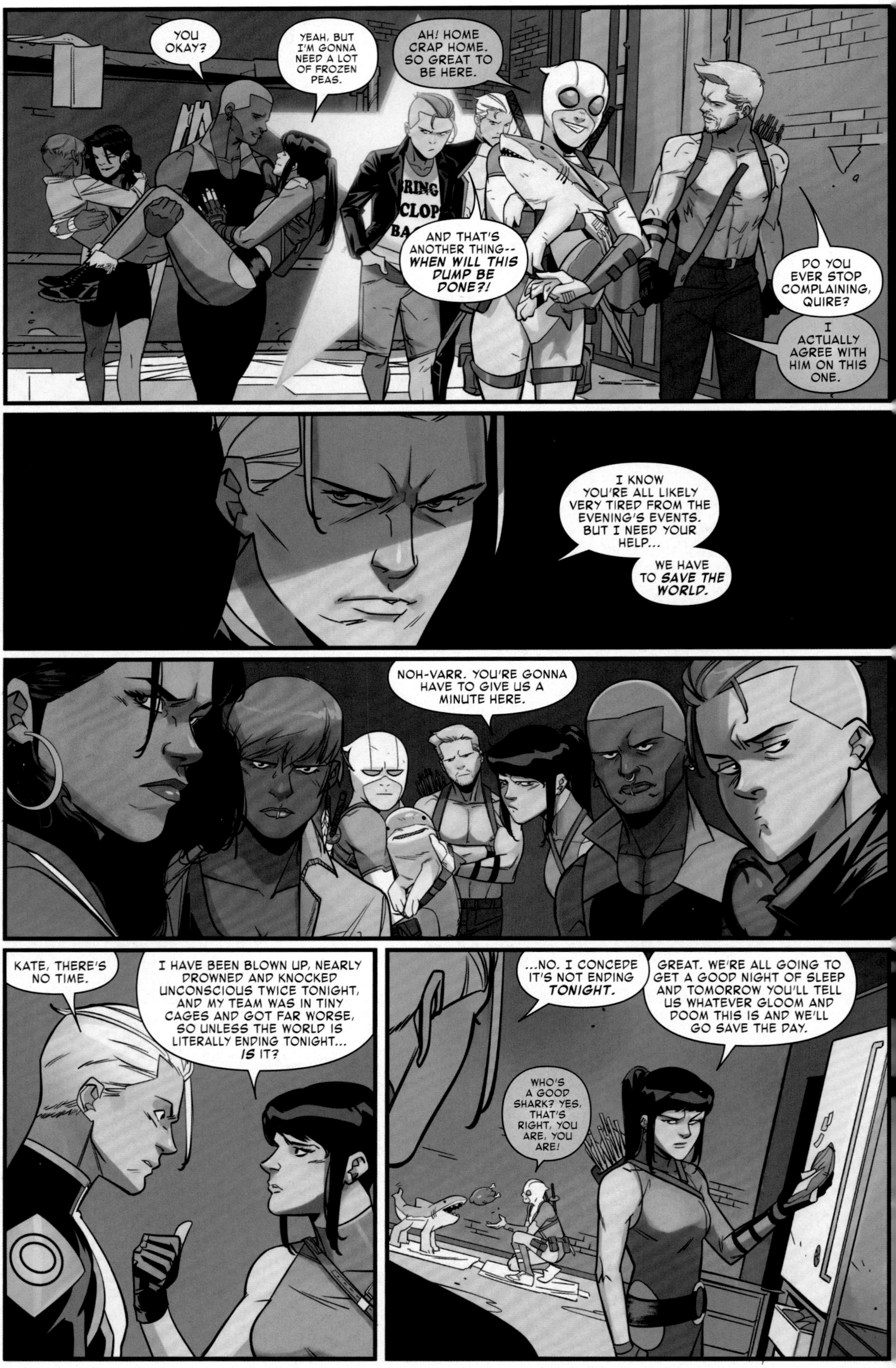
YOU OKAY?
YEAH, BUT I'M GONNA NEED A LOT OF FROZEN PEAS.
AH! HOME CRAP HOME. SO GREAT TO BE HERE.
AND THAT'S ANOTHER THING-- WHEN WILL THIS DUMP BE DONE?!
BRING CLOP BA
DO YOU EVER STOP COMPLAINING, QUIRE?
I ACTUALLY AGREE WITH HIM ON THIS ONE.
I KNOW YOU'RE ALL LIKELY VERY TIRED FROM THE EVENING'S EVENTS. BUT I NEED YOUR HELP...
WE HAVE TO SAVE THE WORLD.
NOH-VARR. YOU'RE GONNA HAVE TO GIVE US A MINUTE HERE.
KATE, THERE'S NO TIME.
I HAVE BEEN BLOWN UP, NEARLY DROWNED AND KNOCKED UNCONSCIOUS TWICE TONIGHT, AND MY TEAM WAS IN TINY CAGES AND GOT FAR WORSE, SO UNLESS THE WORLD IS LITERALLY ENDING TONIGHT... IS IT?
...NO. I CONCEDE IT'S NOT ENDING TONIGHT.
GREAT. WE'RE ALL GOING TO GET A GOOD NIGHT OF SLEEP AND TOMORROW YOU'LL TELL US WHATEVER GLOOM AND DOOM THIS IS AND WE'LL GO SAVE THE DAY.
WHO'S A GOOD SHARK? YES, THAT'S RIGHT, YOU ARE, YOU ARE!

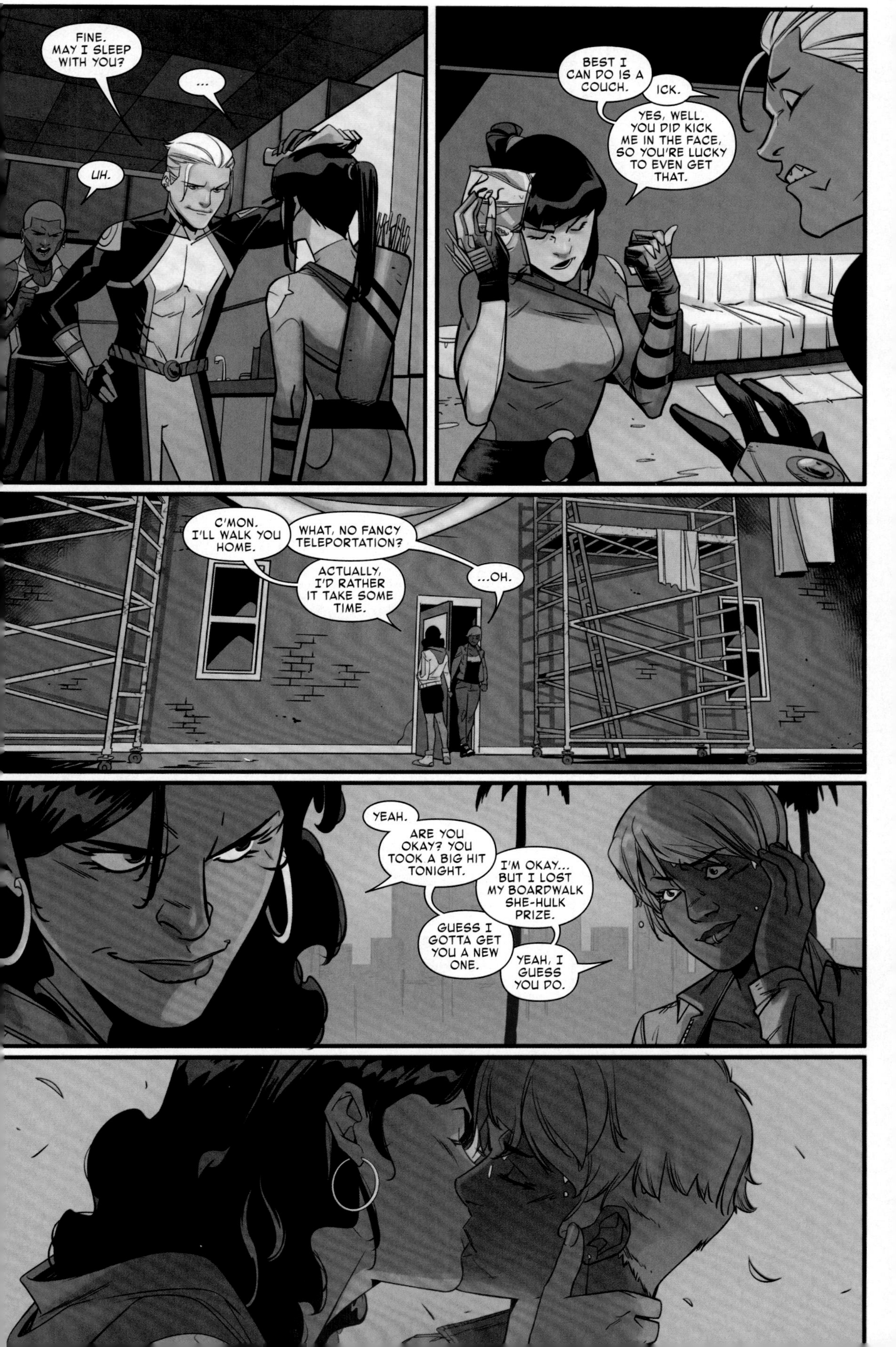
FINE. MAY I SLEEP WITH YOU?
...
UH.
BEST I CAN DO IS A COUCH.
ICK.
YES, WELL. YOU DID KICK ME IN THE FACE, SO YOU'RE LUCKY TO EVEN GET THAT.
C'MON. I'LL WALK YOU HOME.
WHAT, NO FANCY TELEPORTATION?
ACTUALLY, I'D RATHER IT TAKE SOME TIME.
...OH.
YEAH.
ARE YOU OKAY? YOU TOOK A BIG HIT TONIGHT.
I'M OKAY... BUT I LOST MY BOARDWALK SHE-HULK PRIZE.
GUESS I GOTTA GET YOU A NEW ONE.
YEAH, I GUESS YOU DO.

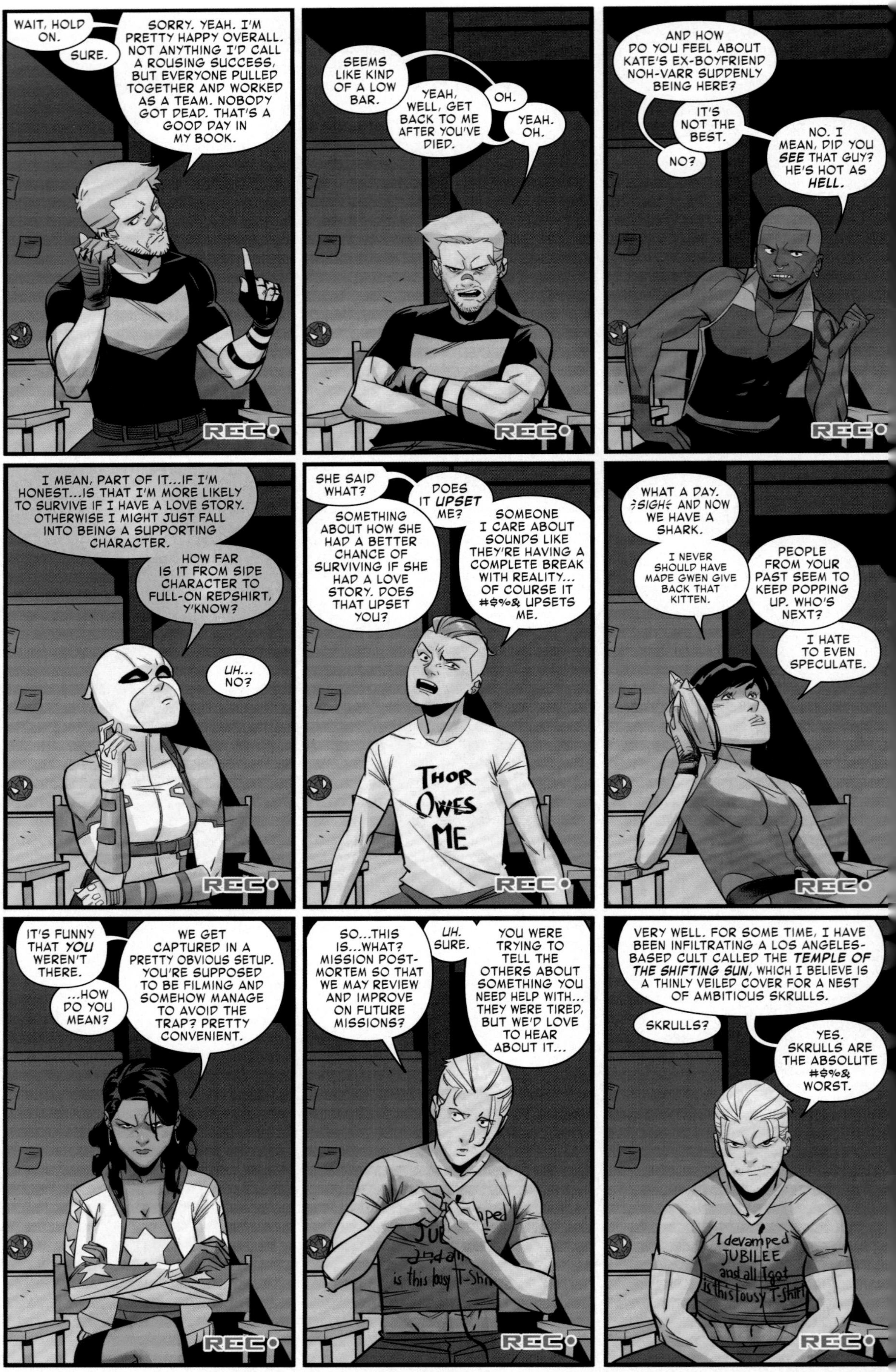
WAIT, HOLD ON.
SORRY. YEAH. I'M PRETTY HAPPY OVERALL. NOT ANYTHING I'D CALL A ROUSING SUCCESS, BUT EVERYONE PULLED TOGETHER AND WORKED AS A TEAM. NOBODY GOT DEAD. THAT'S A GOOD DAY IN MY BOOK.
SURE.
REC
SEEMS LIKE KIND OF A LOW BAR.
YEAH, WELL, GET BACK TO ME AFTER YOU'VE DIED.
OH.
YEAH. OH.
REC
AND HOW DO YOU FEEL ABOUT KATE'S EX-BOYFRIEND NOH-VARR SUDDENLY BEING HERE?
IT'S NOT THE BEST.
NO?
NO. I MEAN, DID YOU SEE THAT GUY? HE'S HOT AS HELL.
REC
I MEAN, PART OF IT...IF I'M HONEST...IS THAT I'M MORE LIKELY TO SURVIVE IF I HAVE A LOVE STORY. OTHERWISE I MIGHT JUST FALL INTO BEING A SUPPORTING CHARACTER.
HOW FAR IS IT FROM SIDE CHARACTER TO FULL-ON REDSHIRT, Y'KNOW?
UH... NO?
REC
SHE SAID WHAT?
DOES IT UPSET ME?
SOMETHING ABOUT HOW SHE HAD A BETTER CHANCE OF SURVIVING IF SHE HAD A LOVE STORY. DOES THAT UPSET YOU?
SOMEONE I CARE ABOUT SOUNDS LIKE THEY'RE HAVING A COMPLETE BREAK WITH REALITY... OF COURSE IT #$%& UPSETS ME.
THOR OWES ME
REC
WHAT A DAY. *SIGH* AND NOW WE HAVE A SHARK.
I NEVER SHOULD HAVE MADE GWEN GIVE BACK THAT KITTEN.
PEOPLE FROM YOUR PAST SEEM TO KEEP POPPING UP. WHO'S NEXT?
I HATE TO EVEN SPECULATE.
REC
IT'S FUNNY THAT YOU WEREN'T THERE.
...HOW DO YOU MEAN?
WE GET CAPTURED IN A PRETTY OBVIOUS SETUP. YOU'RE SUPPOSED TO BE FILMING AND SOMEHOW MANAGE TO AVOID THE TRAP? PRETTY CONVENIENT.
REC
SO...THIS IS...WHAT? MISSION POST-MORTEM SO THAT WE MAY REVIEW AND IMPROVE ON FUTURE MISSIONS?
UH. SURE.
YOU WERE TRYING TO TELL THE OTHERS ABOUT SOMETHING YOU NEED HELP WITH... THEY WERE TIRED, BUT WE'D LOVE TO HEAR ABOUT IT...
is this lousy T-Shirt
REC
VERY WELL. FOR SOME TIME, I HAVE BEEN INFILTRATING A LOS ANGELES-BASED CULT CALLED THE TEMPLE OF THE SHIFTING SUN, WHICH I BELIEVE IS A THINLY VEILED COVER FOR A NEST OF AMBITIOUS SKRULLS.
SKRULLS?
YES. SKRULLS ARE THE ABSOLUTE #$%& WORST.
I devamped JUBILEE and all I got is this lousy T-Shirt
REC

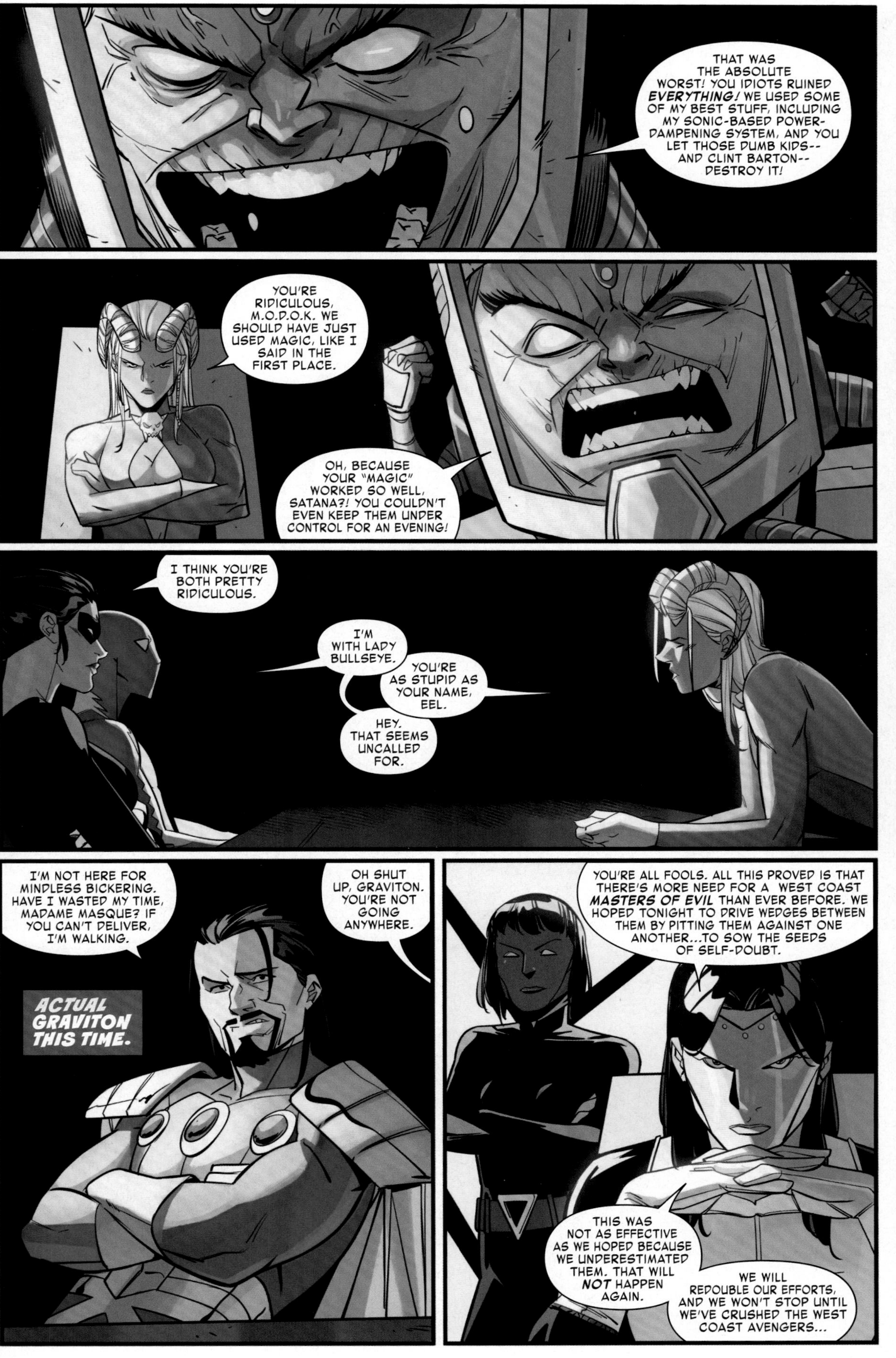
THAT WAS THE ABSOLUTE WORST! YOU IDIOTS RUINED *EVERYTHING!* WE USED SOME OF MY BEST STUFF, INCLUDING MY SONIC-BASED POWER-DAMPENING SYSTEM, AND YOU LET THOSE DUMB KIDS-- AND CLINT BARTON-- DESTROY IT!
YOU'RE RIDICULOUS, M.O.D.O.K. WE SHOULD HAVE JUST USED MAGIC, LIKE I SAID IN THE FIRST PLACE.
OH, BECAUSE YOUR "MAGIC" WORKED SO WELL, SATANA?! YOU COULDN'T EVEN KEEP THEM UNDER CONTROL FOR AN EVENING!
I THINK YOU'RE BOTH PRETTY RIDICULOUS.
I'M WITH LADY BULLSEYE.
YOU'RE AS STUPID AS YOUR NAME, EEL.
HEY. THAT SEEMS UNCALLED FOR.
I'M NOT HERE FOR MINDLESS BICKERING. HAVE I WASTED MY TIME, MADAME MASQUE? IF YOU CAN'T DELIVER, I'M WALKING.
OH SHUT UP, GRAVITON. YOU'RE NOT GOING ANYWHERE.
ACTUAL GRAVITON THIS TIME.
YOU'RE ALL FOOLS. ALL THIS PROVED IS THAT THERE'S MORE NEED FOR A WEST COAST *MASTERS OF EVIL* THAN EVER BEFORE. WE HOPED TONIGHT TO DRIVE WEDGES BETWEEN THEM BY PITTING THEM AGAINST ONE ANOTHER...TO SOW THE SEEDS OF SELF-DOUBT.
THIS WAS NOT AS EFFECTIVE AS WE HOPED BECAUSE WE UNDERESTIMATED THEM. THAT WILL *NOT* HAPPEN AGAIN.
WE WILL REDOUBLE OUR EFFORTS, AND WE WON'T STOP UNTIL WE'VE CRUSHED THE WEST COAST AVENGERS...

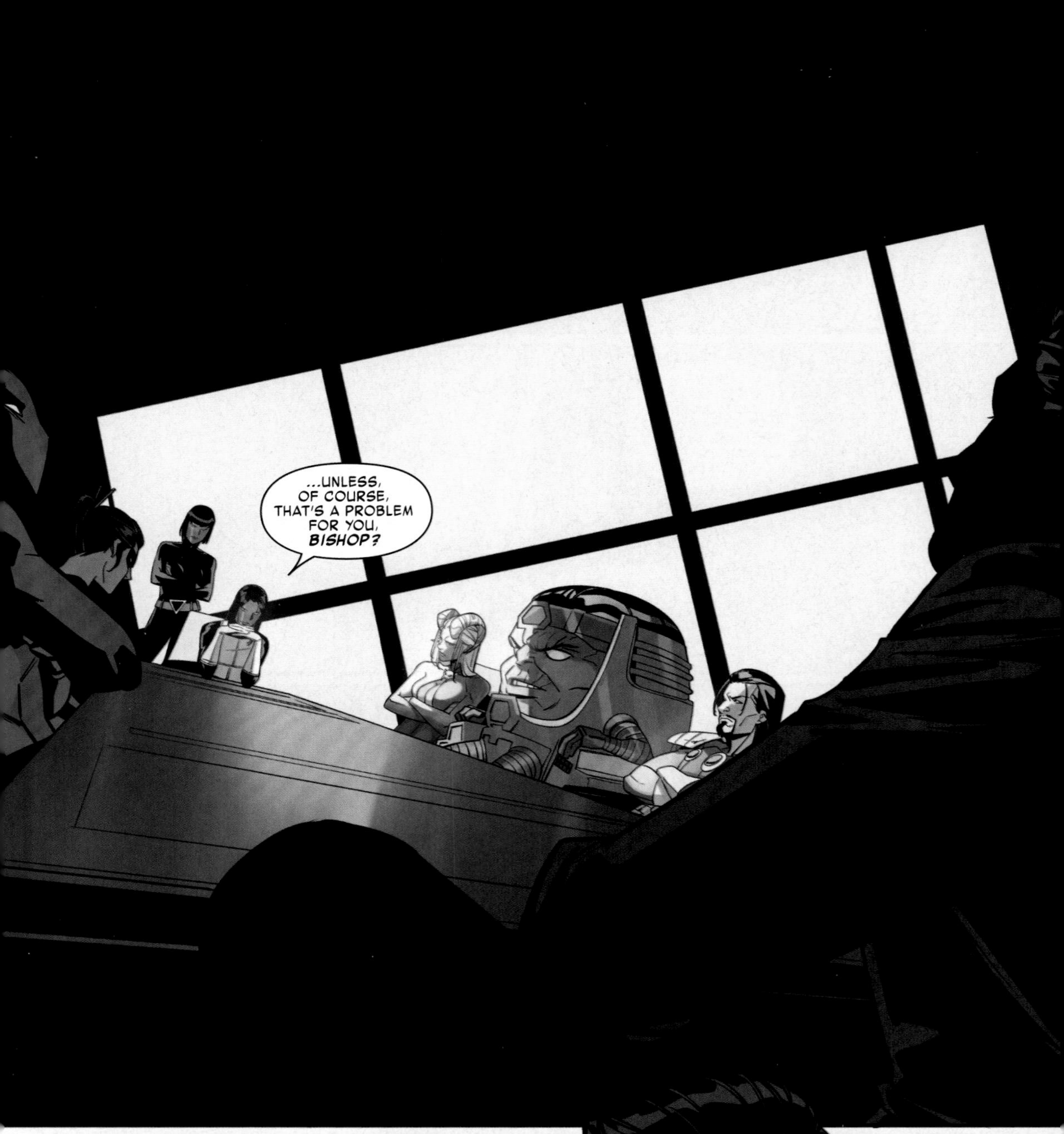
...UNLESS, OF COURSE, THAT'S A PROBLEM FOR YOU, BISHOP?

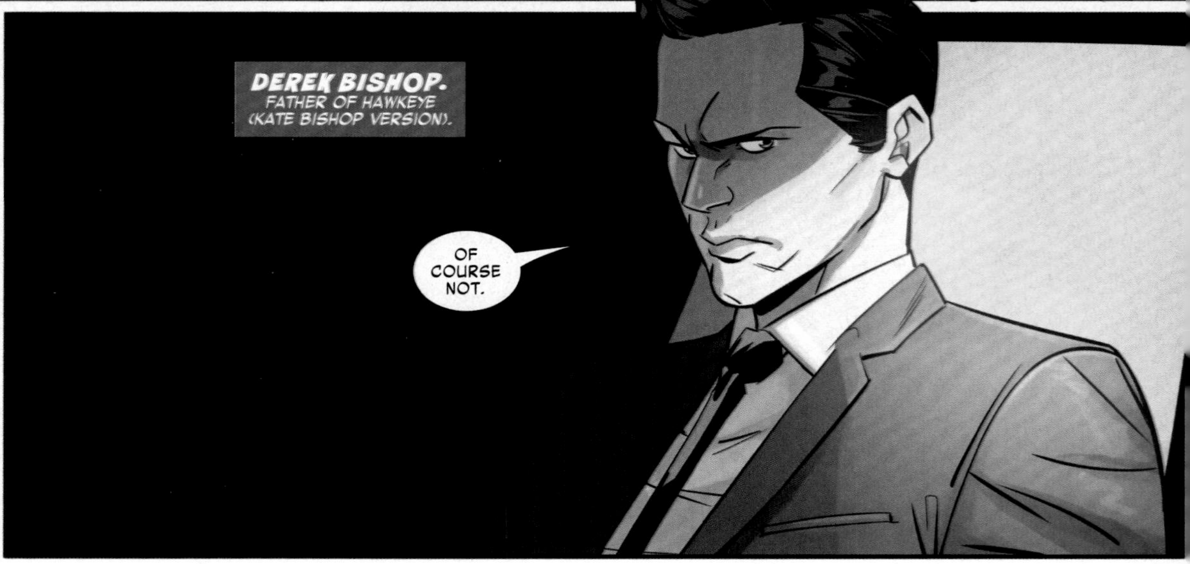
DEREK BISHOP.
FATHER OF HAWKEYE (KATE BISHOP VERSION).
OF COURSE NOT.

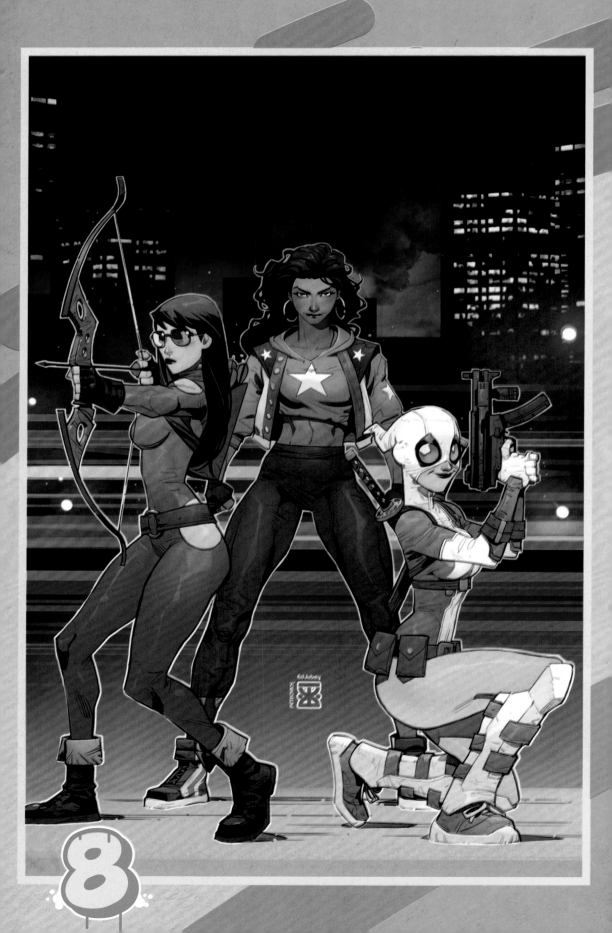

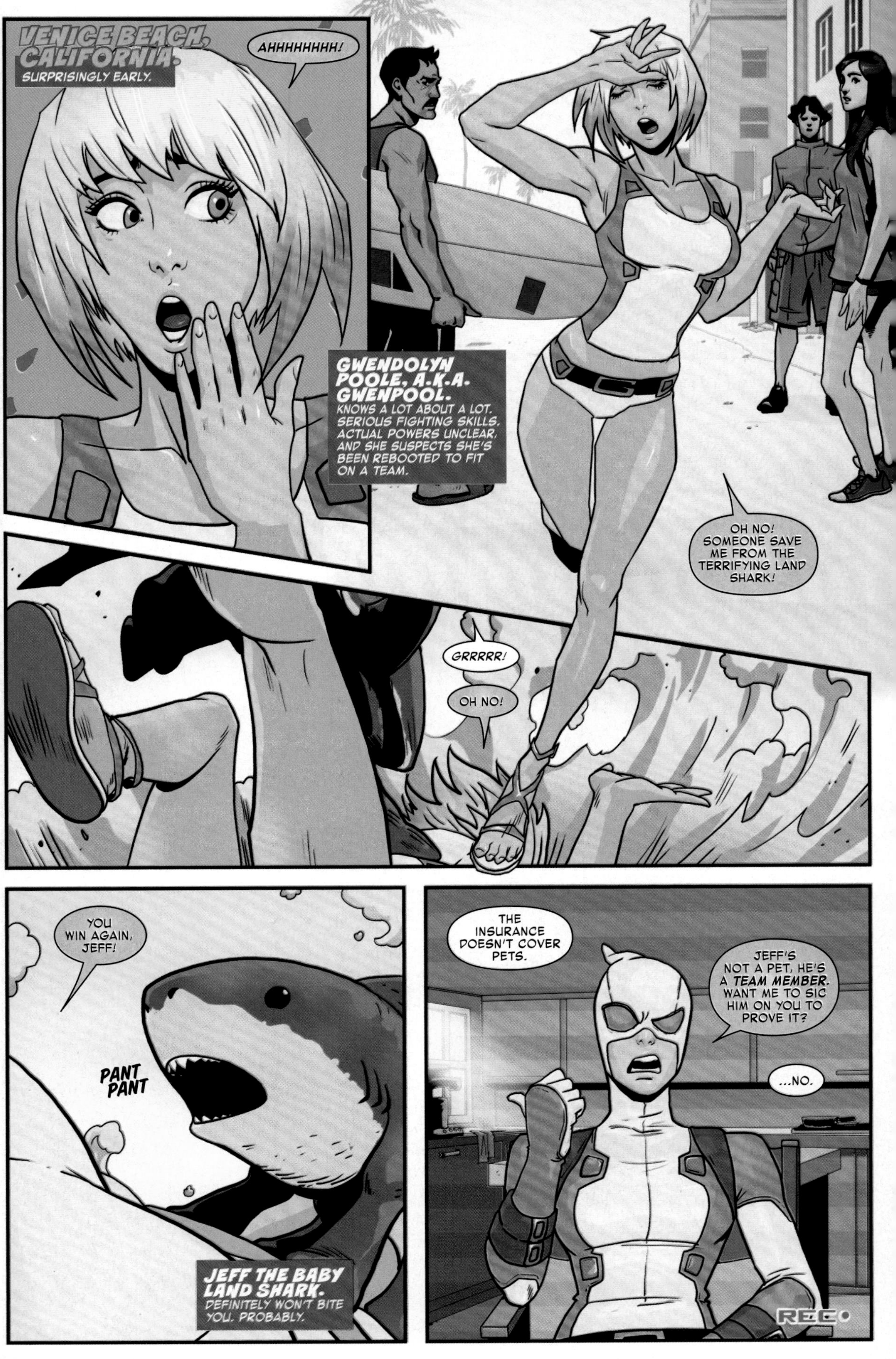
VENICE BEACH, CALIFORNIA.
SURPRISINGLY EARLY.
AHHHHHHHHH!
GWENDOLYN POOLE, A.K.A. GWENPOOL.
KNOWS A LOT ABOUT A LOT. SERIOUS FIGHTING SKILLS. ACTUAL POWERS UNCLEAR, AND SHE SUSPECTS SHE'S BEEN REBOOTED TO FIT ON A TEAM.
OH NO! SOMEONE SAVE ME FROM THE TERRIFYING LAND SHARK!
GRRRRR!
OH NO!
YOU WIN AGAIN, JEFF!
PANT PANT
JEFF THE BABY LAND SHARK.
DEFINITELY WON'T BITE YOU. PROBABLY.
THE INSURANCE DOESN'T COVER PETS.
JEFF'S NOT A PET, HE'S A TEAM MEMBER. WANT ME TO SIC HIM ON YOU TO PROVE IT?
...NO.
REC

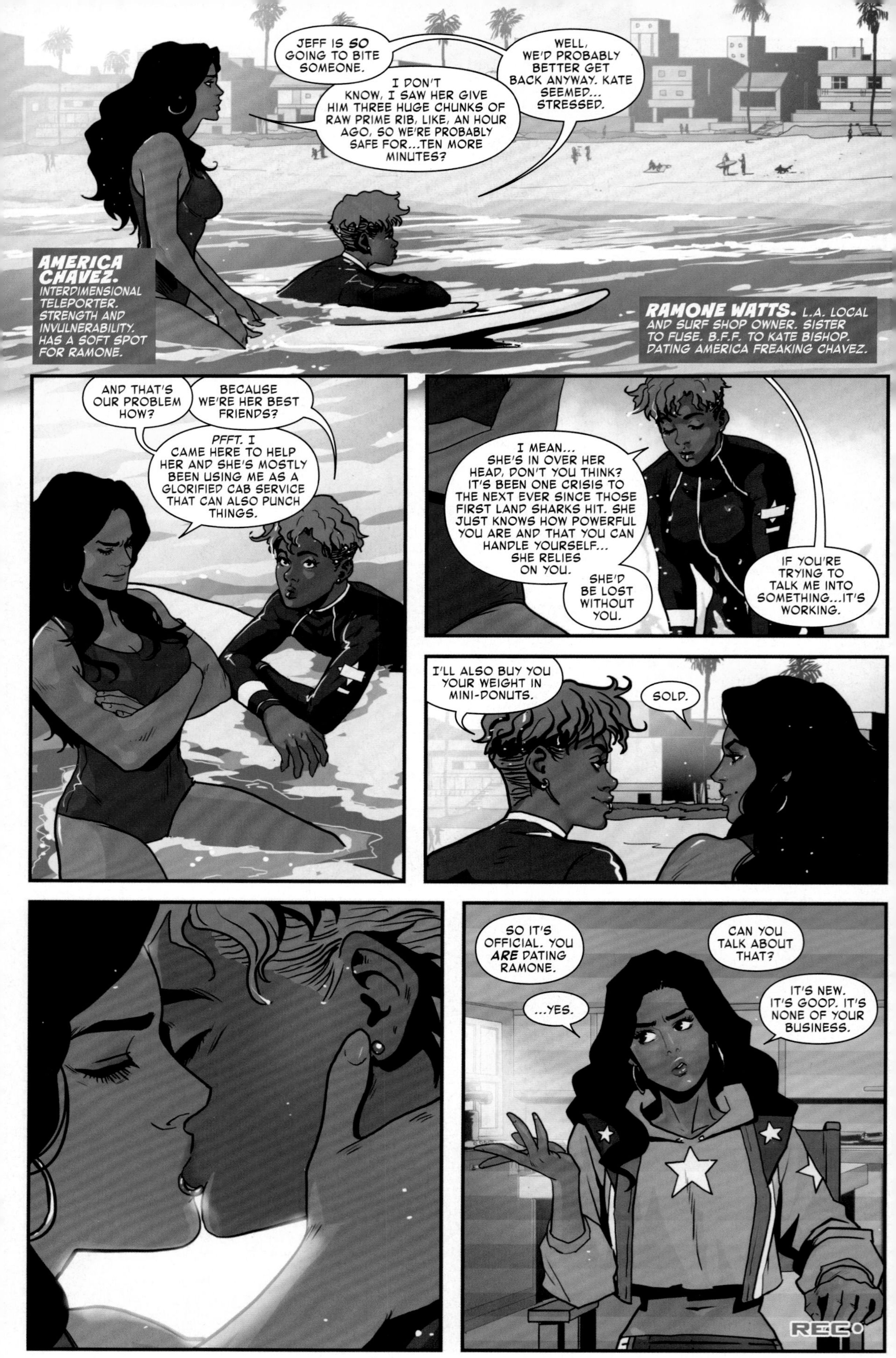
JEFF IS **SO** GOING TO BITE SOMEONE.
I DON'T KNOW, I SAW HER GIVE HIM THREE HUGE CHUNKS OF RAW PRIME RIB, LIKE, AN HOUR AGO, SO WE'RE PROBABLY SAFE FOR...TEN MORE MINUTES?
WELL, WE'D PROBABLY BETTER GET BACK ANYWAY. KATE SEEMED... STRESSED.
AMERICA CHAVEZ. INTERDIMENSIONAL TELEPORTER. STRENGTH AND INVULNERABILITY. HAS A SOFT SPOT FOR RAMONE.
RAMONE WATTS. L.A. LOCAL AND SURF SHOP OWNER. SISTER TO FUSE. B.F.F. TO KATE BISHOP. DATING AMERICA FREAKING CHAVEZ.
AND THAT'S OUR PROBLEM HOW?
BECAUSE WE'RE HER BEST FRIENDS?
PFFT. I CAME HERE TO HELP HER AND SHE'S MOSTLY BEEN USING ME AS A GLORIFIED CAB SERVICE THAT CAN ALSO PUNCH THINGS.
I MEAN... SHE'S IN OVER HER HEAD, DON'T YOU THINK? IT'S BEEN ONE CRISIS TO THE NEXT EVER SINCE THOSE FIRST LAND SHARKS HIT. SHE JUST KNOWS HOW POWERFUL YOU ARE AND THAT YOU CAN HANDLE YOURSELF... SHE RELIES ON YOU.
SHE'D BE LOST WITHOUT YOU.
IF YOU'RE TRYING TO TALK ME INTO SOMETHING...IT'S WORKING.
I'LL ALSO BUY YOU YOUR WEIGHT IN MINI-DONUTS.
SOLD.
SO IT'S OFFICIAL. YOU **ARE** DATING RAMONE.
...YES.
CAN YOU TALK ABOUT THAT?
IT'S NEW. IT'S GOOD. IT'S NONE OF YOUR BUSINESS.
REC

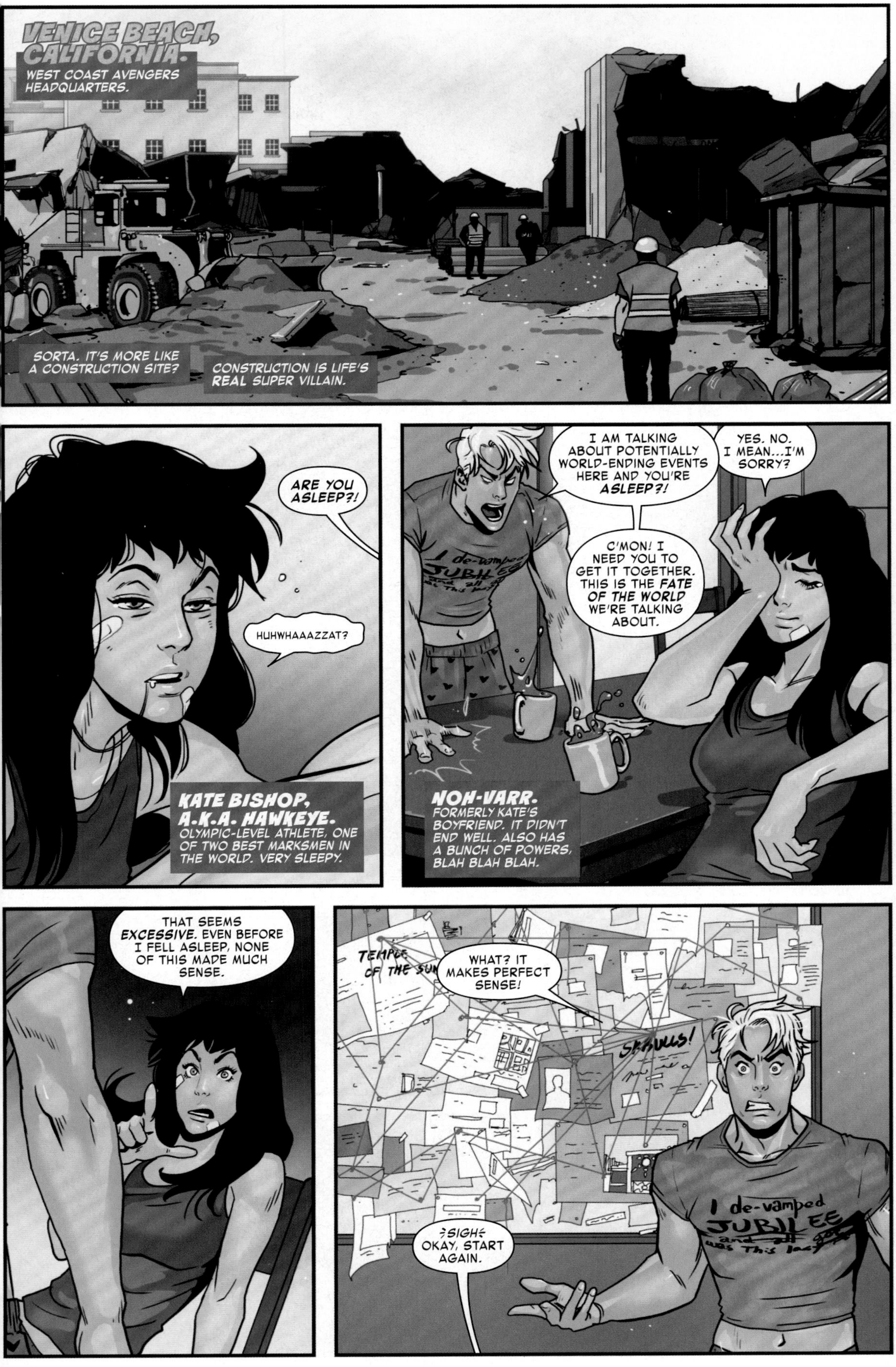
VENICE BEACH, CALIFORNIA.
WEST COAST AVENGERS HEADQUARTERS.
SORTA. IT'S MORE LIKE A CONSTRUCTION SITE?
CONSTRUCTION IS LIFE'S REAL SUPER VILLAIN.
ARE YOU ASLEEP?!
HUHWHAAAZZAT?
KATE BISHOP, A.K.A. HAWKEYE.
OLYMPIC-LEVEL ATHLETE, ONE OF TWO BEST MARKSMEN IN THE WORLD. VERY SLEEPY.
I AM TALKING ABOUT POTENTIALLY WORLD-ENDING EVENTS HERE AND YOU'RE ASLEEP?!
YES. NO. I MEAN...I'M SORRY?
C'MON! I NEED YOU TO GET IT TOGETHER. THIS IS THE FATE OF THE WORLD WE'RE TALKING ABOUT.
NOH-VARR.
FORMERLY KATE'S BOYFRIEND. IT DIDN'T END WELL. ALSO HAS A BUNCH OF POWERS, BLAH BLAH BLAH.
THAT SEEMS EXCESSIVE. EVEN BEFORE I FELL ASLEEP, NONE OF THIS MADE MUCH SENSE.
WHAT? IT MAKES PERFECT SENSE!
SKRULLS!
I de-vamped JUBILEE
SIGH OKAY, START AGAIN.

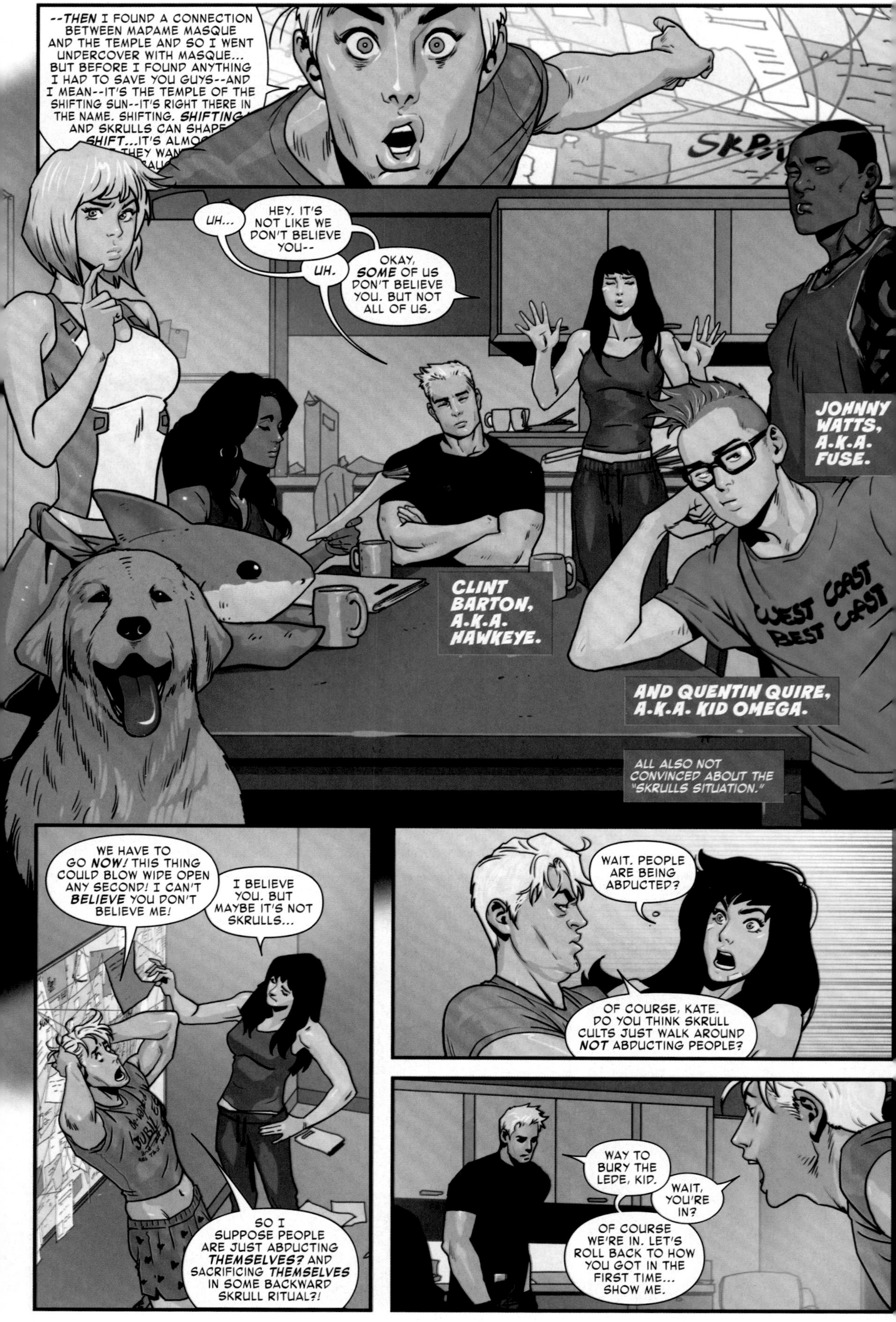

--THEN I FOUND A CONNECTION BETWEEN MADAME MASQUE AND THE TEMPLE AND SO I WENT UNDERCOVER WITH MASQUE... BUT BEFORE I FOUND ANYTHING I HAD TO SAVE YOU GUYS--AND I MEAN--IT'S THE TEMPLE OF THE SHIFTING SUN--IT'S RIGHT THERE IN THE NAME. SHIFTING. SHIFTING! AND SKRULLS CAN SHAPE SHIFT...IT'S ALMO
UH...
HEY. IT'S NOT LIKE WE DON'T BELIEVE YOU--
UH.
OKAY, SOME OF US DON'T BELIEVE YOU. BUT NOT ALL OF US.
JOHNNY WATTS, A.K.A. FUSE.
CLINT BARTON, A.K.A. HAWKEYE.
AND QUENTIN QUIRE, A.K.A. KID OMEGA.
ALL ALSO NOT CONVINCED ABOUT THE "SKRULLS SITUATION."
WEST COAST BEST COAST
WE HAVE TO GO NOW! THIS THING COULD BLOW WIDE OPEN ANY SECOND! I CAN'T BELIEVE YOU DON'T BELIEVE ME!
I BELIEVE YOU. BUT MAYBE IT'S NOT SKRULLS...
SO I SUPPOSE PEOPLE ARE JUST ABDUCTING THEMSELVES? AND SACRIFICING THEMSELVES IN SOME BACKWARD SKRULL RITUAL?!
WAIT. PEOPLE ARE BEING ABDUCTED?
OF COURSE, KATE. DO YOU THINK SKRULL CULTS JUST WALK AROUND NOT ABDUCTING PEOPLE?
WAY TO BURY THE LEDE, KID.
WAIT, YOU'RE IN?
OF COURSE WE'RE IN. LET'S ROLL BACK TO HOW YOU GOT IN THE FIRST TIME... SHOW ME.

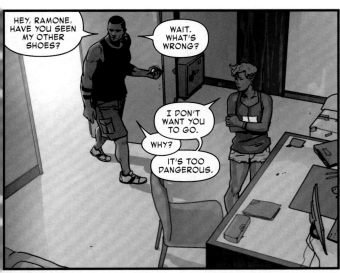

HEY, RAMONE, HAVE YOU SEEN MY OTHER SHOES?

WAIT. WHAT'S WRONG?

I DON'T WANT YOU TO GO.

WHY?

IT'S TOO DANGEROUS.

WHERE'S THIS COMING FROM? I'VE DONE STUFF WAY SCARIER THAN THIS BEFORE...IT'S PROBABLY NOT EVEN SKRULLS. PROBABLY JUST A BUNCH OF HOLLYWOOD SOCIAL CLIMBERS.

SEEING THIS HERO STUFF UP CLOSE LIKE I DID IN THAT STUPID FUN HOUSE OF HORRORS WAS TOO REAL, JOHNNY. YOU COULD REALLY DIE DOING THIS.

NOT GONNA HAPPEN.

OH, COME ON! THAT'S SO NOT A THING YOU'RE IN CONTROL OF!

KATE, AMERICA AND CLINT WON'T LET ANYTHING HAPPEN TO ME.

AND NOH-VARR?

HOPEFULLY IT WON'T COME DOWN TO HIM.

ANNNND YOU JUST JINXED YOURSELF, JOHNNY.

NEITHER OF US BELIEVES IN THAT, SIS, AND YOU KNOW IT!

YEAH... RIGHT.

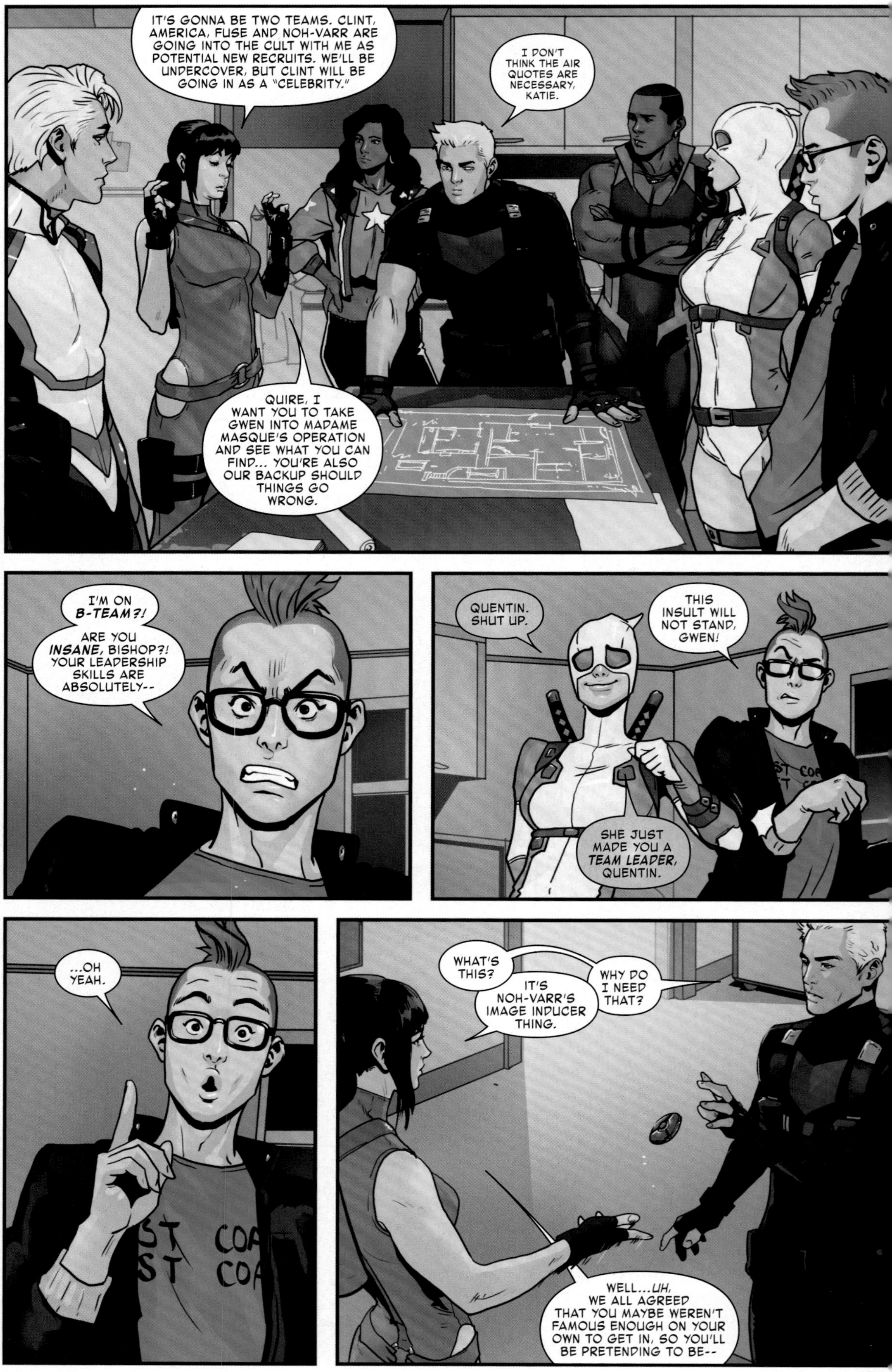
IT'S GONNA BE TWO TEAMS. CLINT, AMERICA, FUSE AND NOH-VARR ARE GOING INTO THE CULT WITH ME AS POTENTIAL NEW RECRUITS. WE'LL BE UNDERCOVER, BUT CLINT WILL BE GOING IN AS A "CELEBRITY."
I DON'T THINK THE AIR QUOTES ARE NECESSARY, KATIE.
QUIRE, I WANT YOU TO TAKE GWEN INTO MADAME MASQUE'S OPERATION AND SEE WHAT YOU CAN FIND... YOU'RE ALSO OUR BACKUP SHOULD THINGS GO WRONG.
I'M ON B-TEAM?!
ARE YOU INSANE, BISHOP?! YOUR LEADERSHIP SKILLS ARE ABSOLUTELY--
QUENTIN. SHUT UP.
THIS INSULT WILL NOT STAND, GWEN!
SHE JUST MADE YOU A TEAM LEADER, QUENTIN.
...OH YEAH.
WHAT'S THIS?
IT'S NOH-VARR'S IMAGE INDUCER THING.
WHY DO I NEED THAT?
WELL...UH, WE ALL AGREED THAT YOU MAYBE WEREN'T FAMOUS ENOUGH ON YOUR OWN TO GET IN, SO YOU'LL BE PRETENDING TO BE--

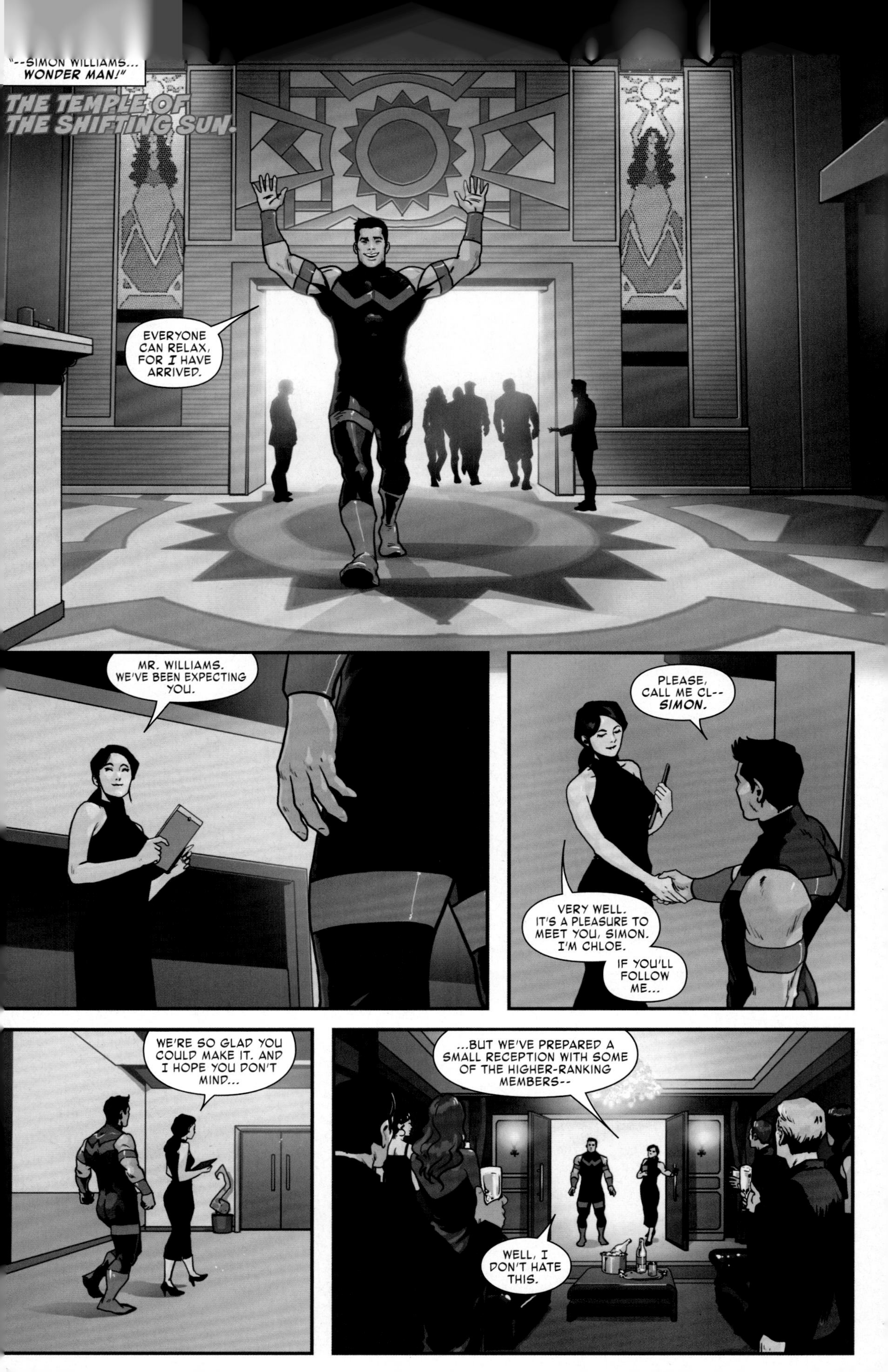
"--SIMON WILLIAMS... WONDER MAN!"
THE TEMPLE OF THE SHIFTING SUN.
EVERYONE CAN RELAX, FOR I HAVE ARRIVED.
MR. WILLIAMS. WE'VE BEEN EXPECTING YOU.
PLEASE, CALL ME CL-- SIMON.
VERY WELL. IT'S A PLEASURE TO MEET YOU, SIMON. I'M CHLOE.
IF YOU'LL FOLLOW ME...
WE'RE SO GLAD YOU COULD MAKE IT. AND I HOPE YOU DON'T MIND...
...BUT WE'VE PREPARED A SMALL RECEPTION WITH SOME OF THE HIGHER-RANKING MEMBERS--
WELL, I DON'T HATE THIS.

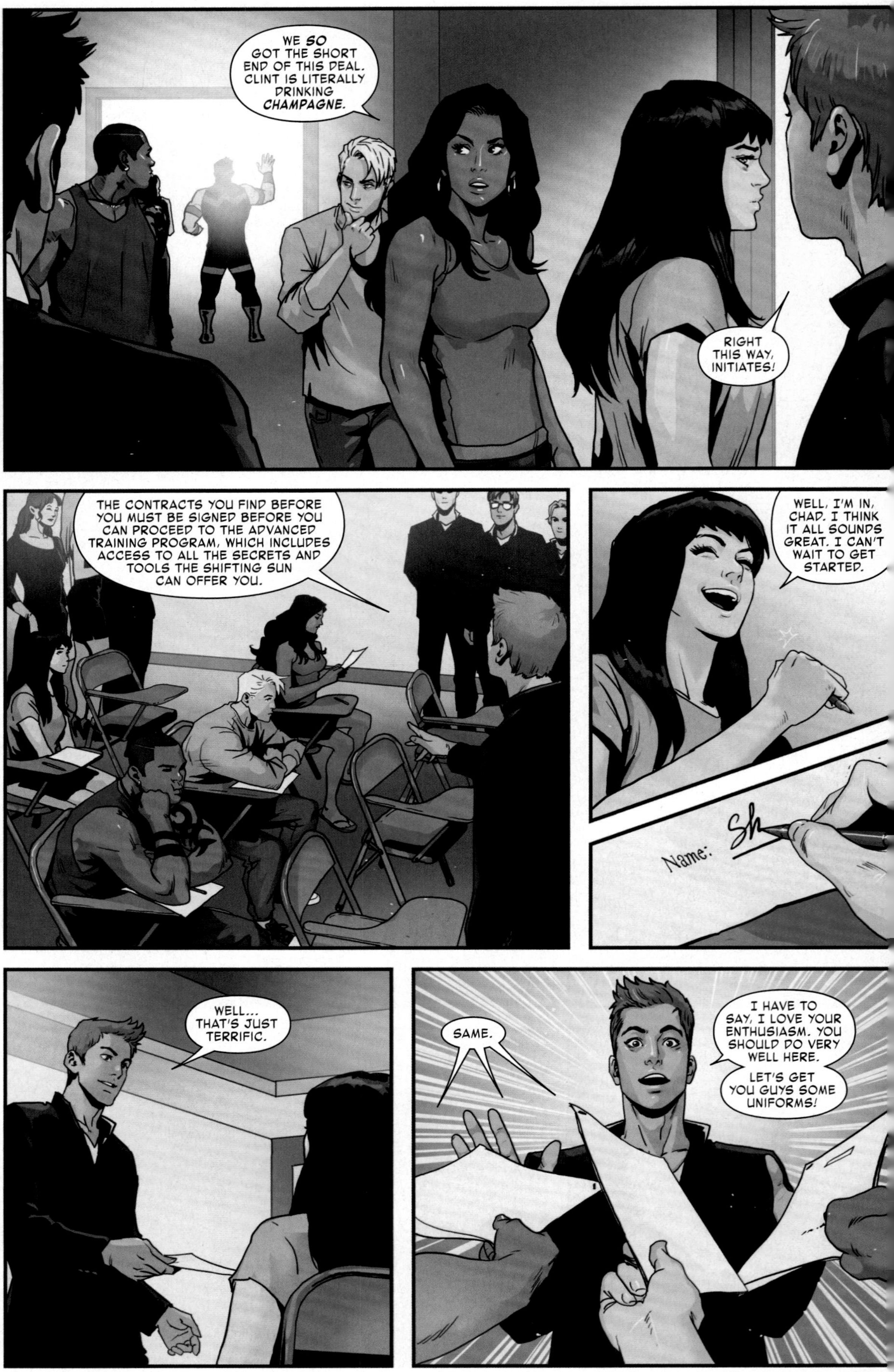
WE SO GOT THE SHORT END OF THIS DEAL. CLINT IS LITERALLY DRINKING CHAMPAGNE.
RIGHT THIS WAY, INITIATES!
THE CONTRACTS YOU FIND BEFORE YOU MUST BE SIGNED BEFORE YOU CAN PROCEED TO THE ADVANCED TRAINING PROGRAM, WHICH INCLUDES ACCESS TO ALL THE SECRETS AND TOOLS THE SHIFTING SUN CAN OFFER YOU.
WELL, I'M IN, CHAD. I THINK IT ALL SOUNDS GREAT. I CAN'T WAIT TO GET STARTED.
Name:
WELL... THAT'S JUST TERRIFIC.
SAME.
I HAVE TO SAY, I LOVE YOUR ENTHUSIASM. YOU SHOULD DO VERY WELL HERE.
LET'S GET YOU GUYS SOME UNIFORMS!

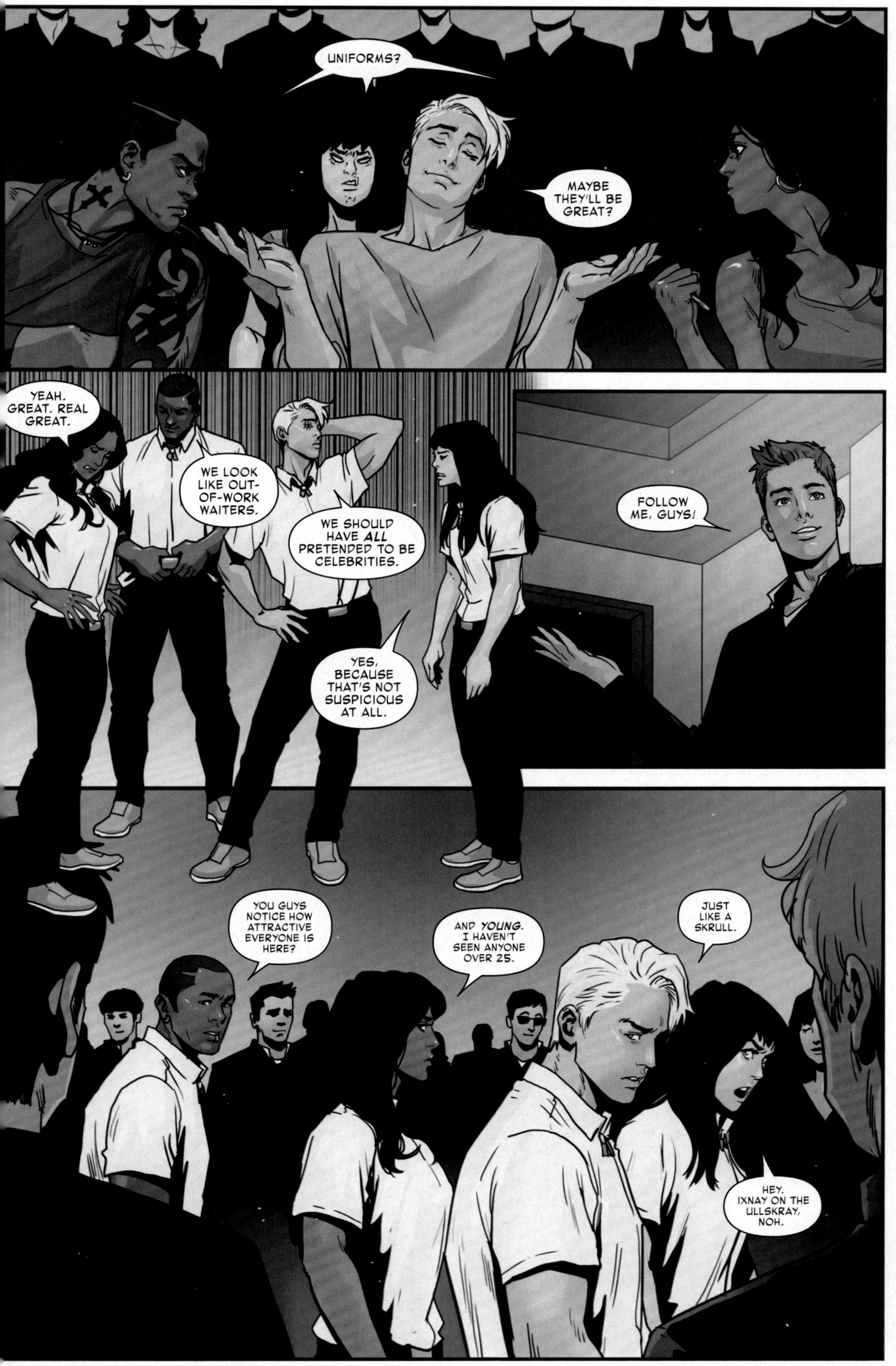
UNIFORMS?
MAYBE THEY'LL BE GREAT?
YEAH. GREAT. REAL GREAT.
WE LOOK LIKE OUT-OF-WORK WAITERS.
WE SHOULD HAVE ALL PRETENDED TO BE CELEBRITIES.
YES, BECAUSE THAT'S NOT SUSPICIOUS AT ALL.
FOLLOW ME, GUYS!
YOU GUYS NOTICE HOW ATTRACTIVE EVERYONE IS HERE?
AND YOUNG. I HAVEN'T SEEN ANYONE OVER 25.
JUST LIKE A SKRULL.
HEY. IXNAY ON THE ULLSKRAY, NOH.

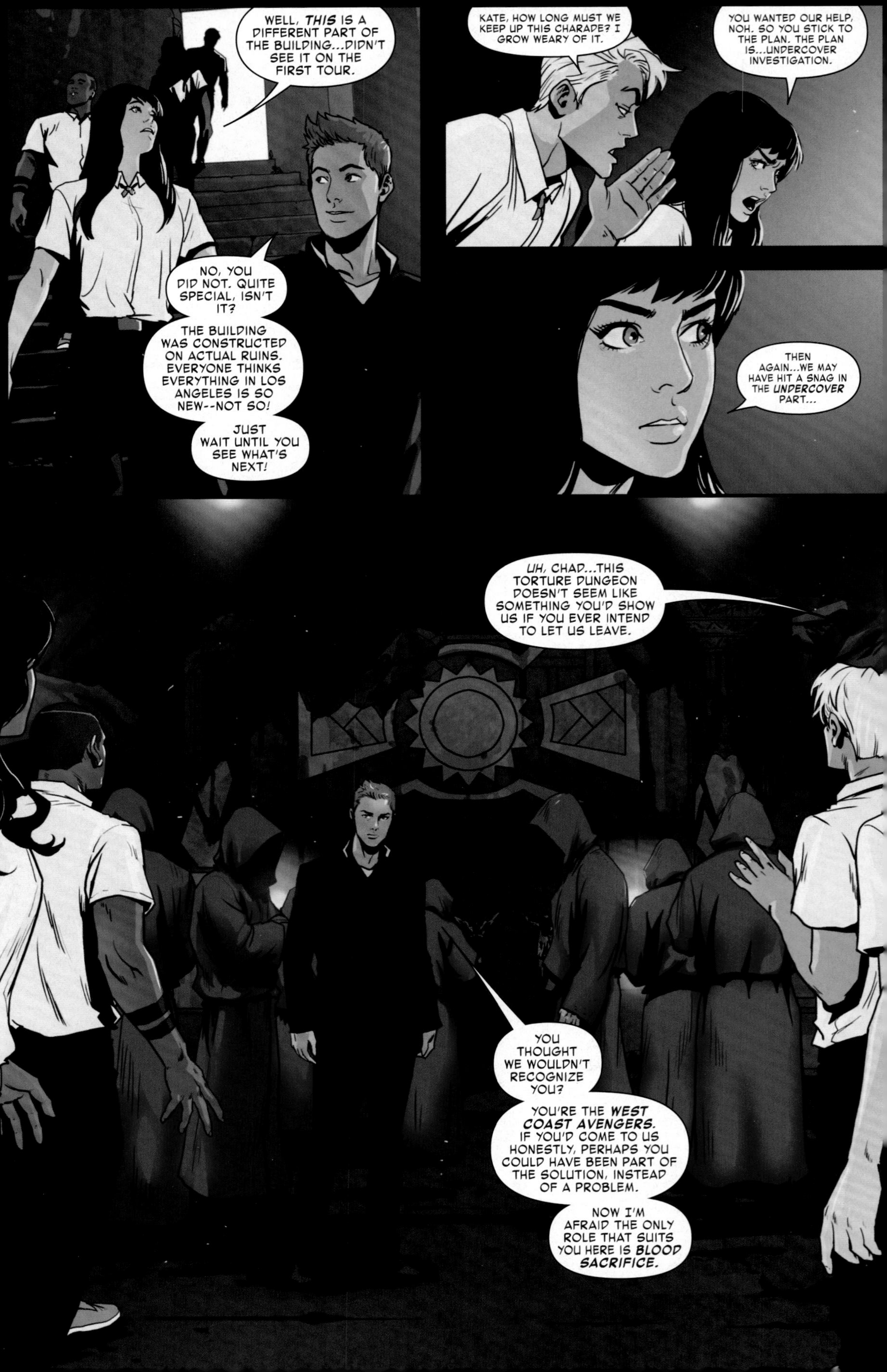

WELL, THIS IS A DIFFERENT PART OF THE BUILDING...DIDN'T SEE IT ON THE FIRST TOUR.
NO, YOU DID NOT. QUITE SPECIAL, ISN'T IT?
THE BUILDING WAS CONSTRUCTED ON ACTUAL RUINS. EVERYONE THINKS EVERYTHING IN LOS ANGELES IS SO NEW--NOT SO!
JUST WAIT UNTIL YOU SEE WHAT'S NEXT!
KATE, HOW LONG MUST WE KEEP UP THIS CHARADE? I GROW WEARY OF IT.
YOU WANTED OUR HELP, NOH. SO YOU STICK TO THE PLAN. THE PLAN IS...UNDERCOVER INVESTIGATION.
THEN AGAIN...WE MAY HAVE HIT A SNAG IN THE UNDERCOVER PART...
UH, CHAD...THIS TORTURE DUNGEON DOESN'T SEEM LIKE SOMETHING YOU'D SHOW US IF YOU EVER INTEND TO LET US LEAVE.
YOU THOUGHT WE WOULDN'T RECOGNIZE YOU?
YOU'RE THE WEST COAST AVENGERS. IF YOU'D COME TO US HONESTLY, PERHAPS YOU COULD HAVE BEEN PART OF THE SOLUTION, INSTEAD OF A PROBLEM.
NOW I'M AFRAID THE ONLY ROLE THAT SUITS YOU HERE IS BLOOD SACRIFICE.

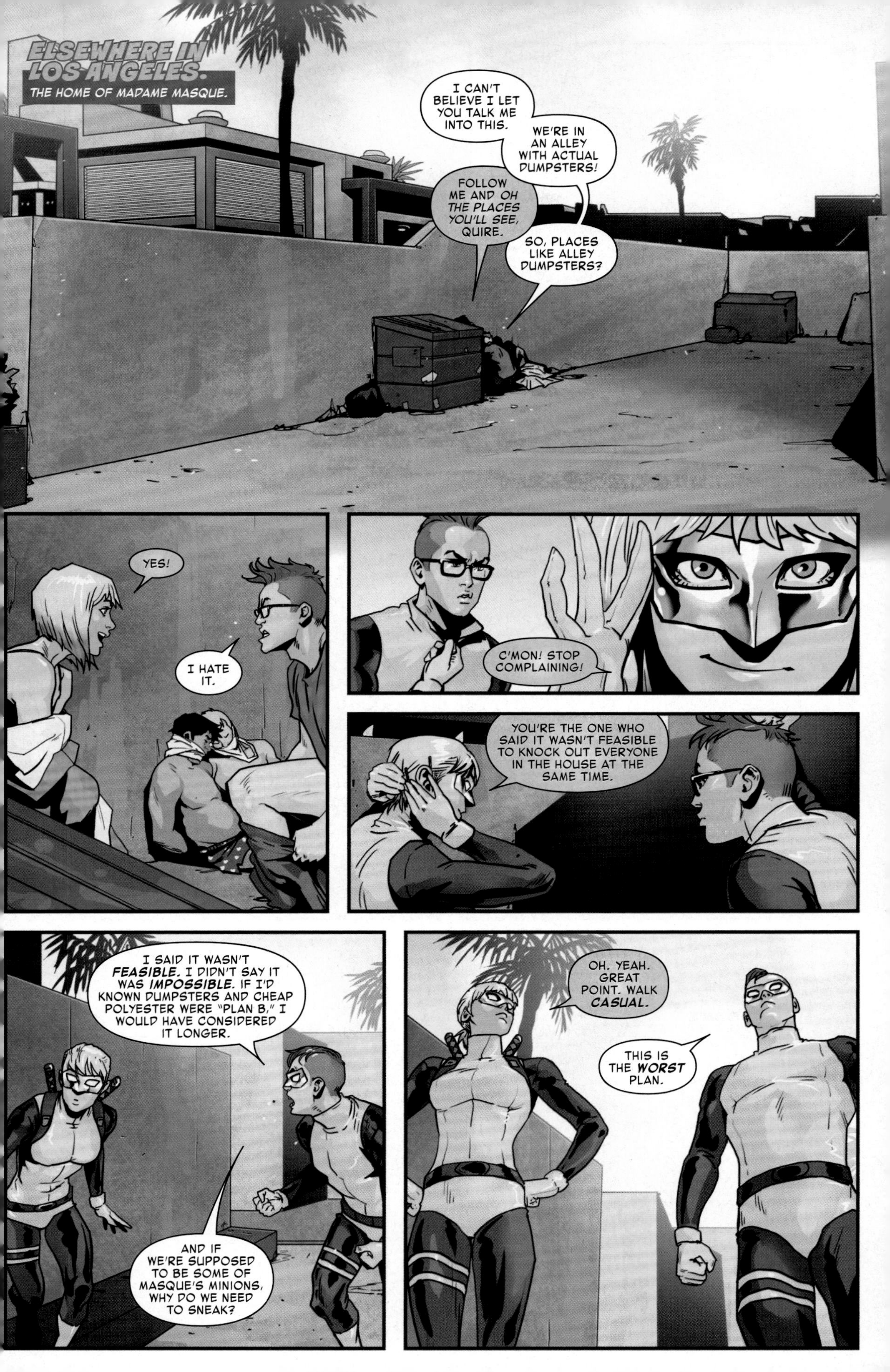
ELSEWHERE IN LOS ANGELES.
THE HOME OF MADAME MASQUE.
I CAN'T BELIEVE I LET YOU TALK ME INTO THIS.
WE'RE IN AN ALLEY WITH ACTUAL DUMPSTERS!
FOLLOW ME AND OH THE PLACES YOU'LL SEE, QUIRE.
SO, PLACES LIKE ALLEY DUMPSTERS?
YES!
I HATE IT.
C'MON! STOP COMPLAINING!
YOU'RE THE ONE WHO SAID IT WASN'T FEASIBLE TO KNOCK OUT EVERYONE IN THE HOUSE AT THE SAME TIME.
I SAID IT WASN'T FEASIBLE. I DIDN'T SAY IT WAS IMPOSSIBLE. IF I'D KNOWN DUMPSTERS AND CHEAP POLYESTER WERE "PLAN B," I WOULD HAVE CONSIDERED IT LONGER.
AND IF WE'RE SUPPOSED TO BE SOME OF MASQUE'S MINIONS, WHY DO WE NEED TO SNEAK?
OH. YEAH. GREAT POINT. WALK CASUAL.
THIS IS THE WORST PLAN.

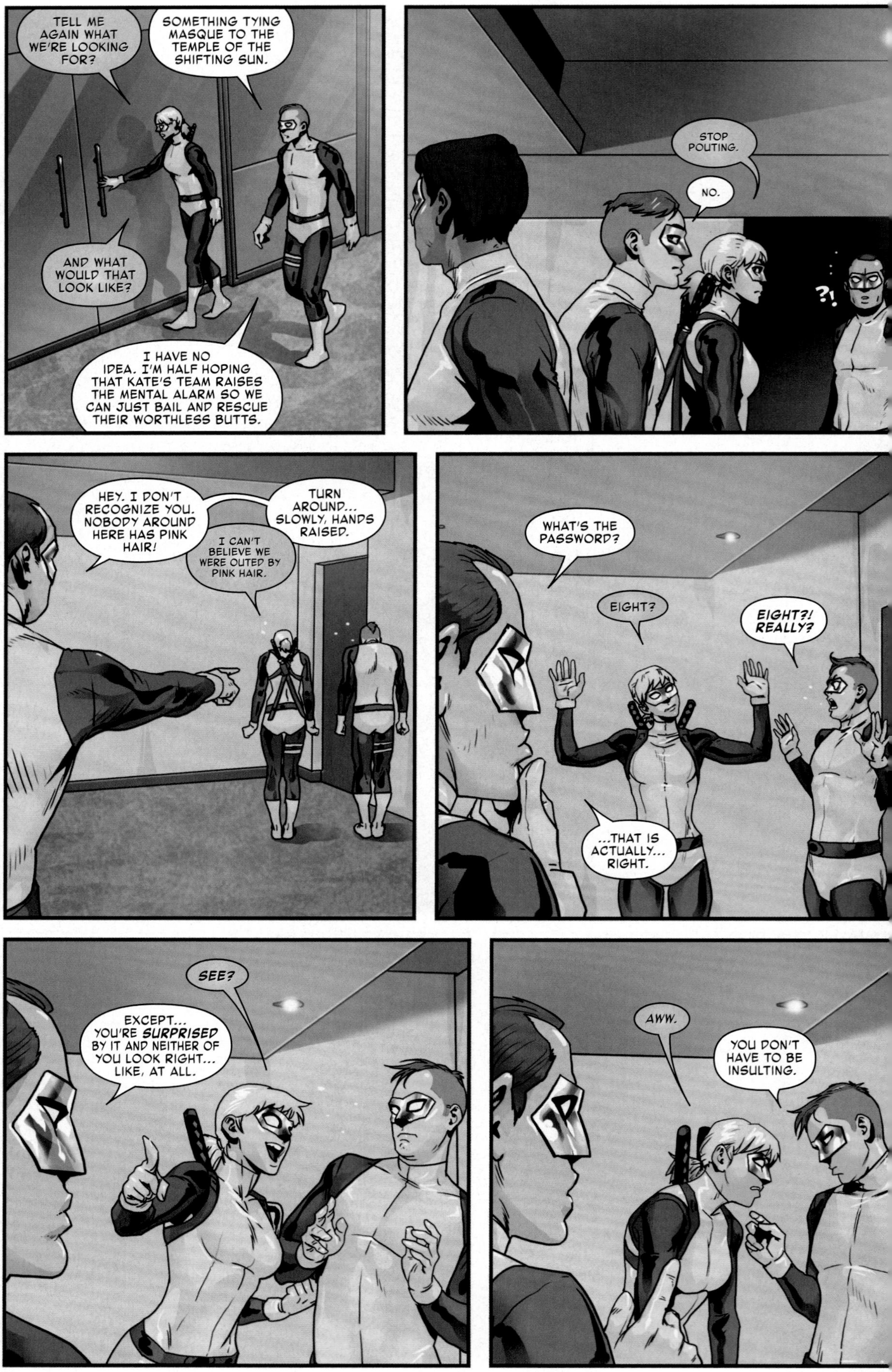
TELL ME AGAIN WHAT WE'RE LOOKING FOR?
SOMETHING TYING MASQUE TO THE TEMPLE OF THE SHIFTING SUN.
AND WHAT WOULD THAT LOOK LIKE?
I HAVE NO IDEA. I'M HALF HOPING THAT KATE'S TEAM RAISES THE MENTAL ALARM SO WE CAN JUST BAIL AND RESCUE THEIR WORTHLESS BUTTS.
STOP POUTING.
NO.
?!
HEY. I DON'T RECOGNIZE YOU. NOBODY AROUND HERE HAS PINK HAIR!
TURN AROUND... SLOWLY, HANDS RAISED.
I CAN'T BELIEVE WE WERE OUTED BY PINK HAIR.
WHAT'S THE PASSWORD?
EIGHT?
EIGHT?! REALLY?
...THAT IS ACTUALLY... RIGHT.
SEE?
EXCEPT... YOU'RE SURPRISED BY IT AND NEITHER OF YOU LOOK RIGHT... LIKE, AT ALL.
AWW.
YOU DON'T HAVE TO BE INSULTING.

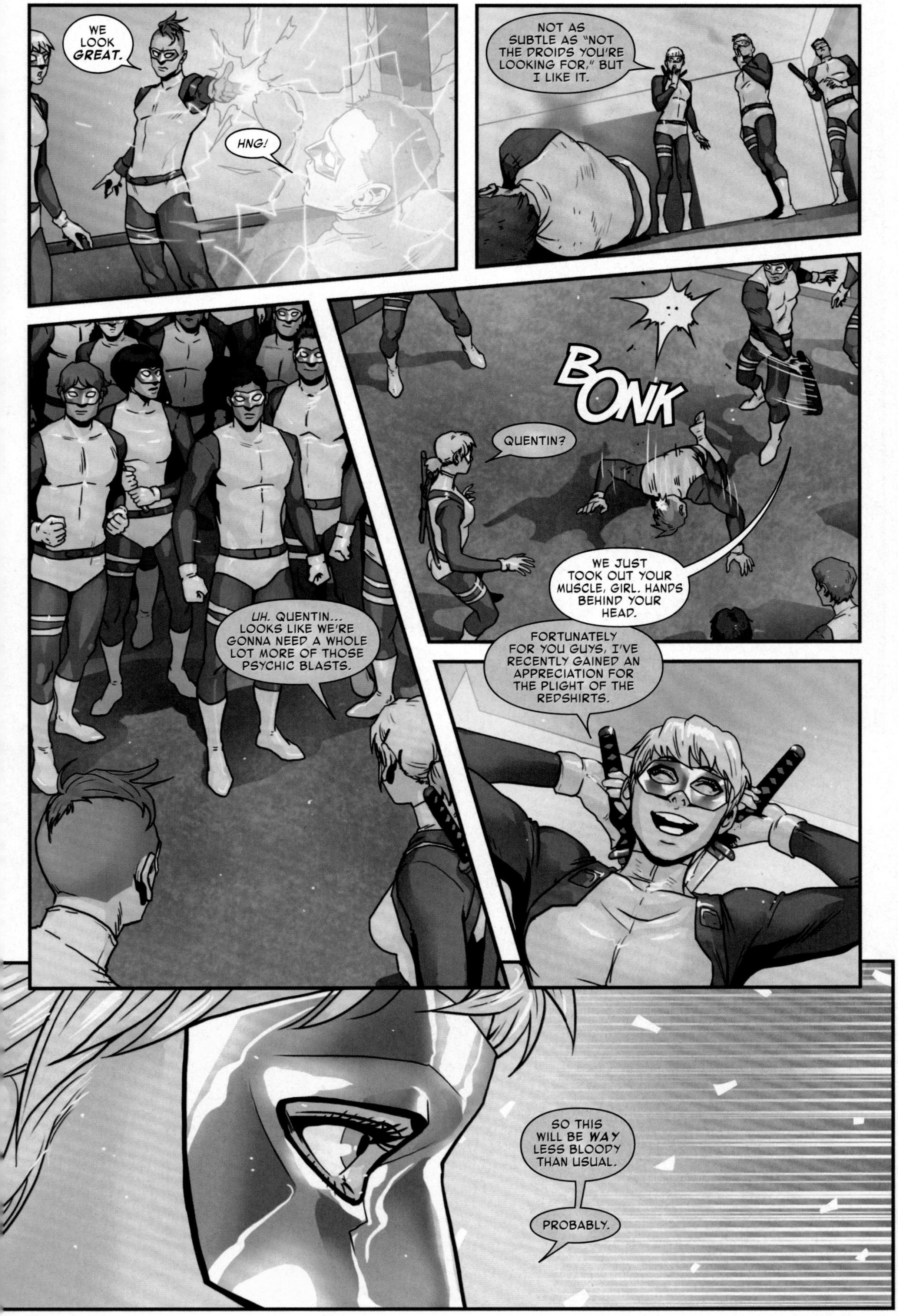
WE LOOK GREAT.
HNG!
NOT AS SUBTLE AS "NOT THE DROIDS YOU'RE LOOKING FOR," BUT I LIKE IT.
UH. QUENTIN... LOOKS LIKE WE'RE GONNA NEED A WHOLE LOT MORE OF THOSE PSYCHIC BLASTS.
BONK
QUENTIN?
WE JUST TOOK OUT YOUR MUSCLE, GIRL. HANDS BEHIND YOUR HEAD.
FORTUNATELY FOR YOU GUYS, I'VE RECENTLY GAINED AN APPRECIATION FOR THE PLIGHT OF THE REDSHIRTS.
SO THIS WILL BE WAY LESS BLOODY THAN USUAL.
PROBABLY.

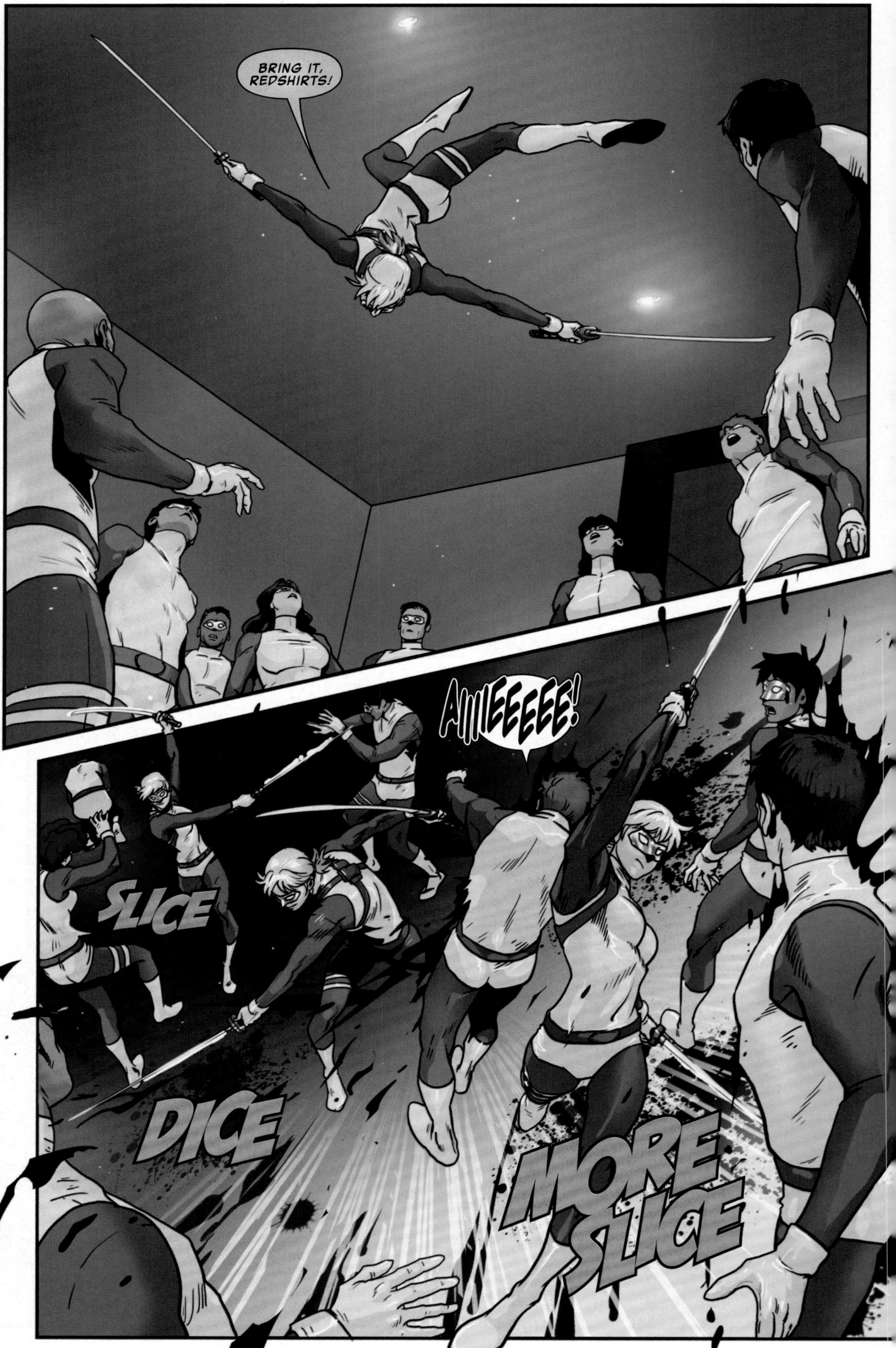
BRING IT, REDSHIRTS!
AIIIIEEEEE!
SLICE
DICE
MORE SLICE

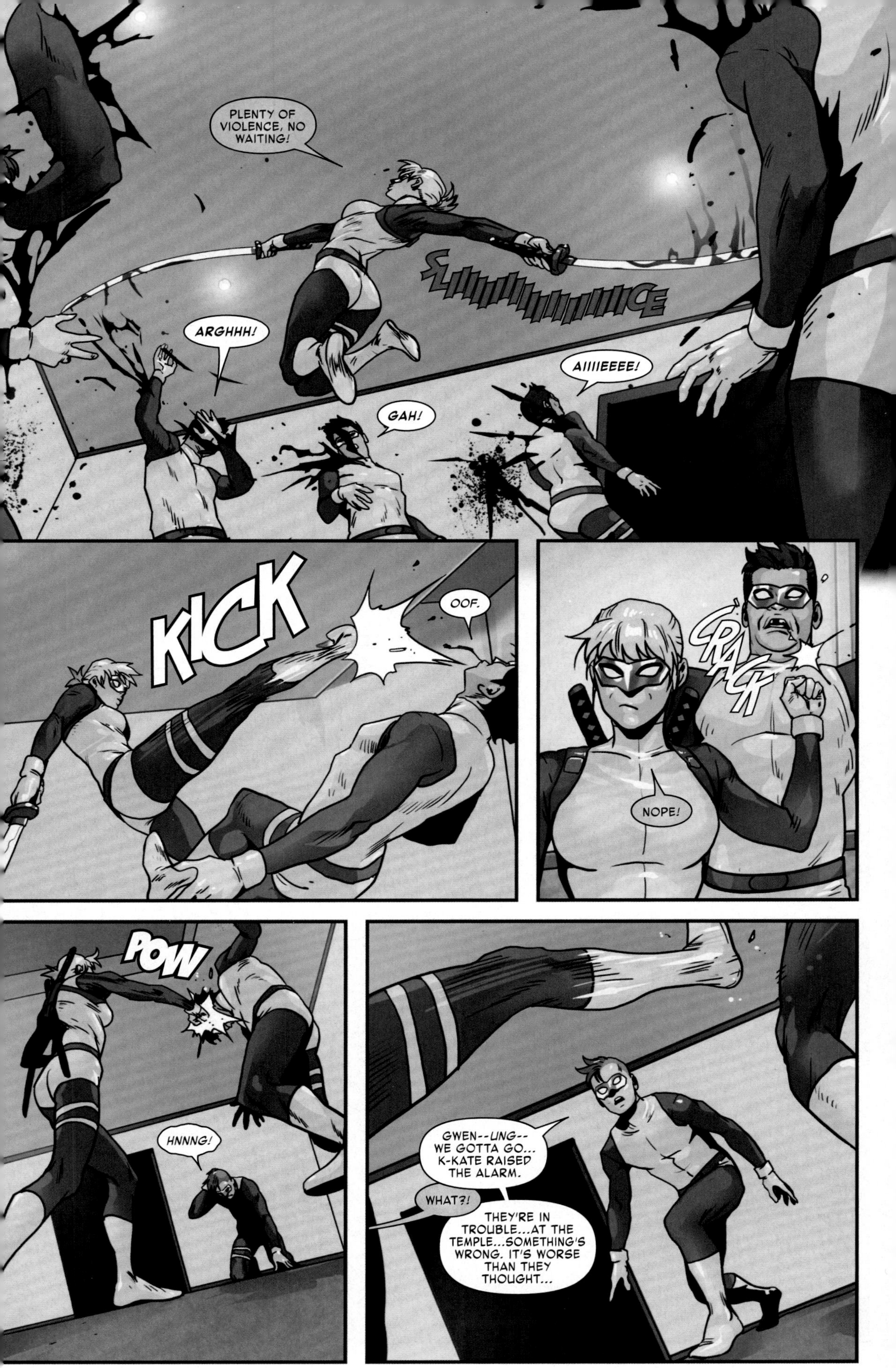
PLENTY OF VIOLENCE, NO WAITING!
SLIIIIIIIIIIIIIICE
ARGHHH!
GAH!
AIIIEEEE!
KICK
OOF.
CRACK
NOPE!
POW
HNNNG!
GWEN--UNG-- WE GOTTA GO... K-KATE RAISED THE ALARM.
WHAT?!
THEY'RE IN TROUBLE...AT THE TEMPLE...SOMETHING'S WRONG. IT'S WORSE THAN THEY THOUGHT...

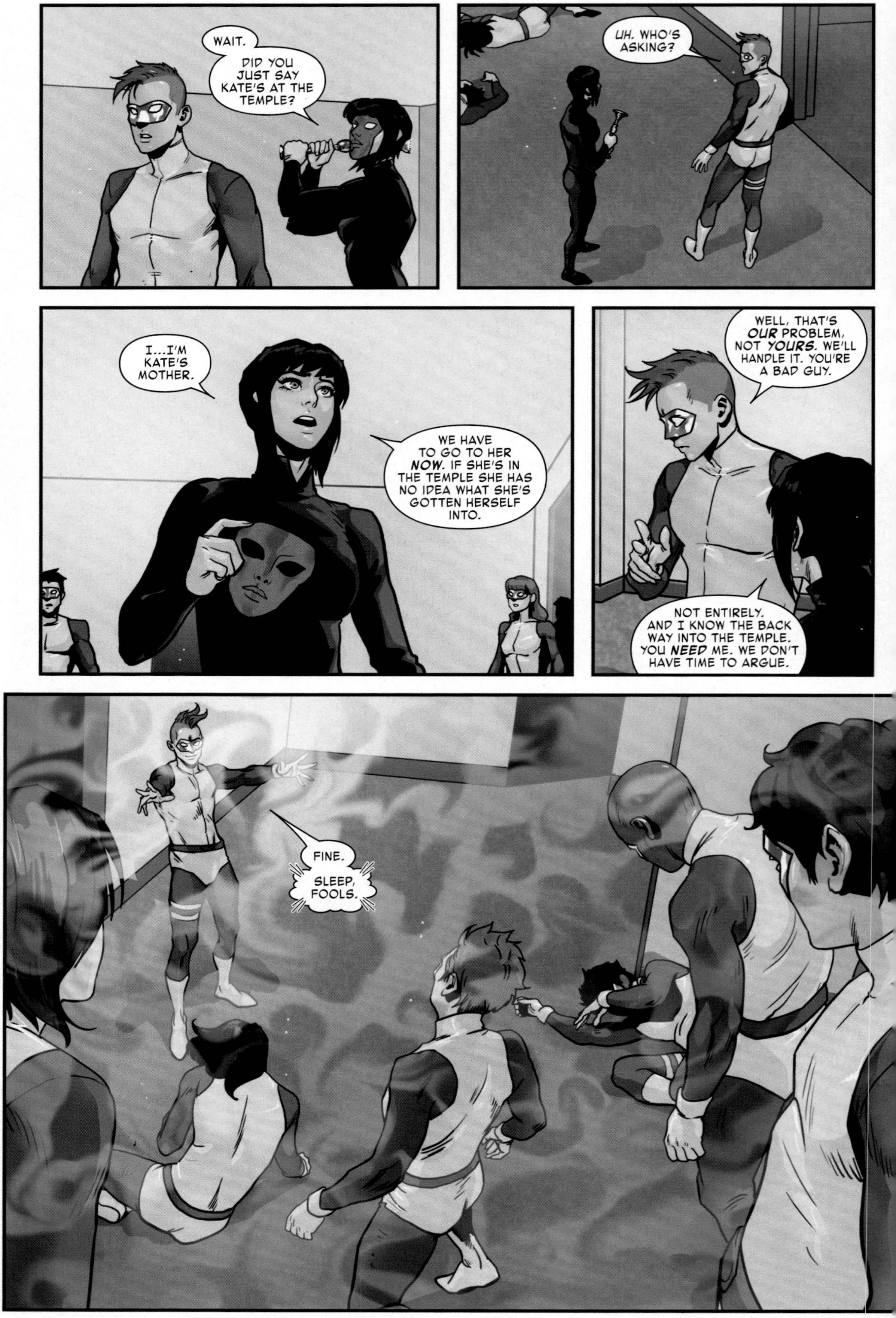
WAIT.
DID YOU JUST SAY KATE'S AT THE TEMPLE?
UH. WHO'S ASKING?
I...I'M KATE'S MOTHER.
WE HAVE TO GO TO HER NOW. IF SHE'S IN THE TEMPLE SHE HAS NO IDEA WHAT SHE'S GOTTEN HERSELF INTO.
WELL, THAT'S OUR PROBLEM, NOT YOURS. WE'LL HANDLE IT. YOU'RE A BAD GUY.
NOT ENTIRELY. AND I KNOW THE BACK WAY INTO THE TEMPLE. YOU NEED ME. WE DON'T HAVE TIME TO ARGUE.
FINE.
SLEEP, FOOLS.

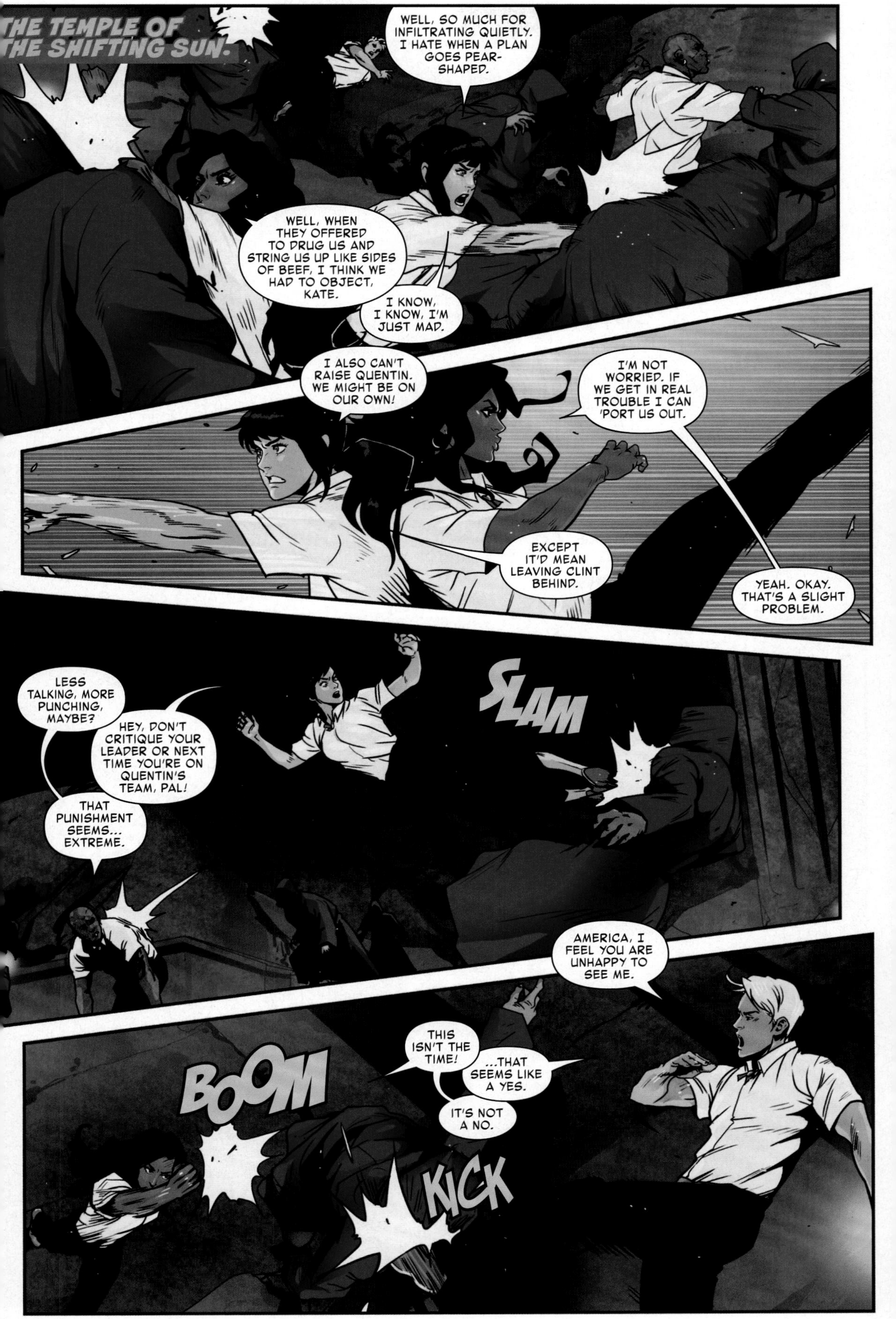
THE TEMPLE OF THE SHIFTING SUN.
WELL, SO MUCH FOR INFILTRATING QUIETLY. I HATE WHEN A PLAN GOES PEAR-SHAPED.
WELL, WHEN THEY OFFERED TO DRUG US AND STRING US UP LIKE SIDES OF BEEF, I THINK WE HAD TO OBJECT, KATE.
I KNOW, I KNOW, I'M JUST MAD.
I ALSO CAN'T RAISE QUENTIN. WE MIGHT BE ON OUR OWN!
I'M NOT WORRIED. IF WE GET IN REAL TROUBLE I CAN 'PORT US OUT.
EXCEPT IT'D MEAN LEAVING CLINT BEHIND.
YEAH. OKAY. THAT'S A SLIGHT PROBLEM.
SLAM
LESS TALKING, MORE PUNCHING, MAYBE?
HEY, DON'T CRITIQUE YOUR LEADER OR NEXT TIME YOU'RE ON QUENTIN'S TEAM, PAL!
THAT PUNISHMENT SEEMS... EXTREME.
AMERICA, I FEEL YOU ARE UNHAPPY TO SEE ME.
BOOM
THIS ISN'T THE TIME!
...THAT SEEMS LIKE A YES.
IT'S NOT A NO.
KICK

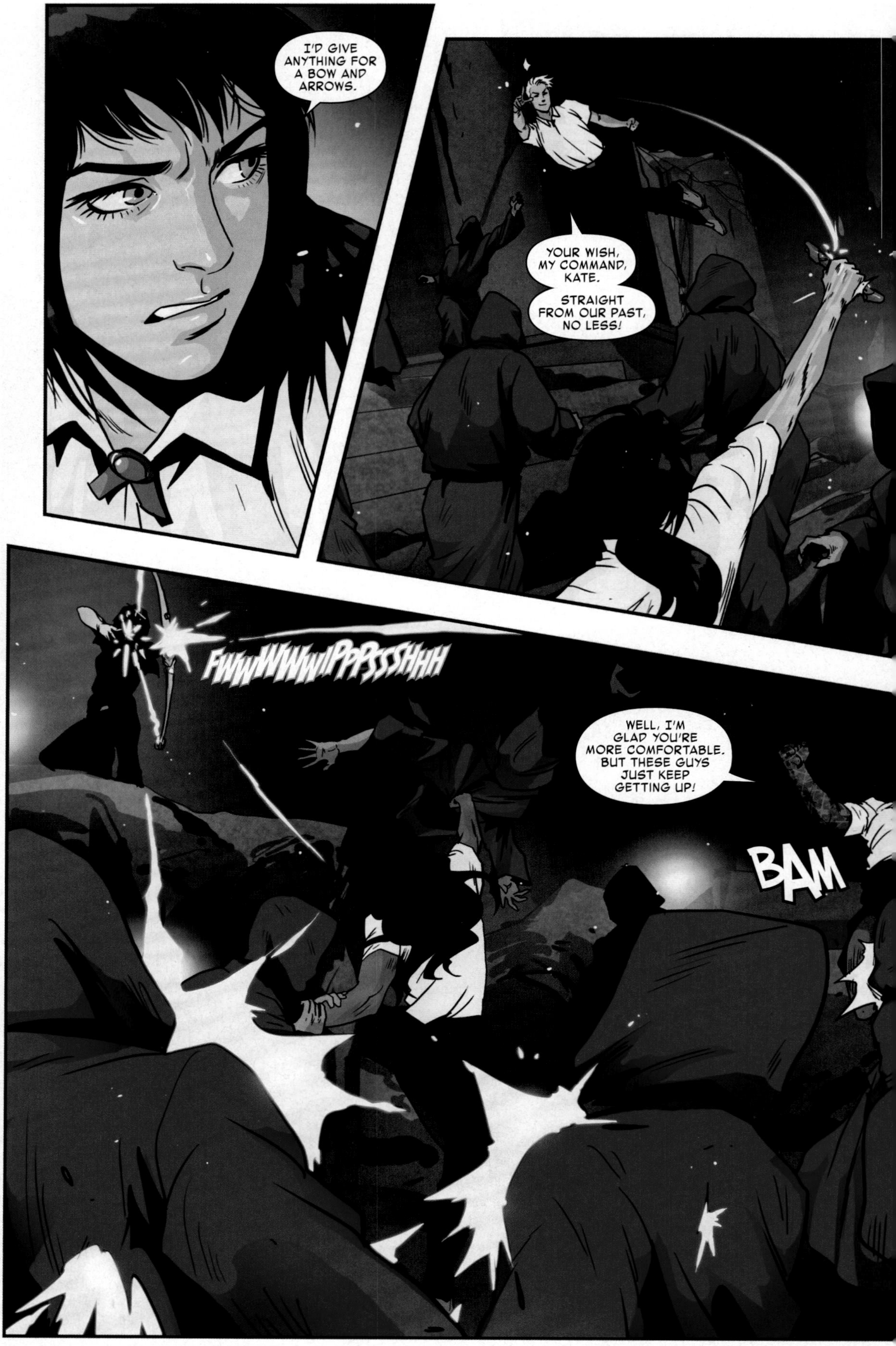
I'D GIVE ANYTHING FOR A BOW AND ARROWS.
YOUR WISH, MY COMMAND, KATE.
STRAIGHT FROM OUR PAST, NO LESS!
FWWWWWWIPPPSSSHHH
WELL, I'M GLAD YOU'RE MORE COMFORTABLE. BUT THESE GUYS JUST KEEP GETTING UP!
BAM

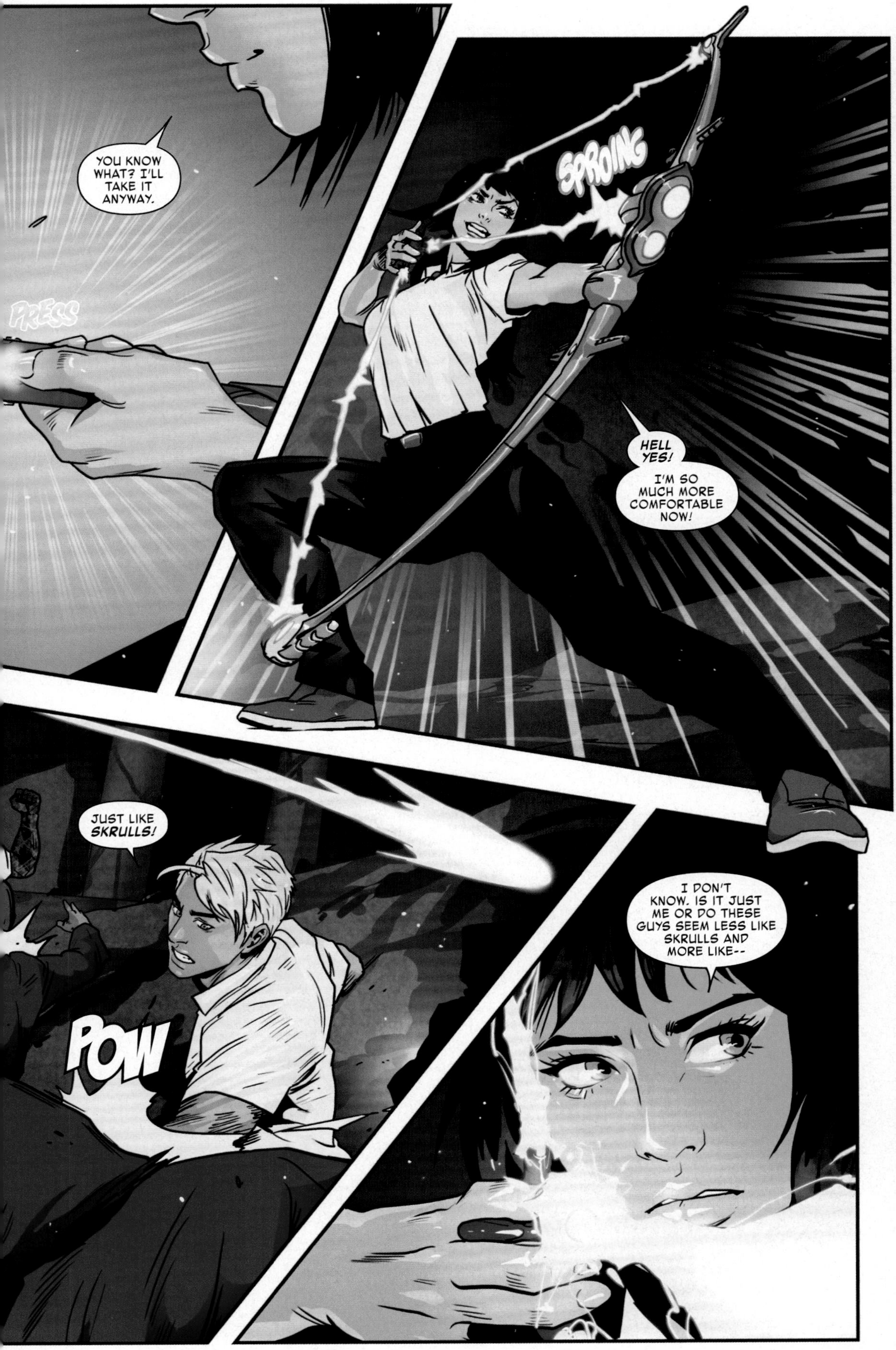
YOU KNOW WHAT? I'LL TAKE IT ANYWAY.
PRESS
SPROING
HELL YES!
I'M SO MUCH MORE COMFORTABLE NOW!
JUST LIKE SKRULLS!
POW
I DON'T KNOW. IS IT JUST ME OR DO THESE GUYS SEEM LESS LIKE SKRULLS AND MORE LIKE--

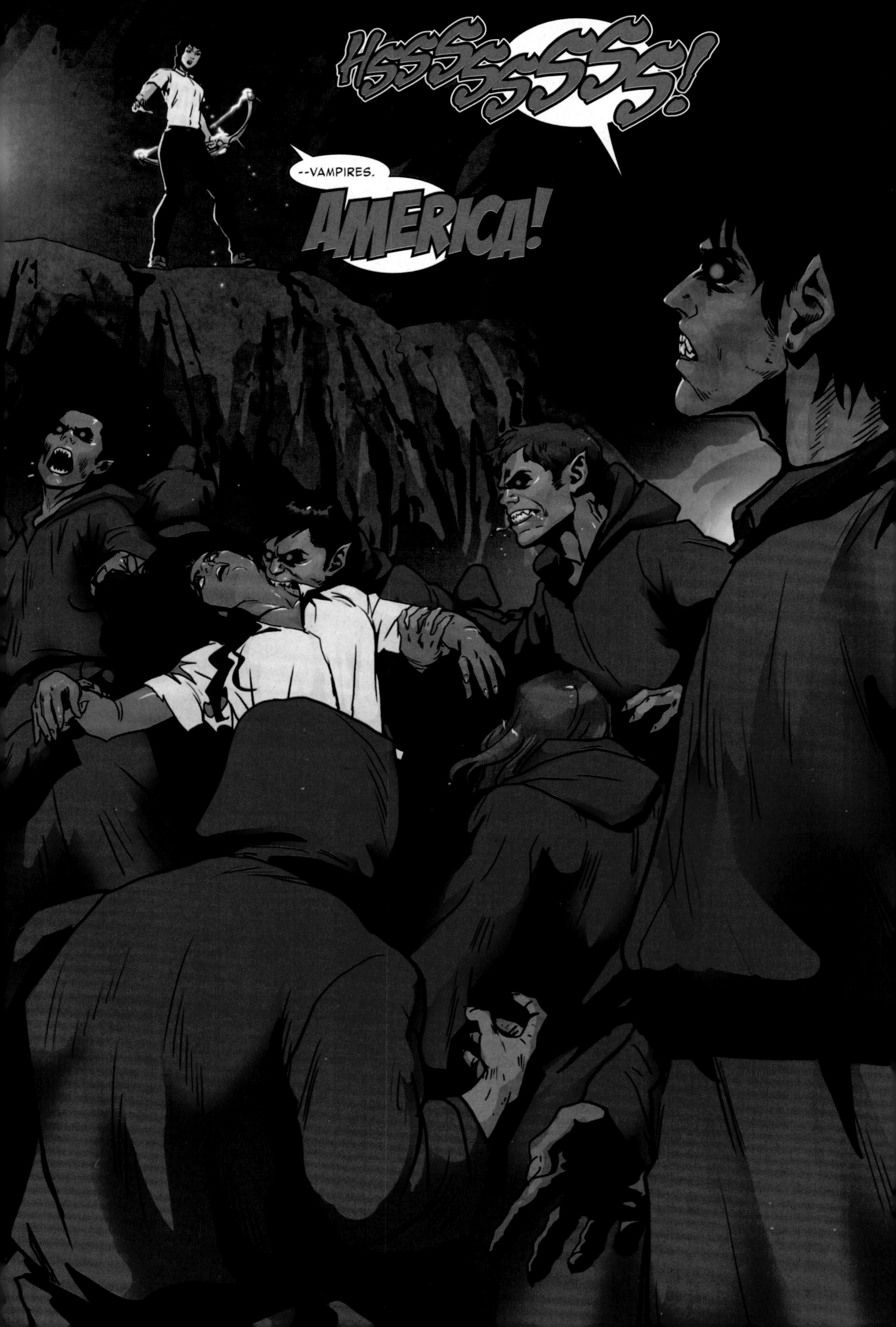
HSSSSSSSS!
--VAMPIRES.
AMERICA!

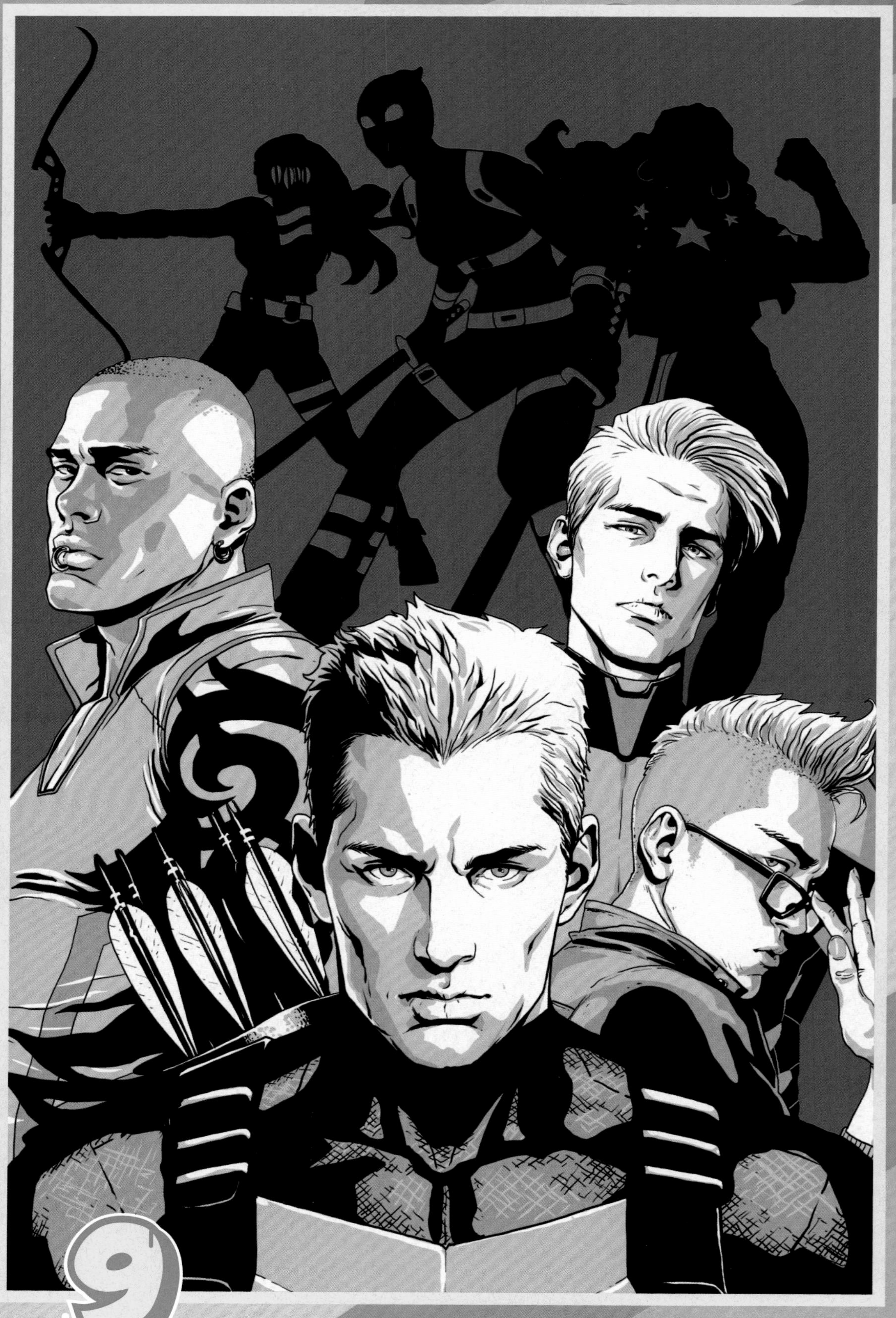
9

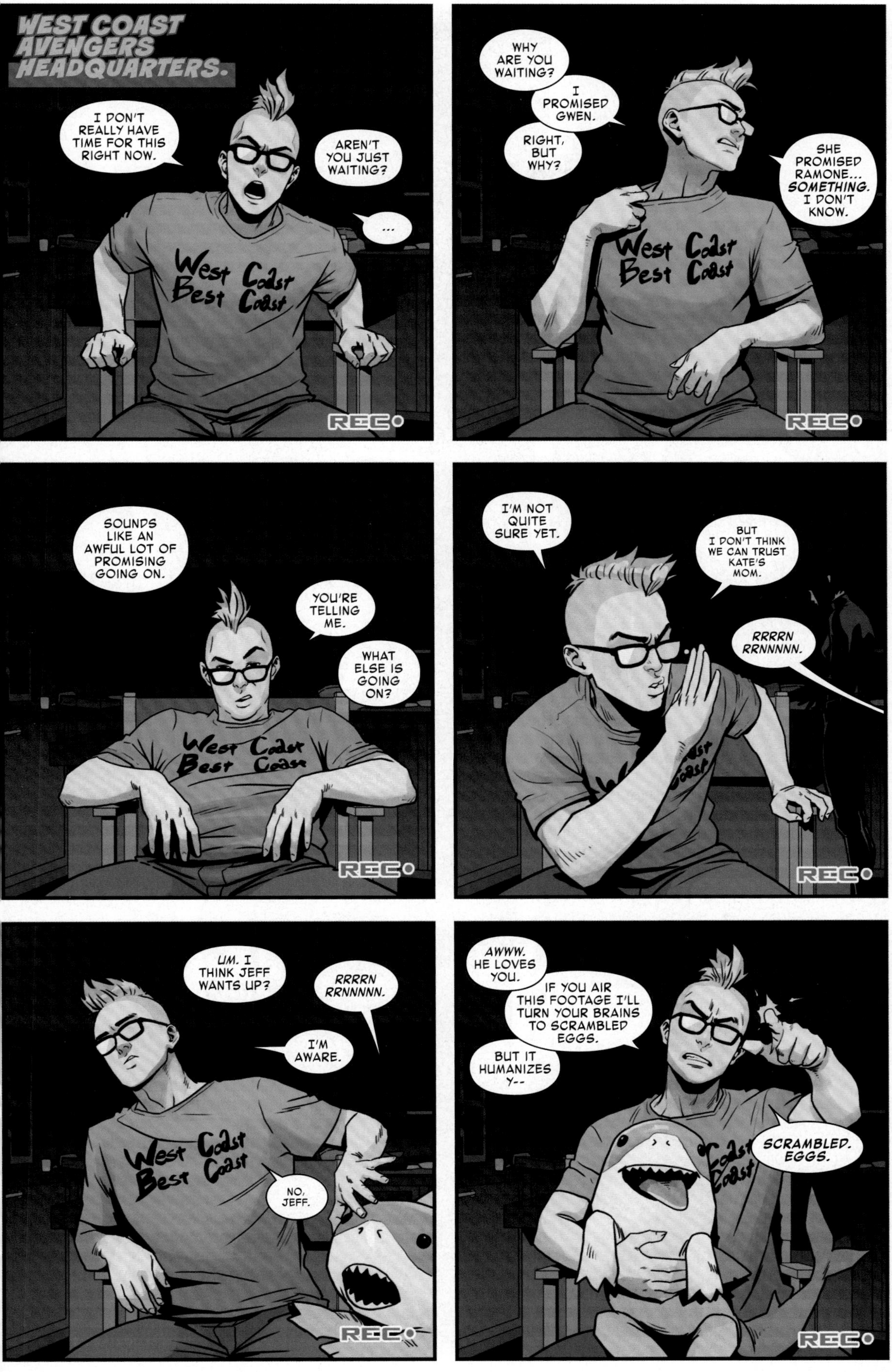
WEST COAST AVENGERS HEADQUARTERS.
I DON'T REALLY HAVE TIME FOR THIS RIGHT NOW.
AREN'T YOU JUST WAITING?
...
West Coast Best Coast
REC
WHY ARE YOU WAITING?
I PROMISED GWEN.
RIGHT, BUT WHY?
SHE PROMISED RAMONE... SOMETHING. I DON'T KNOW.
West Coast Best Coast
REC
SOUNDS LIKE AN AWFUL LOT OF PROMISING GOING ON.
YOU'RE TELLING ME.
WHAT ELSE IS GOING ON?
West Coast Best Coast
REC
I'M NOT QUITE SURE YET.
BUT I DON'T THINK WE CAN TRUST KATE'S MOM.
RRRRN RRNNNNN.
REC
UM. I THINK JEFF WANTS UP?
RRRRN RRNNNNN.
I'M AWARE.
West Coast Best Coast
NO, JEFF.
REC
AWWW. HE LOVES YOU.
IF YOU AIR THIS FOOTAGE I'LL TURN YOUR BRAINS TO SCRAMBLED EGGS.
BUT IT HUMANIZES Y--
SCRAMBLED. EGGS.
REC

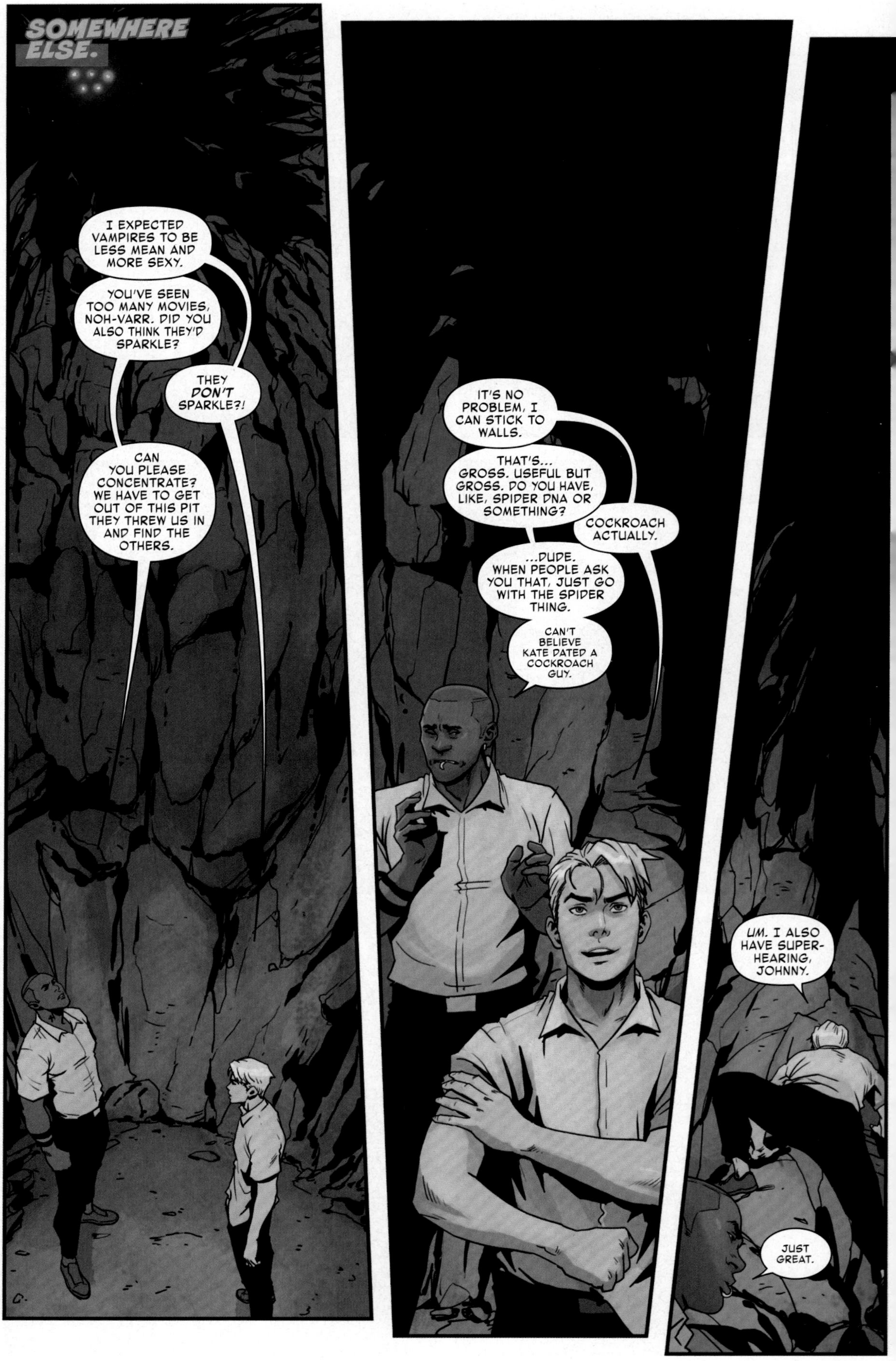
SOMEWHERE ELSE.
I EXPECTED VAMPIRES TO BE LESS MEAN AND MORE SEXY.
YOU'VE SEEN TOO MANY MOVIES, NOH-VARR. DID YOU ALSO THINK THEY'D SPARKLE?
THEY DON'T SPARKLE?!
CAN YOU PLEASE CONCENTRATE? WE HAVE TO GET OUT OF THIS PIT THEY THREW US IN AND FIND THE OTHERS.
IT'S NO PROBLEM, I CAN STICK TO WALLS.
THAT'S... GROSS. USEFUL BUT GROSS. DO YOU HAVE, LIKE, SPIDER DNA OR SOMETHING?
COCKROACH ACTUALLY.
...DUDE. WHEN PEOPLE ASK YOU THAT, JUST GO WITH THE SPIDER THING.
CAN'T BELIEVE KATE DATED A COCKROACH GUY.
UM. I ALSO HAVE SUPER-HEARING, JOHNNY.
JUST GREAT.

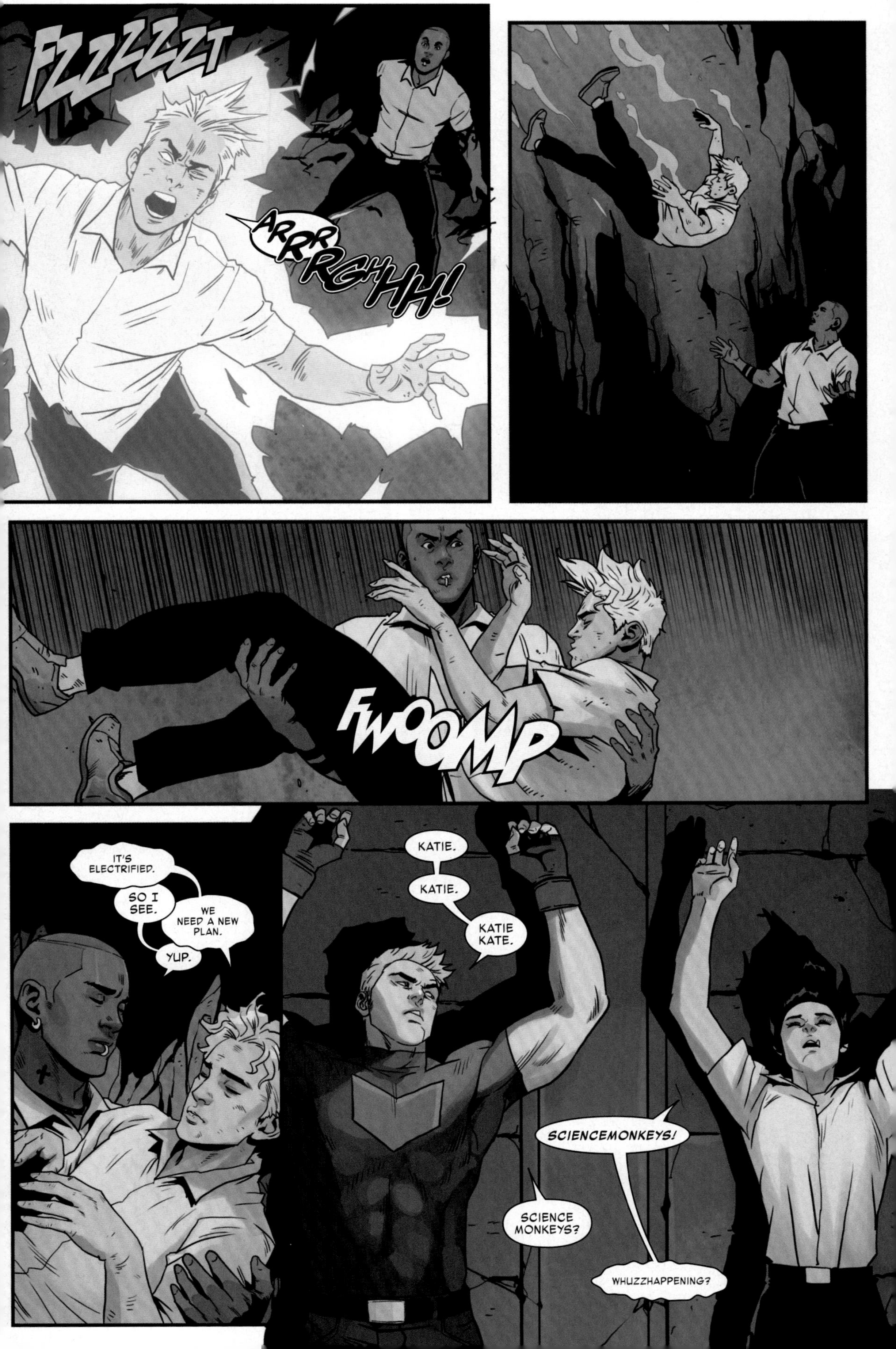
FZZZZZT
ARRRRGHHH!
FWOOMP
IT'S ELECTRIFIED.
SO I SEE.
WE NEED A NEW PLAN.
YUP.
KATIE.
KATIE.
KATIE KATE.
SCIENCEMONKEYS!
SCIENCE MONKEYS?
WHUZZHAPPENING?

KATE, I DON'T KNOW WHAT THE HELL SCIENCE MONKEYS ARE BUT CAN YOU PLEASE WAKE UP ALREADY? BECAUSE--

WE'RE STRUNG UP LIKE WE'RE ON THE MENU.

YEAH. THAT.

THE BOWELS OF THE TEMPLE OF THE SHIFTING SUN.

WHAT HAPPENED TO YOU? HOW DID YOU GET HERE? YOU WERE SUPPOSED TO BE UNDERCOVER.

I DON'T WANT TO TALK ABOUT IT.

CLINT.

ALL RIGHT, ALL RIGHT. YOU SEE ANY OF THE OTHERS?

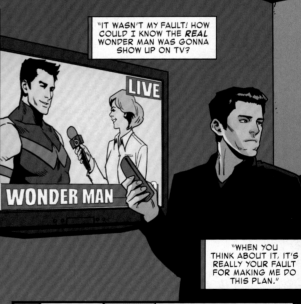

"IT WASN'T MY FAULT! HOW COULD I KNOW THE REAL WONDER MAN WAS GONNA SHOW UP ON TV?"

LIVE

WONDER MAN

"WHEN YOU THINK ABOUT IT, IT'S REALLY YOUR FAULT FOR MAKING ME DO THIS PLAN."

NO. AND I'M TRYING TO NOT BE OFFENDED THAT YOU AND I ARE STRUNG UP WITH WHAT I ASSUME ARE THE REST OF THE APPETIZERS, WHILE OUR MORE "POWERED" FRIENDS SEEM TO BE ELSEWHERE.

DON'T BE OFFENDED, JUST BE GRATEFUL.

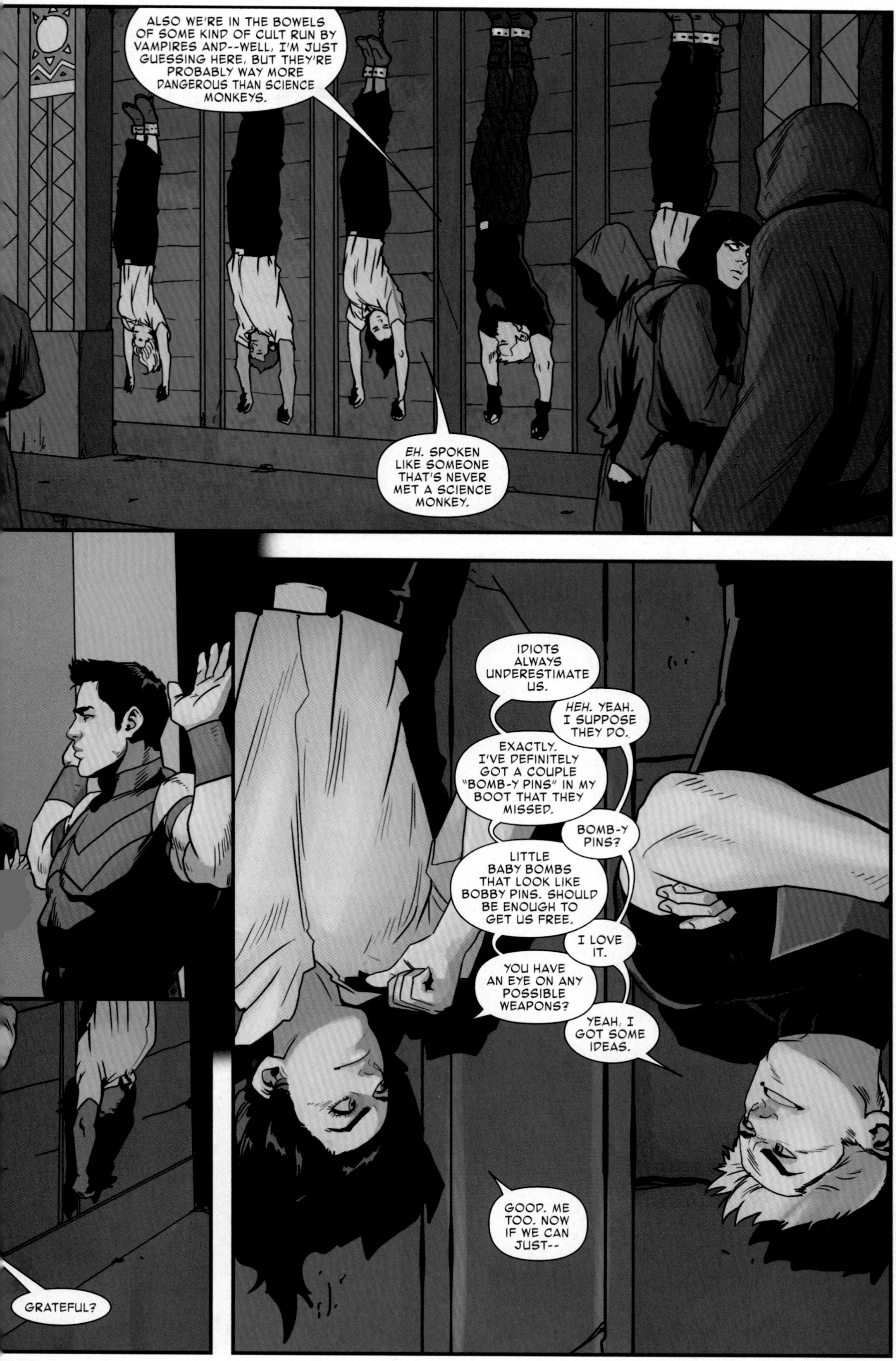
ALSO WE'RE IN THE BOWELS OF SOME KIND OF CULT RUN BY VAMPIRES AND--WELL, I'M JUST GUESSING HERE, BUT THEY'RE PROBABLY WAY MORE DANGEROUS THAN SCIENCE MONKEYS.
EH. SPOKEN LIKE SOMEONE THAT'S NEVER MET A SCIENCE MONKEY.
GRATEFUL?
IDIOTS ALWAYS UNDERESTIMATE US.
HEH. YEAH. I SUPPOSE THEY DO.
EXACTLY. I'VE DEFINITELY GOT A COUPLE "BOMB-Y PINS" IN MY BOOT THAT THEY MISSED.
BOMB-Y PINS?
LITTLE BABY BOMBS THAT LOOK LIKE BOBBY PINS. SHOULD BE ENOUGH TO GET US FREE.
I LOVE IT.
YOU HAVE AN EYE ON ANY POSSIBLE WEAPONS?
YEAH, I GOT SOME IDEAS.
GOOD. ME TOO. NOW IF WE CAN JUST--

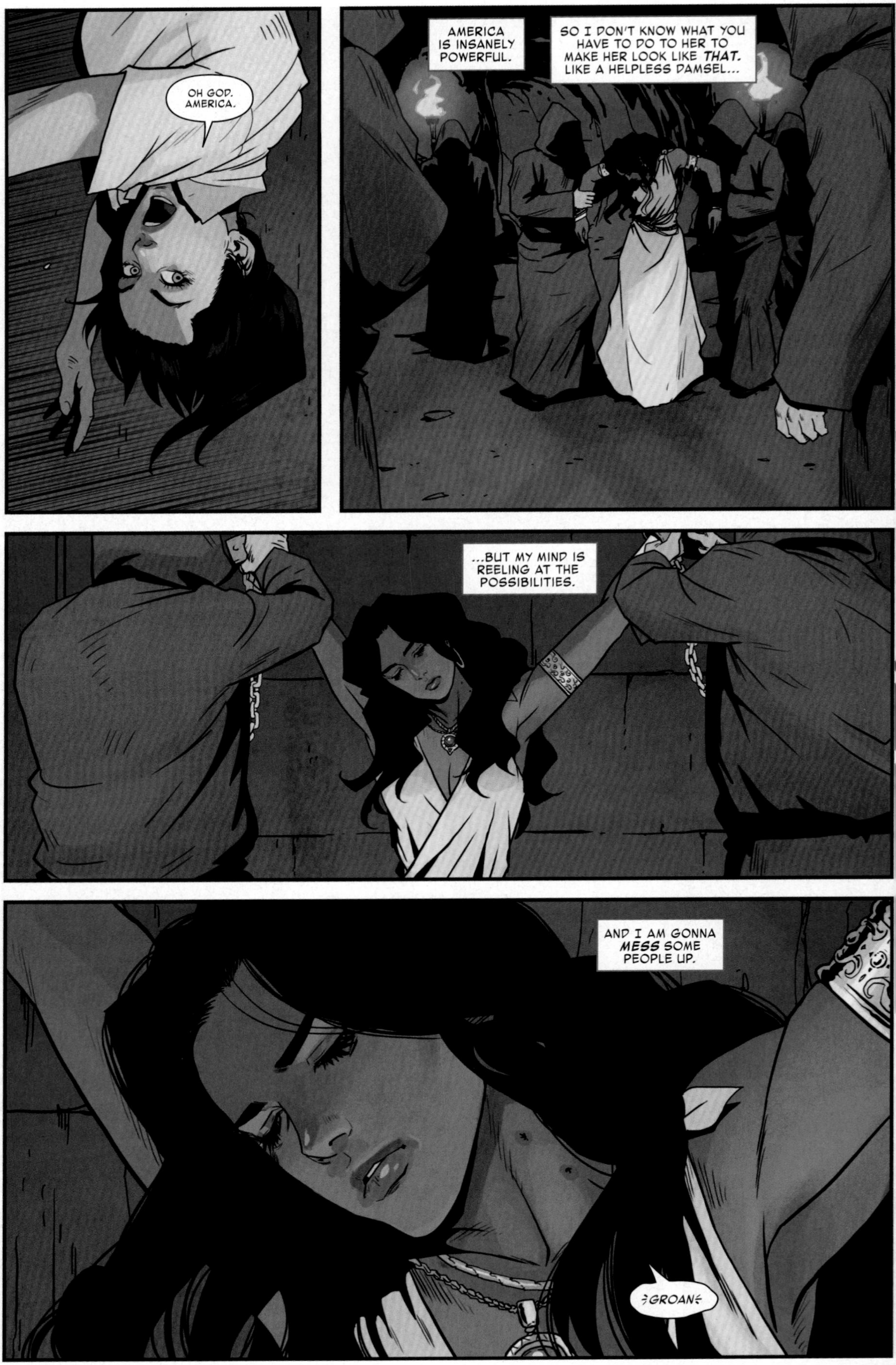
OH GOD. AMERICA.
AMERICA IS INSANELY POWERFUL.
SO I DON'T KNOW WHAT YOU HAVE TO DO TO HER TO MAKE HER LOOK LIKE *THAT.* LIKE A HELPLESS DAMSEL...
...BUT MY MIND IS REELING AT THE POSSIBILITIES.
AND I AM GONNA *MESS* SOME PEOPLE UP.
GROAN

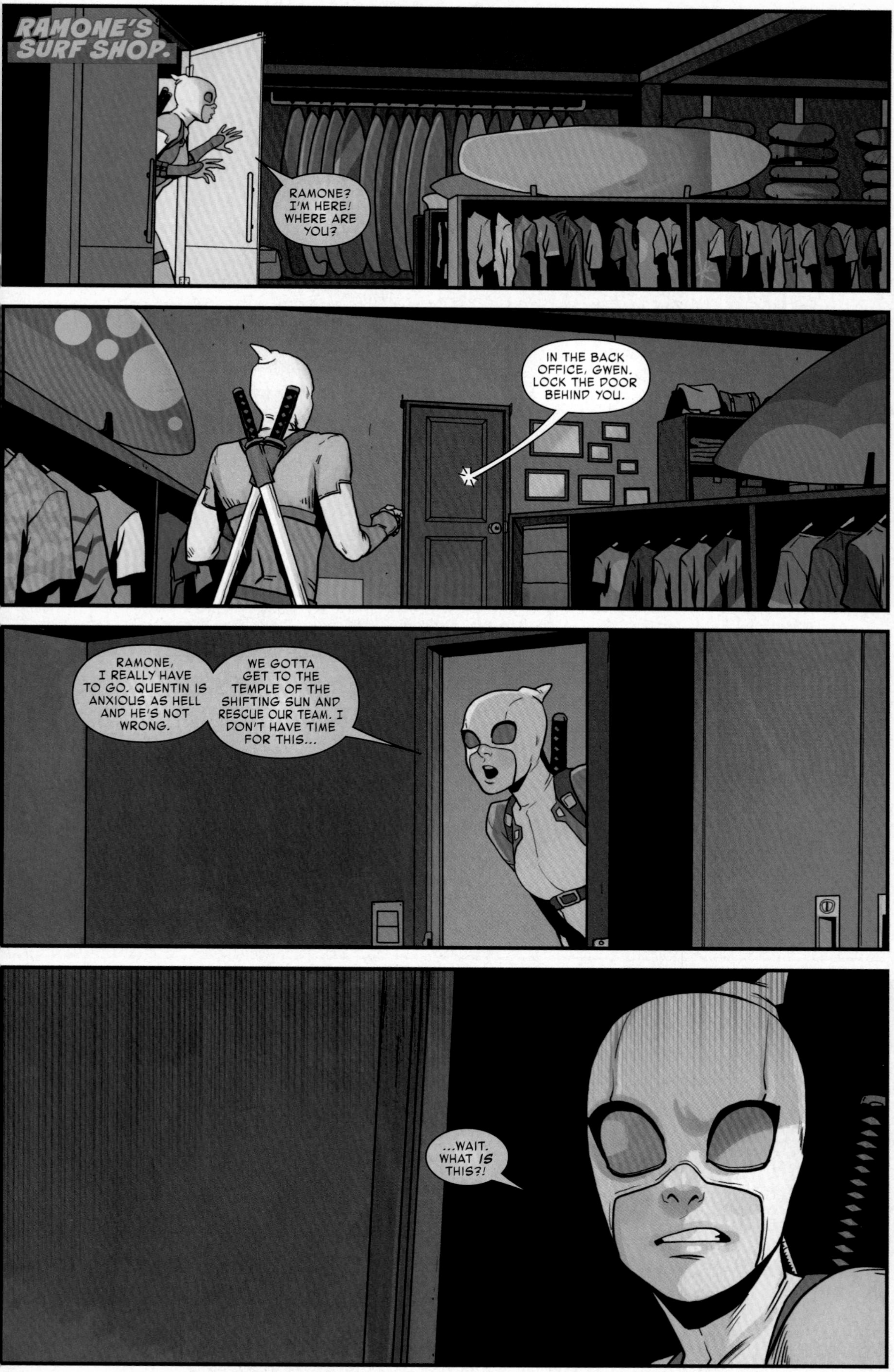
RAMONE'S SURF SHOP.
RAMONE? I'M HERE! WHERE ARE YOU?
IN THE BACK OFFICE, GWEN. LOCK THE DOOR BEHIND YOU.
RAMONE, I REALLY HAVE TO GO. QUENTIN IS ANXIOUS AS HELL AND HE'S NOT WRONG.
WE GOTTA GET TO THE TEMPLE OF THE SHIFTING SUN AND RESCUE OUR TEAM. I DON'T HAVE TIME FOR THIS...
...WAIT. WHAT *IS* THIS?!

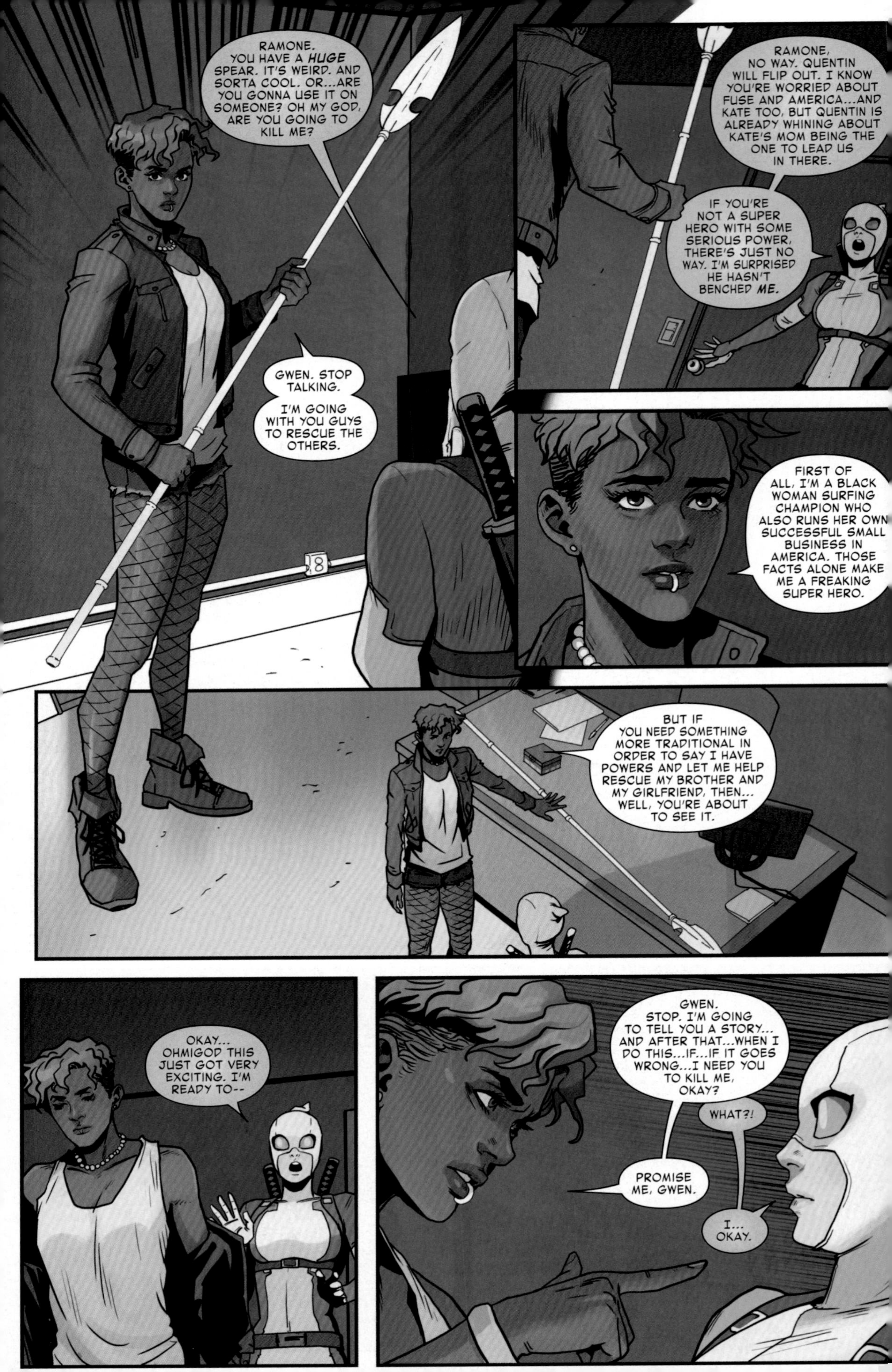
RAMONE. YOU HAVE A HUGE SPEAR. IT'S WEIRD. AND SORTA COOL. OR...ARE YOU GONNA USE IT ON SOMEONE? OH MY GOD, ARE YOU GOING TO KILL ME?
GWEN. STOP TALKING.
I'M GOING WITH YOU GUYS TO RESCUE THE OTHERS.
RAMONE, NO WAY. QUENTIN WILL FLIP OUT. I KNOW YOU'RE WORRIED ABOUT FUSE AND AMERICA...AND KATE TOO, BUT QUENTIN IS ALREADY WHINING ABOUT KATE'S MOM BEING THE ONE TO LEAD US IN THERE.
IF YOU'RE NOT A SUPER HERO WITH SOME SERIOUS POWER, THERE'S JUST NO WAY. I'M SURPRISED HE HASN'T BENCHED ME.
FIRST OF ALL, I'M A BLACK WOMAN SURFING CHAMPION WHO ALSO RUNS HER OWN SUCCESSFUL SMALL BUSINESS IN AMERICA. THOSE FACTS ALONE MAKE ME A FREAKING SUPER HERO.
BUT IF YOU NEED SOMETHING MORE TRADITIONAL IN ORDER TO SAY I HAVE POWERS AND LET ME HELP RESCUE MY BROTHER AND MY GIRLFRIEND, THEN... WELL, YOU'RE ABOUT TO SEE IT.
OKAY... OHMIGOD THIS JUST GOT VERY EXCITING. I'M READY TO--
GWEN. STOP. I'M GOING TO TELL YOU A STORY... AND AFTER THAT...WHEN I DO THIS...IF...IF IT GOES WRONG...I NEED YOU TO KILL ME, OKAY?
WHAT?!
PROMISE ME, GWEN.
I... OKAY.

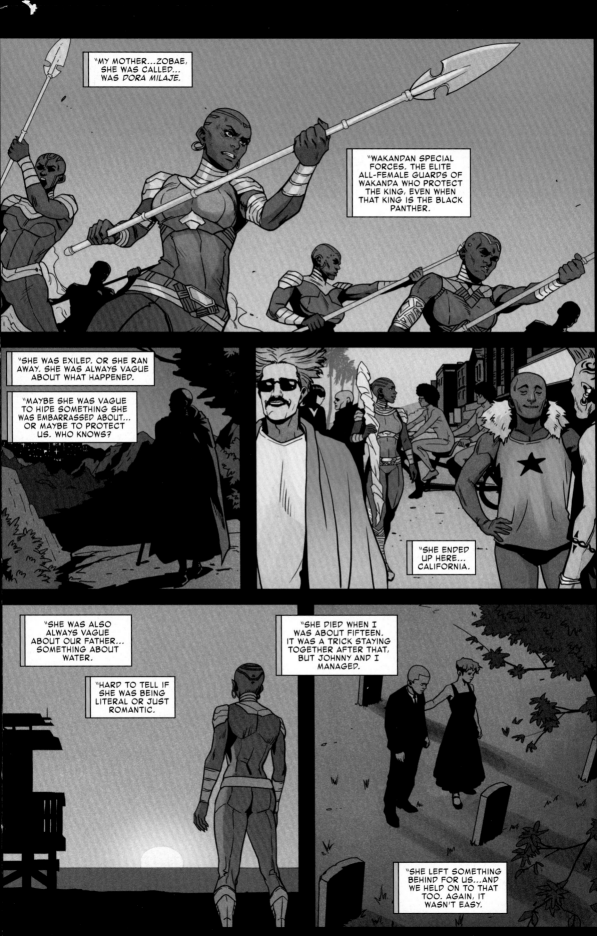

"MY MOTHER...ZOBAE, SHE WAS CALLED... WAS DORA MILAJE.

"WAKANDAN SPECIAL FORCES. THE ELITE ALL-FEMALE GUARDS OF WAKANDA WHO PROTECT THE KING, EVEN WHEN THAT KING IS THE BLACK PANTHER.

"SHE WAS EXILED. OR SHE RAN AWAY. SHE WAS ALWAYS VAGUE ABOUT WHAT HAPPENED.

"MAYBE SHE WAS VAGUE TO HIDE SOMETHING SHE WAS EMBARRASSED ABOUT... OR MAYBE TO PROTECT US. WHO KNOWS?

"SHE ENDED UP HERE... CALIFORNIA.

"SHE WAS ALSO ALWAYS VAGUE ABOUT OUR FATHER... SOMETHING ABOUT WATER.

"HARD TO TELL IF SHE WAS BEING LITERAL OR JUST ROMANTIC.

"SHE DIED WHEN I WAS ABOUT FIFTEEN. IT WAS A TRICK STAYING TOGETHER AFTER THAT, BUT JOHNNY AND I MANAGED.

"SHE LEFT SOMETHING BEHIND FOR US...AND WE HELD ON TO THAT TOO. AGAIN, IT WASN'T EASY.

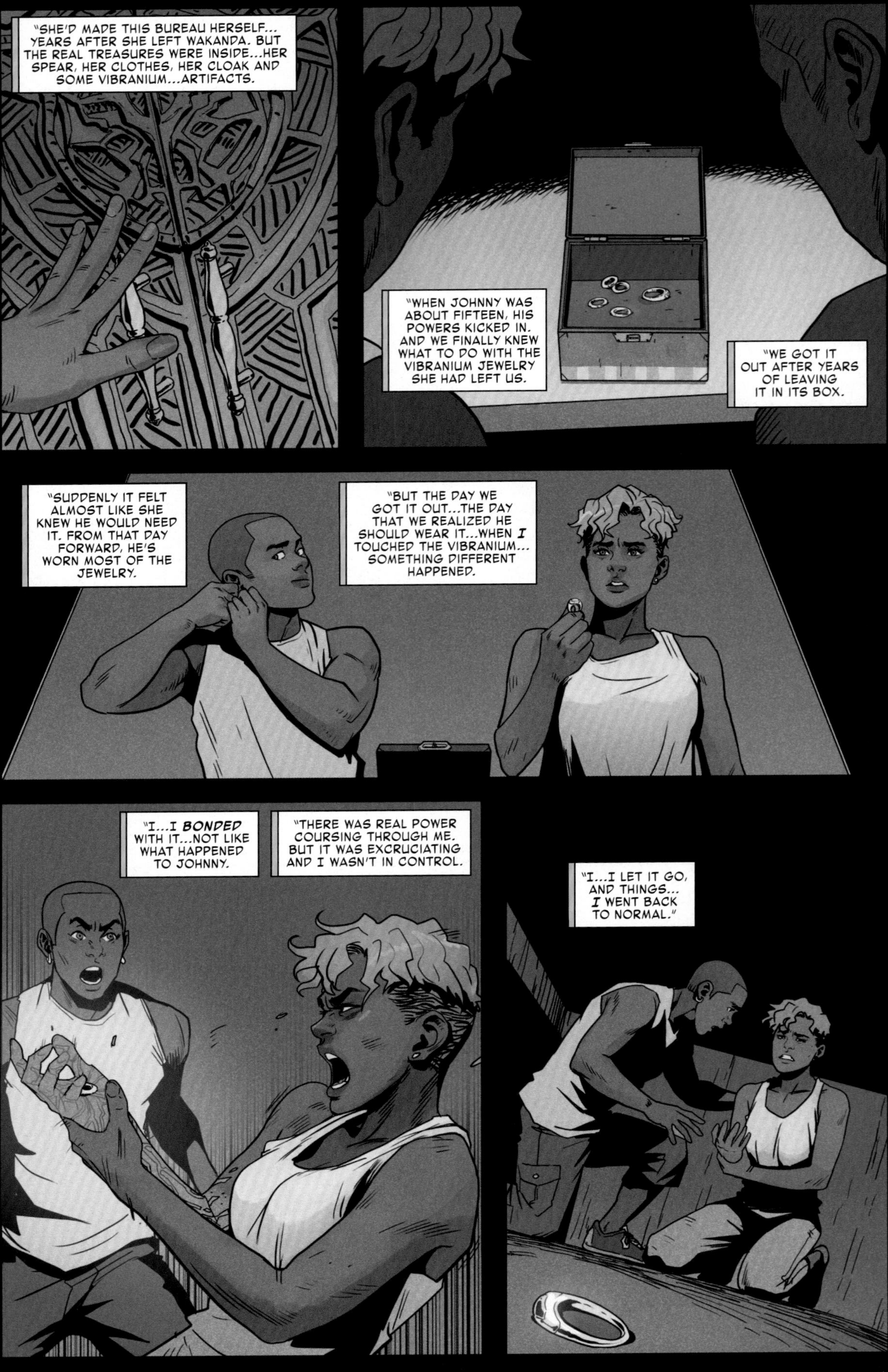
"SHE'D MADE THIS BUREAU HERSELF... YEARS AFTER SHE LEFT WAKANDA. BUT THE REAL TREASURES WERE INSIDE...HER SPEAR, HER CLOTHES, HER CLOAK AND SOME VIBRANIUM...ARTIFACTS.
"WHEN JOHNNY WAS ABOUT FIFTEEN, HIS POWERS KICKED IN. AND WE FINALLY KNEW WHAT TO DO WITH THE VIBRANIUM JEWELRY SHE HAD LEFT US.
"WE GOT IT OUT AFTER YEARS OF LEAVING IT IN ITS BOX.
"SUDDENLY IT FELT ALMOST LIKE SHE KNEW HE WOULD NEED IT. FROM THAT DAY FORWARD, HE'S WORN MOST OF THE JEWELRY.
"BUT THE DAY WE GOT IT OUT...THE DAY THAT WE REALIZED HE SHOULD WEAR IT...WHEN *I* TOUCHED THE VIBRANIUM... SOMETHING DIFFERENT HAPPENED.
"I...I *BONDED* WITH IT...NOT LIKE WHAT HAPPENED TO JOHNNY.
"THERE WAS REAL POWER COURSING THROUGH ME. BUT IT WAS EXCRUCIATING AND I WASN'T IN CONTROL.
"I...I LET IT GO, AND THINGS... *I* WENT BACK TO NORMAL."

WELL... MOST OF ME.

I NEVER TOUCHED THE RING AGAIN.

RAMONE...YOU DON'T HAVE TO DO THIS.

DON'T I? MY WHOLE WORLD IS TRAPPED IN THAT STUPID CULT, GWEN.

I KNOW. BUT WE...WE CAN HANDLE IT. QUENTIN AND I WILL BRING THEM BACK, I PROMISE.

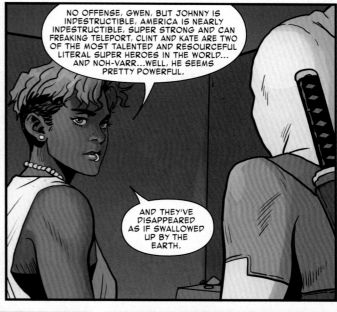

NO OFFENSE, GWEN, BUT JOHNNY IS INDESTRUCTIBLE, AMERICA IS NEARLY INDESTRUCTIBLE, SUPER STRONG AND CAN FREAKING TELEPORT, CLINT AND KATE ARE TWO OF THE MOST TALENTED AND RESOURCEFUL LITERAL SUPER HEROES IN THE WORLD... AND NOH-VARR...WELL, HE SEEMS PRETTY POWERFUL.

AND THEY'VE DISAPPEARED AS IF SWALLOWED UP BY THE EARTH.

SO FORGIVE ME IF I THINK YOU NEED REINFORCEMENTS.

ARE YOU ABSOLUTELY SURE ABOUT THIS?

I USED TO THINK I WAS PUTTING THIS OFF BECAUSE I WAS AFRAID...TURNS OUT I JUST NEEDED TO BE... *INSPIRED.*

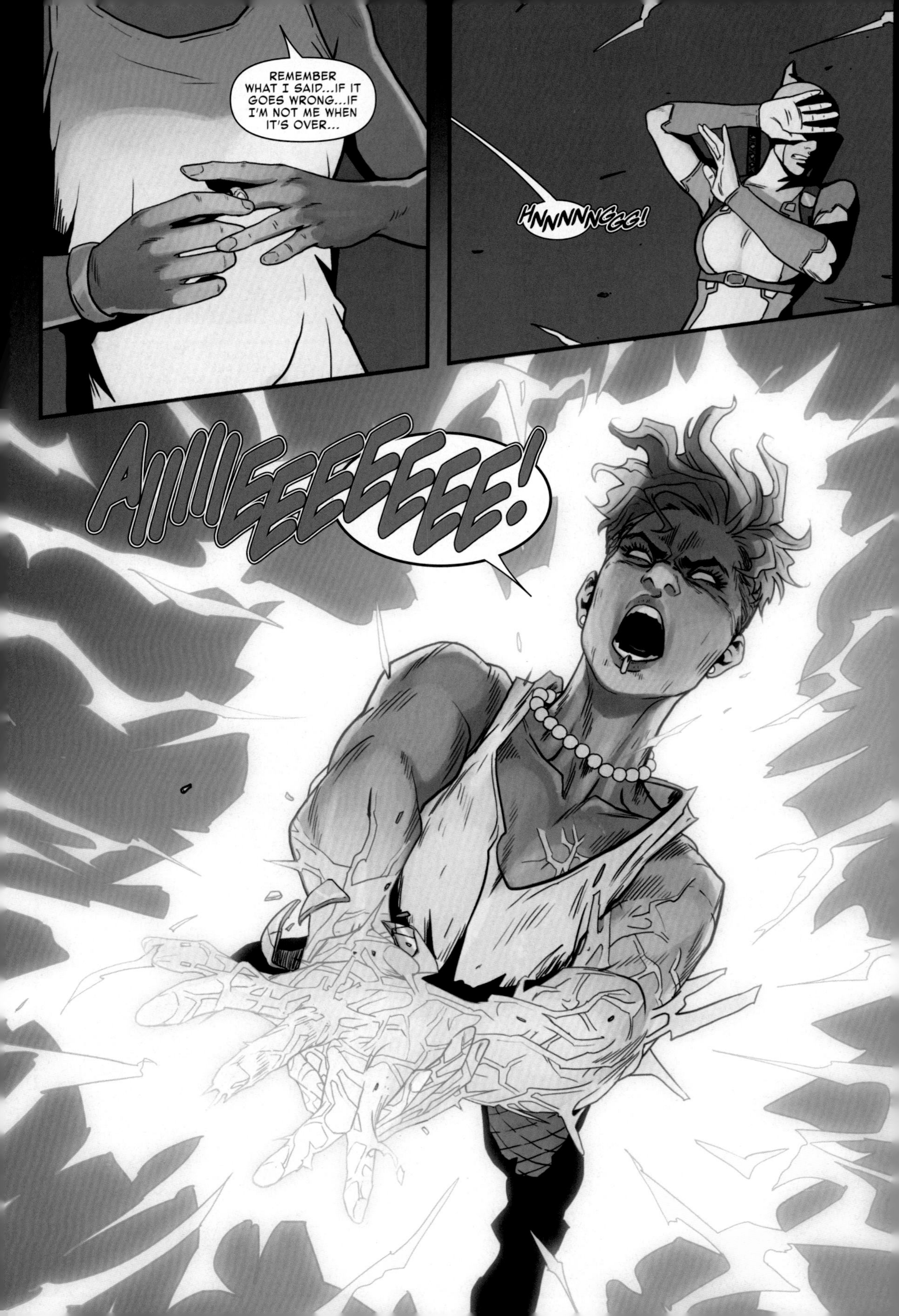
REMEMBER WHAT I SAID...IF IT GOES WRONG...IF I'M NOT ME WHEN IT'S OVER...
HNNNNNGGG!
AIIIIEEEEEEEE!

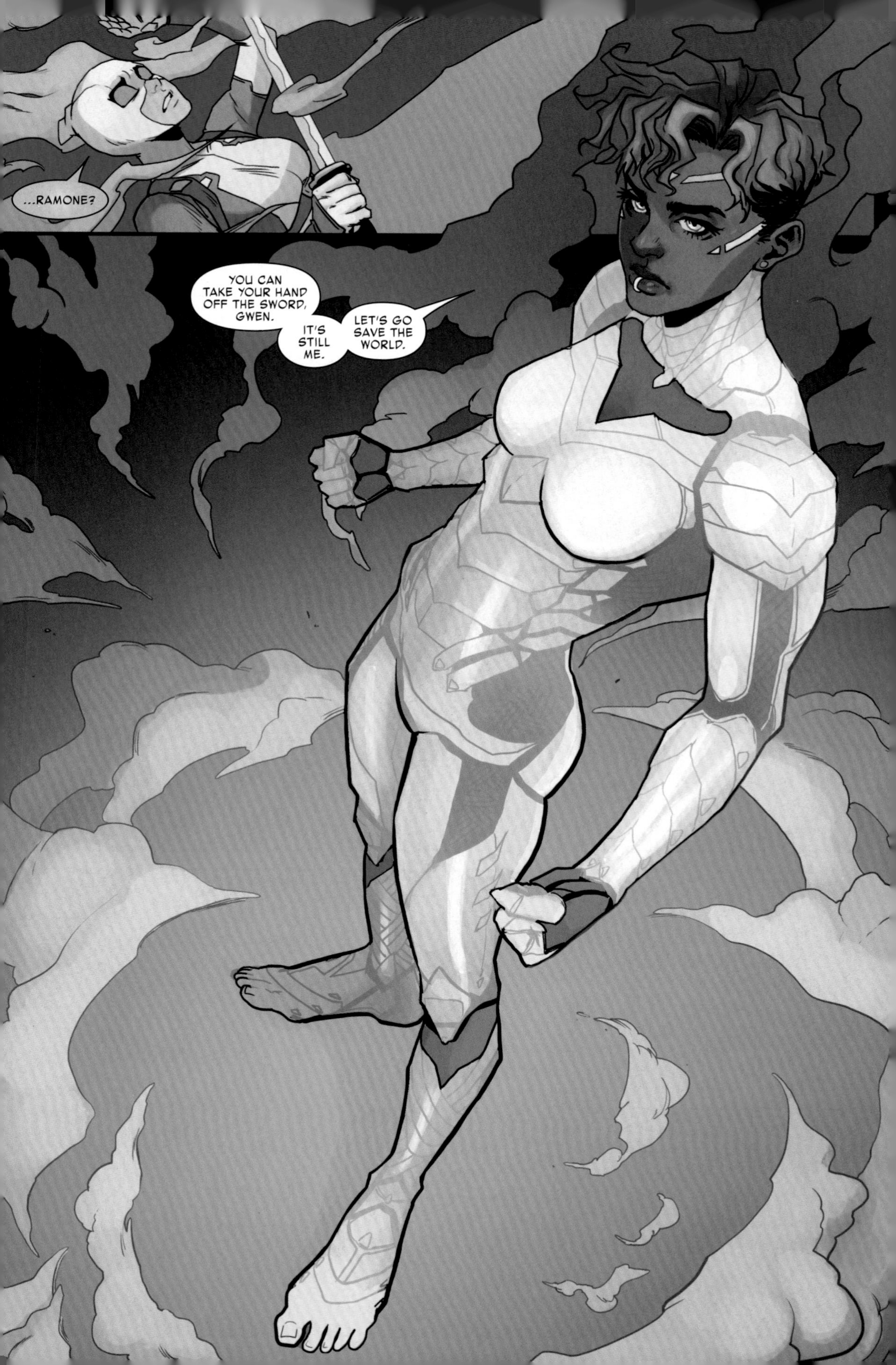
...RAMONE?
YOU CAN TAKE YOUR HAND OFF THE SWORD, GWEN.
IT'S STILL ME.
LET'S GO SAVE THE WORLD.

WHAT... WHAT HAPPENED TO THE RING?

IT MERGED WITH ME.

BUT IF YOU CAN'T TAKE IT OFF...

THIS IS PERMANENT. I KNEW IT WOULD BE.

TIME TO RESCUE MY WHOLE WORLD, GWEN.

...

OKAY, WE'RE HERE. I'M SORRY!

WHAT THE HELL TOOK-- OH. UH. IS THAT YOU, RAMONE?

IT IS.

I'm Ready For The Reboot

WELL, HELL. YES.

I'm Ready For The Reboot

THESE ARE THE KIND OF REINFORCEMENTS I'M TALKING ABOUT.

NEARLY UNIRONIC "GO TEAM" THUMBS-UP!

I'm Ready For

DID YOU... CHANGE YOUR T-SHIRT?

I'm Ready For The Reboot

YOU TOOK A VERY LONG TIME.

ALL RIGHT, LET'S GET THIS RESCUE MISSION STARTED!

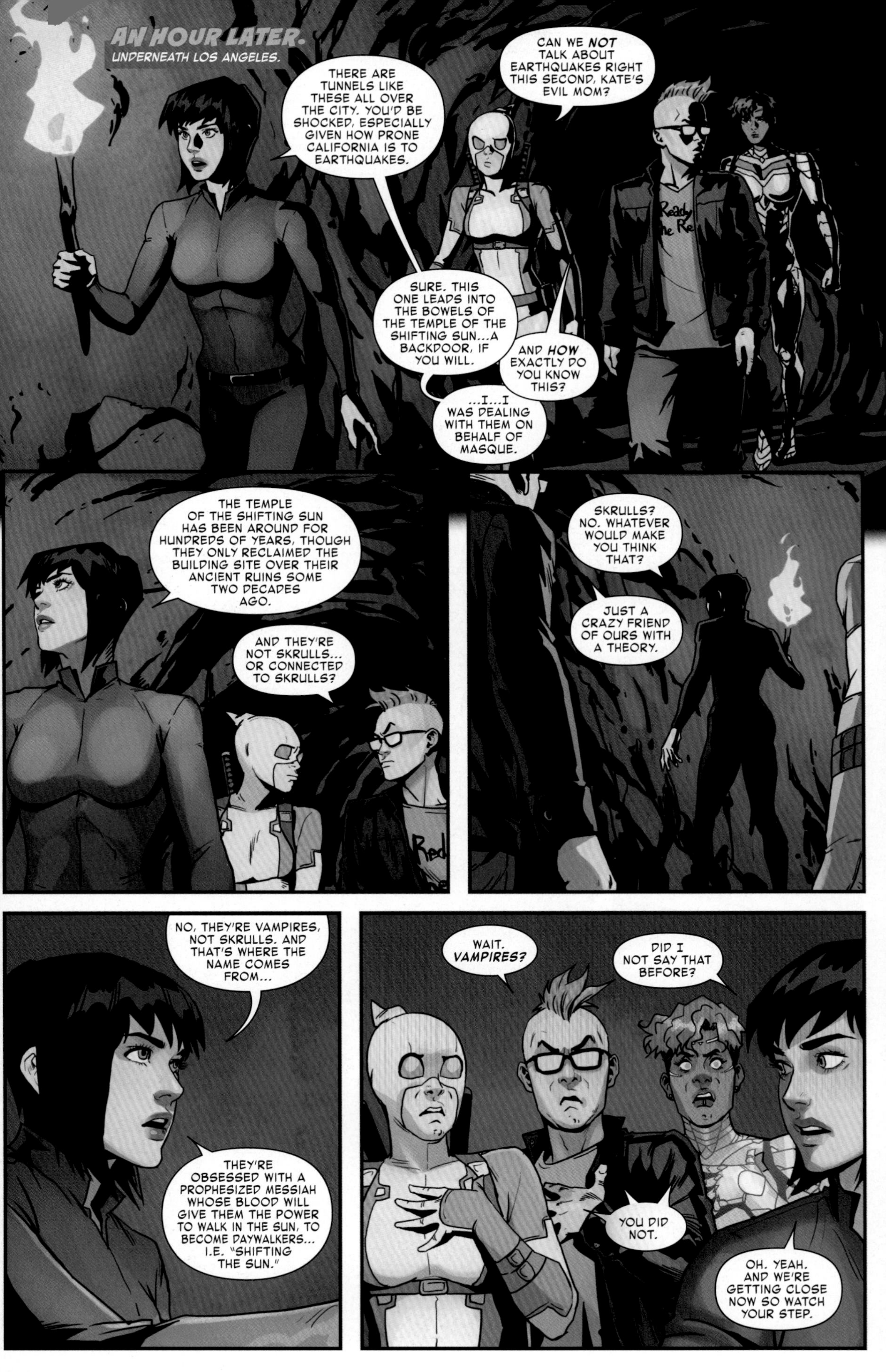
AN HOUR LATER.
UNDERNEATH LOS ANGELES.
THERE ARE TUNNELS LIKE THESE ALL OVER THE CITY. YOU'D BE SHOCKED, ESPECIALLY GIVEN HOW PRONE CALIFORNIA IS TO EARTHQUAKES.
CAN WE NOT TALK ABOUT EARTHQUAKES RIGHT THIS SECOND, KATE'S EVIL MOM?
SURE. THIS ONE LEADS INTO THE BOWELS OF THE TEMPLE OF THE SHIFTING SUN...A BACKDOOR, IF YOU WILL.
AND HOW EXACTLY DO YOU KNOW THIS?
...I...I WAS DEALING WITH THEM ON BEHALF OF MASQUE.
THE TEMPLE OF THE SHIFTING SUN HAS BEEN AROUND FOR HUNDREDS OF YEARS, THOUGH THEY ONLY RECLAIMED THE BUILDING SITE OVER THEIR ANCIENT RUINS SOME TWO DECADES AGO.
AND THEY'RE NOT SKRULLS... OR CONNECTED TO SKRULLS?
SKRULLS? NO. WHATEVER WOULD MAKE YOU THINK THAT?
JUST A CRAZY FRIEND OF OURS WITH A THEORY.
NO, THEY'RE VAMPIRES, NOT SKRULLS. AND THAT'S WHERE THE NAME COMES FROM...
THEY'RE OBSESSED WITH A PROPHESIZED MESSIAH WHOSE BLOOD WILL GIVE THEM THE POWER TO WALK IN THE SUN, TO BECOME DAYWALKERS... I.E. "SHIFTING THE SUN."
WAIT. VAMPIRES?
DID I NOT SAY THAT BEFORE?
YOU DID NOT.
OH. YEAH. AND WE'RE GETTING CLOSE NOW SO WATCH YOUR STEP.

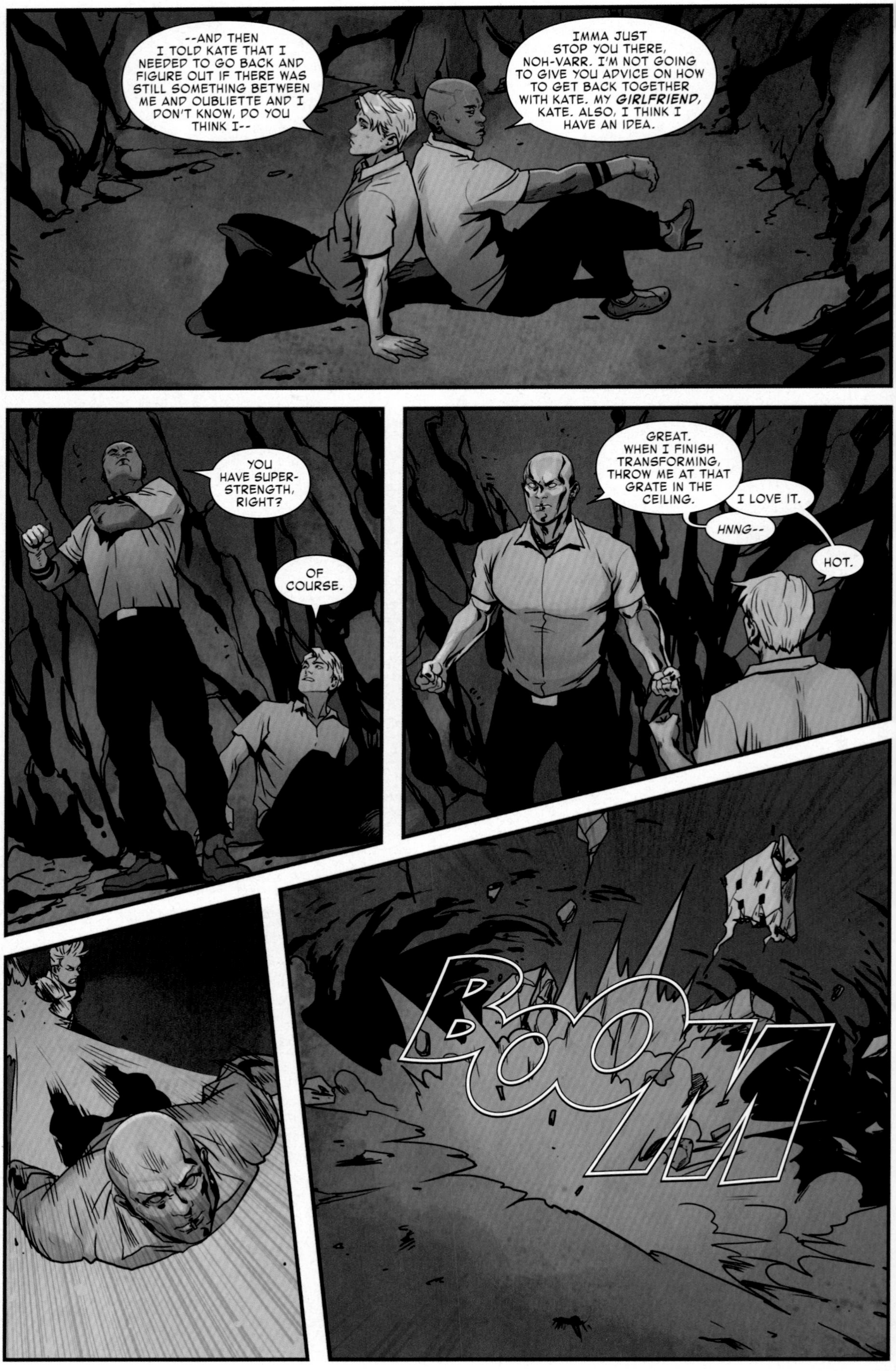
--AND THEN I TOLD KATE THAT I NEEDED TO GO BACK AND FIGURE OUT IF THERE WAS STILL SOMETHING BETWEEN ME AND OUBLIETTE AND I DON'T KNOW, DO YOU THINK I--
IMMA JUST STOP YOU THERE, NOH-VARR. I'M NOT GOING TO GIVE YOU ADVICE ON HOW TO GET BACK TOGETHER WITH KATE. MY *GIRLFRIEND,* KATE. ALSO, I THINK I HAVE AN IDEA.
YOU HAVE SUPER-STRENGTH, RIGHT?
OF COURSE.
GREAT. WHEN I FINISH TRANSFORMING, THROW ME AT THAT GRATE IN THE CEILING.
HNNG--
I LOVE IT.
HOT.
BOOM

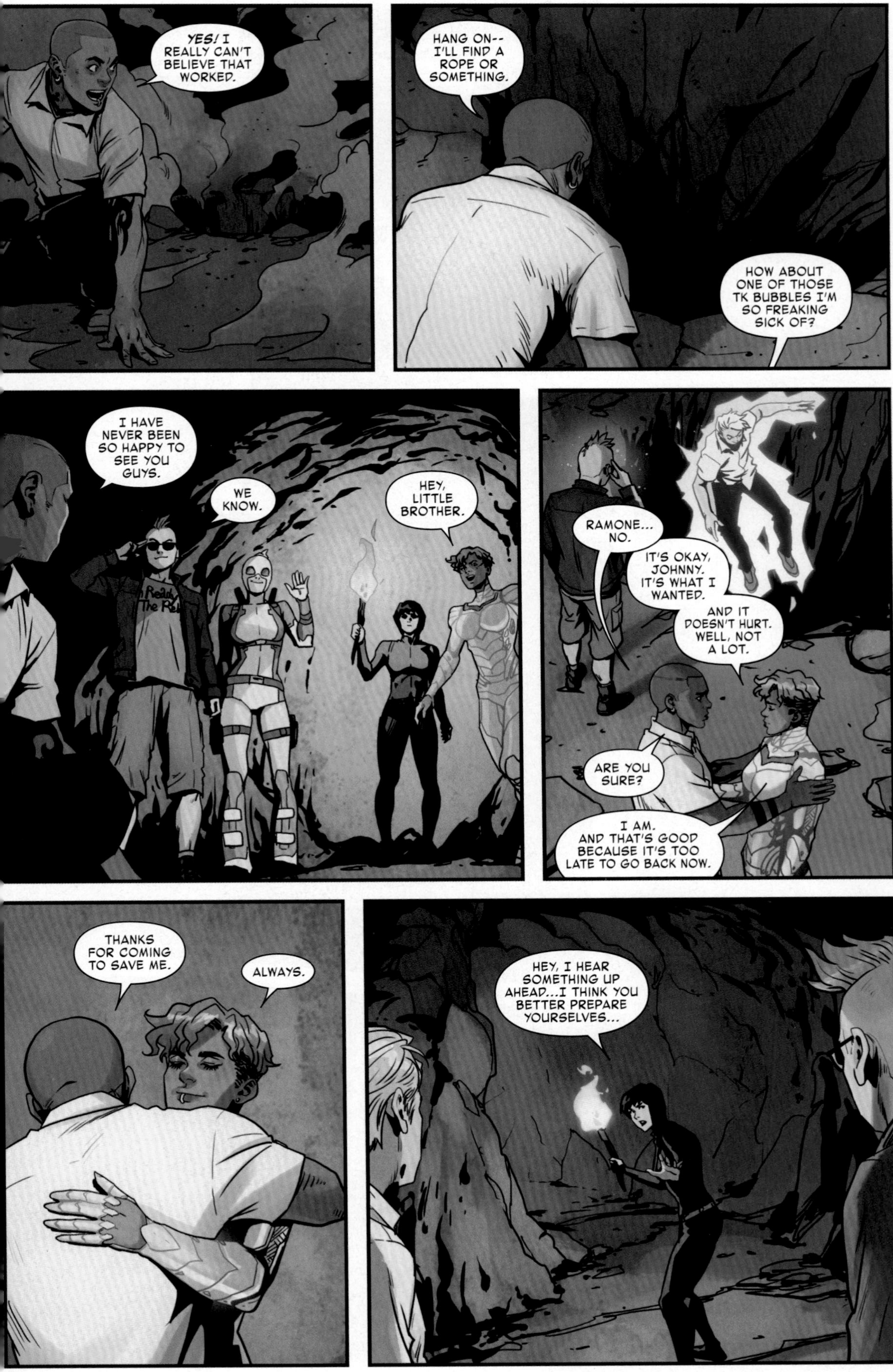
YES! I REALLY CAN'T BELIEVE THAT WORKED.
HANG ON-- I'LL FIND A ROPE OR SOMETHING.
HOW ABOUT ONE OF THOSE TK BUBBLES I'M SO FREAKING SICK OF?
I HAVE NEVER BEEN SO HAPPY TO SEE YOU GUYS.
WE KNOW.
HEY, LITTLE BROTHER.
RAMONE... NO.
IT'S OKAY, JOHNNY. IT'S WHAT I WANTED.
AND IT DOESN'T HURT. WELL, NOT A LOT.
ARE YOU SURE?
I AM. AND THAT'S GOOD BECAUSE IT'S TOO LATE TO GO BACK NOW.
THANKS FOR COMING TO SAVE ME.
ALWAYS.
HEY, I HEAR SOMETHING UP AHEAD...I THINK YOU BETTER PREPARE YOURSELVES...

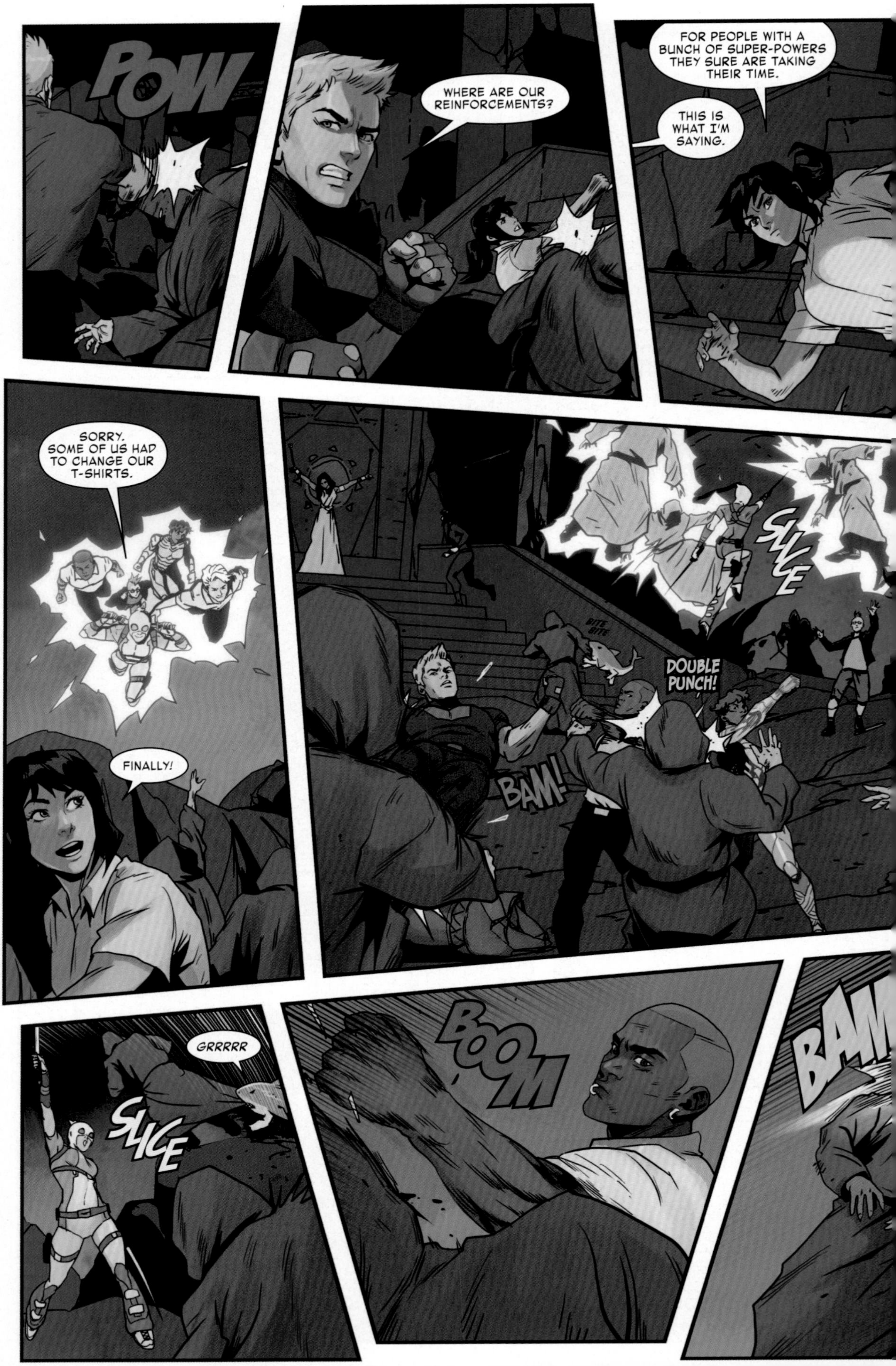
POW
WHERE ARE OUR REINFORCEMENTS?
FOR PEOPLE WITH A BUNCH OF SUPER-POWERS THEY SURE ARE TAKING THEIR TIME.
THIS IS WHAT I'M SAYING.
SORRY. SOME OF US HAD TO CHANGE OUR T-SHIRTS.
FINALLY!
SLICE
BITE BITE
DOUBLE PUNCH!
BAM!
GRRRRR
SLICE
BOOM
BAM

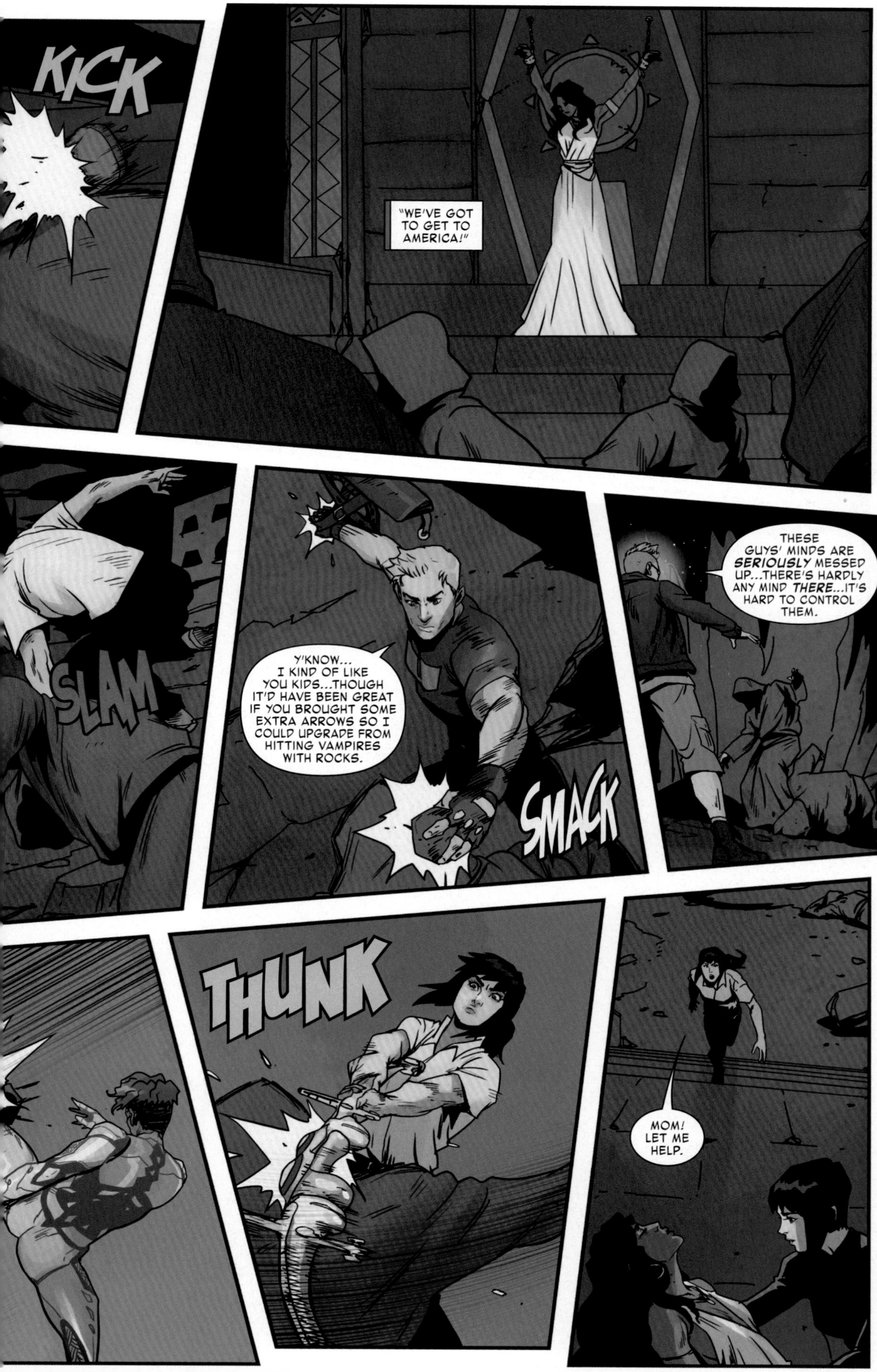
KICK
"WE'VE GOT TO GET TO AMERICA!"
SLAM
Y'KNOW... I KIND OF LIKE YOU KIDS...THOUGH IT'D HAVE BEEN GREAT IF YOU BROUGHT SOME EXTRA ARROWS SO I COULD UPGRADE FROM HITTING VAMPIRES WITH ROCKS.
SMACK
THESE GUYS' MINDS ARE SERIOUSLY MESSED UP...THERE'S HARDLY ANY MIND THERE...IT'S HARD TO CONTROL THEM.
THUNK
MOM! LET ME HELP.

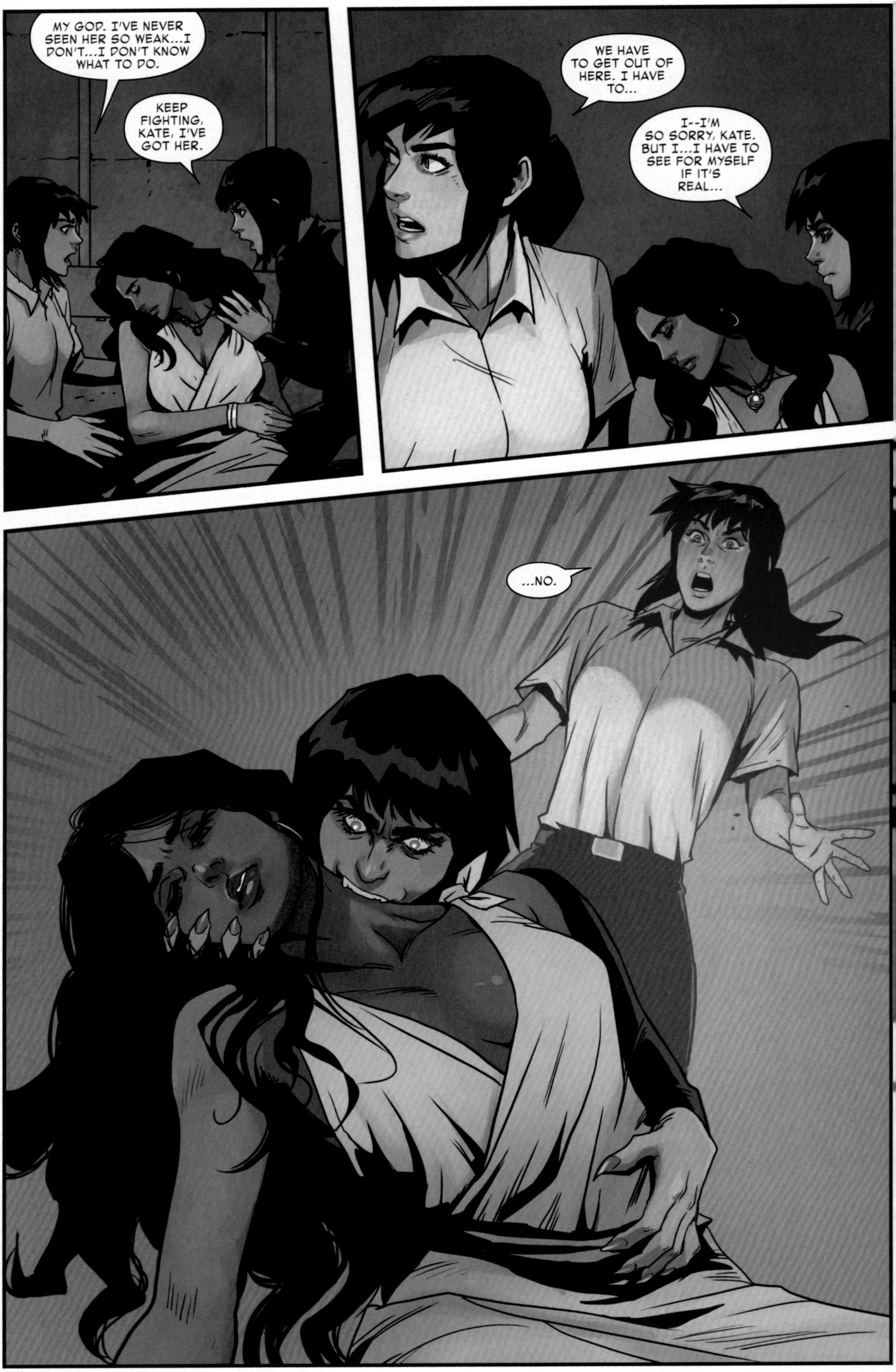
MY GOD. I'VE NEVER SEEN HER SO WEAK...I DON'T...I DON'T KNOW WHAT TO DO.
KEEP FIGHTING, KATE, I'VE GOT HER.
WE HAVE TO GET OUT OF HERE. I HAVE TO...
I--I'M SO SORRY, KATE. BUT I...I HAVE TO SEE FOR MYSELF IF IT'S REAL...
...NO.

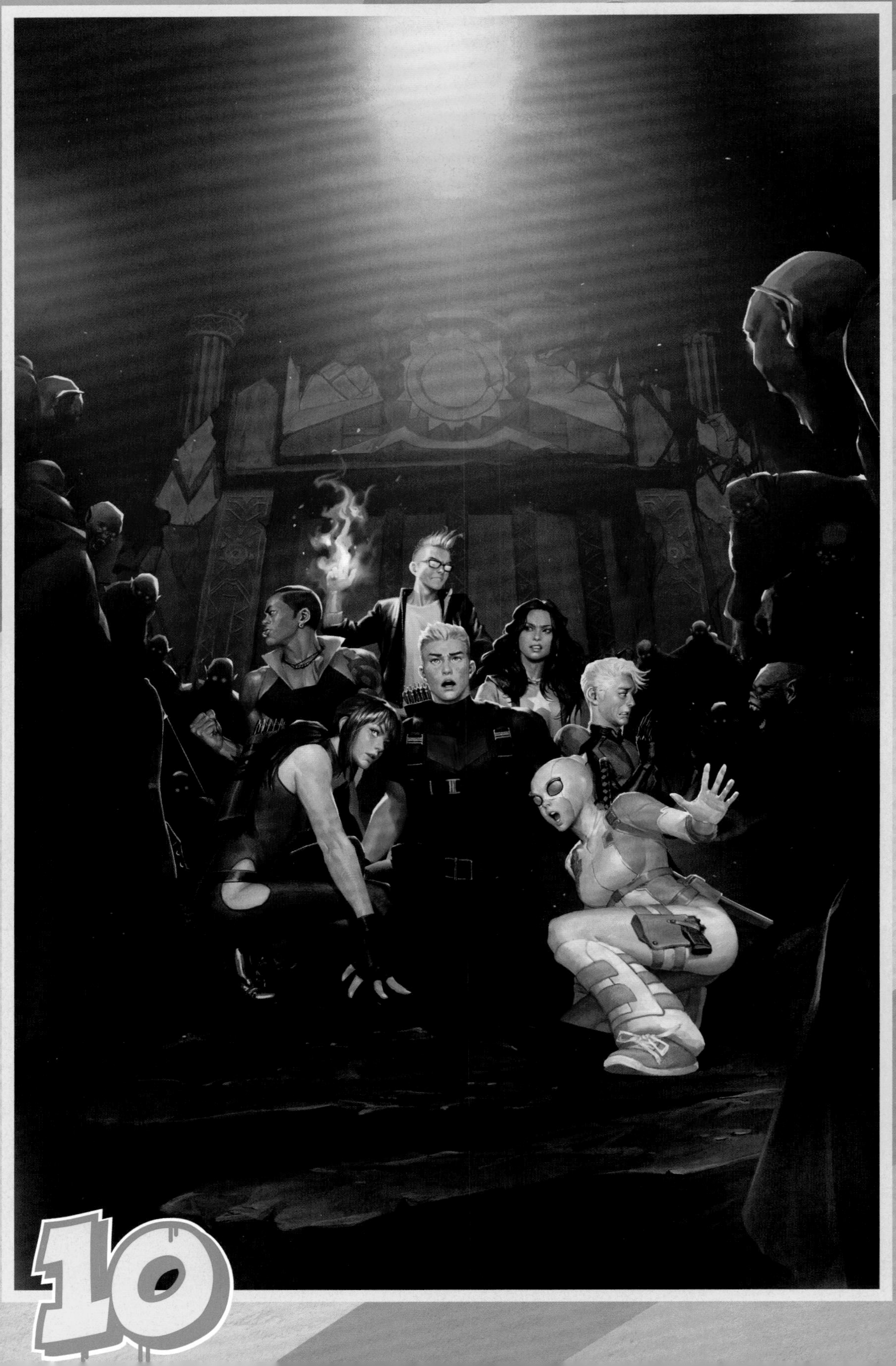
10

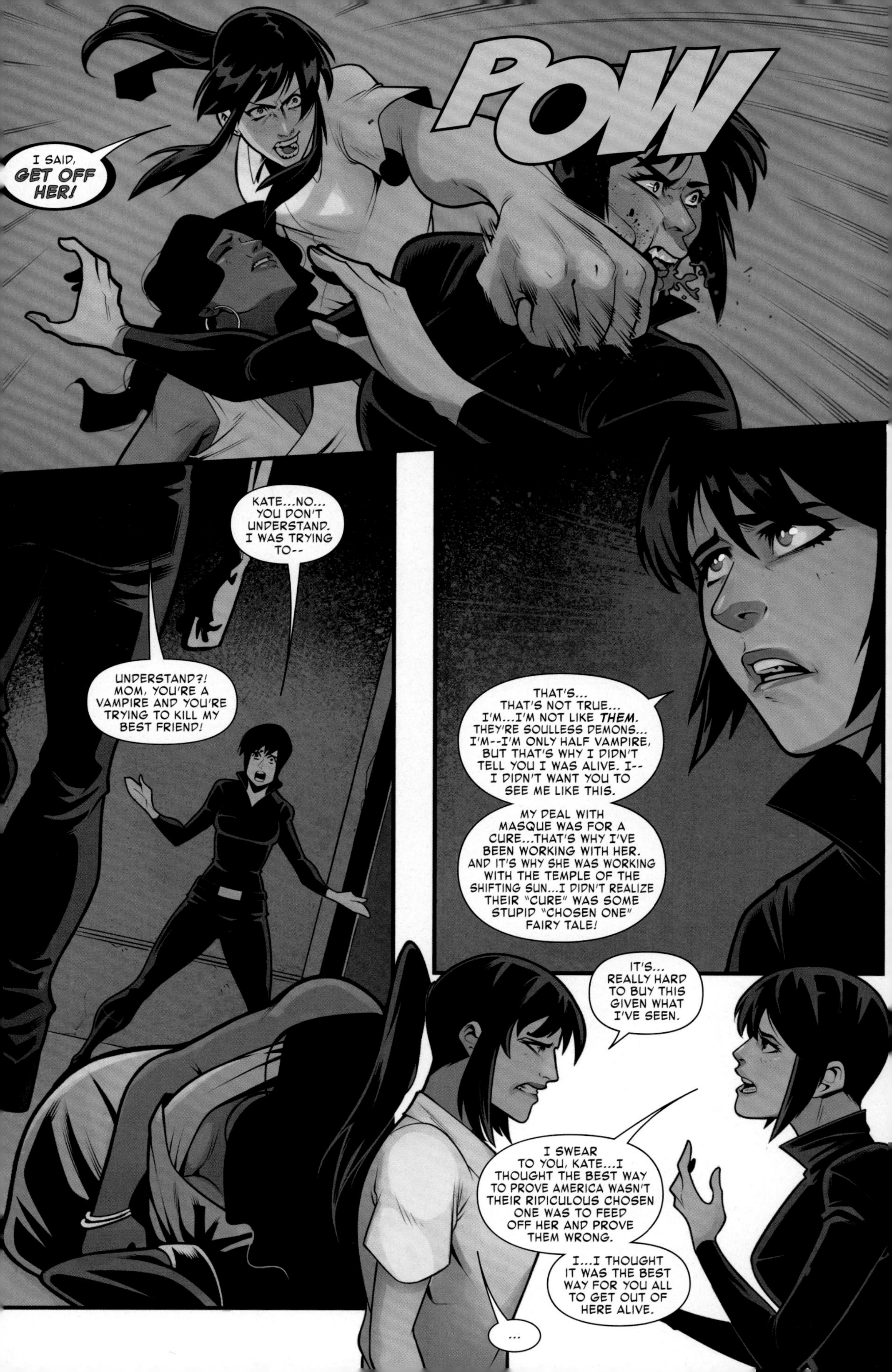
I SAID, GET OFF HER!
POW
KATE...NO... YOU DON'T UNDERSTAND. I WAS TRYING TO--
UNDERSTAND?! MOM, YOU'RE A VAMPIRE AND YOU'RE TRYING TO KILL MY BEST FRIEND!
THAT'S... THAT'S NOT TRUE... I'M...I'M NOT LIKE THEM. THEY'RE SOULLESS DEMONS... I'M--I'M ONLY HALF VAMPIRE, BUT THAT'S WHY I DIDN'T TELL YOU I WAS ALIVE. I-- I DIDN'T WANT YOU TO SEE ME LIKE THIS.
MY DEAL WITH MASQUE WAS FOR A CURE...THAT'S WHY I'VE BEEN WORKING WITH HER. AND IT'S WHY SHE WAS WORKING WITH THE TEMPLE OF THE SHIFTING SUN...I DIDN'T REALIZE THEIR "CURE" WAS SOME STUPID "CHOSEN ONE" FAIRY TALE!
IT'S... REALLY HARD TO BUY THIS GIVEN WHAT I'VE SEEN.
I SWEAR TO YOU, KATE...I THOUGHT THE BEST WAY TO PROVE AMERICA WASN'T THEIR RIDICULOUS CHOSEN ONE WAS TO FEED OFF HER AND PROVE THEM WRONG.
I...I THOUGHT IT WAS THE BEST WAY FOR YOU ALL TO GET OUT OF HERE ALIVE.
...

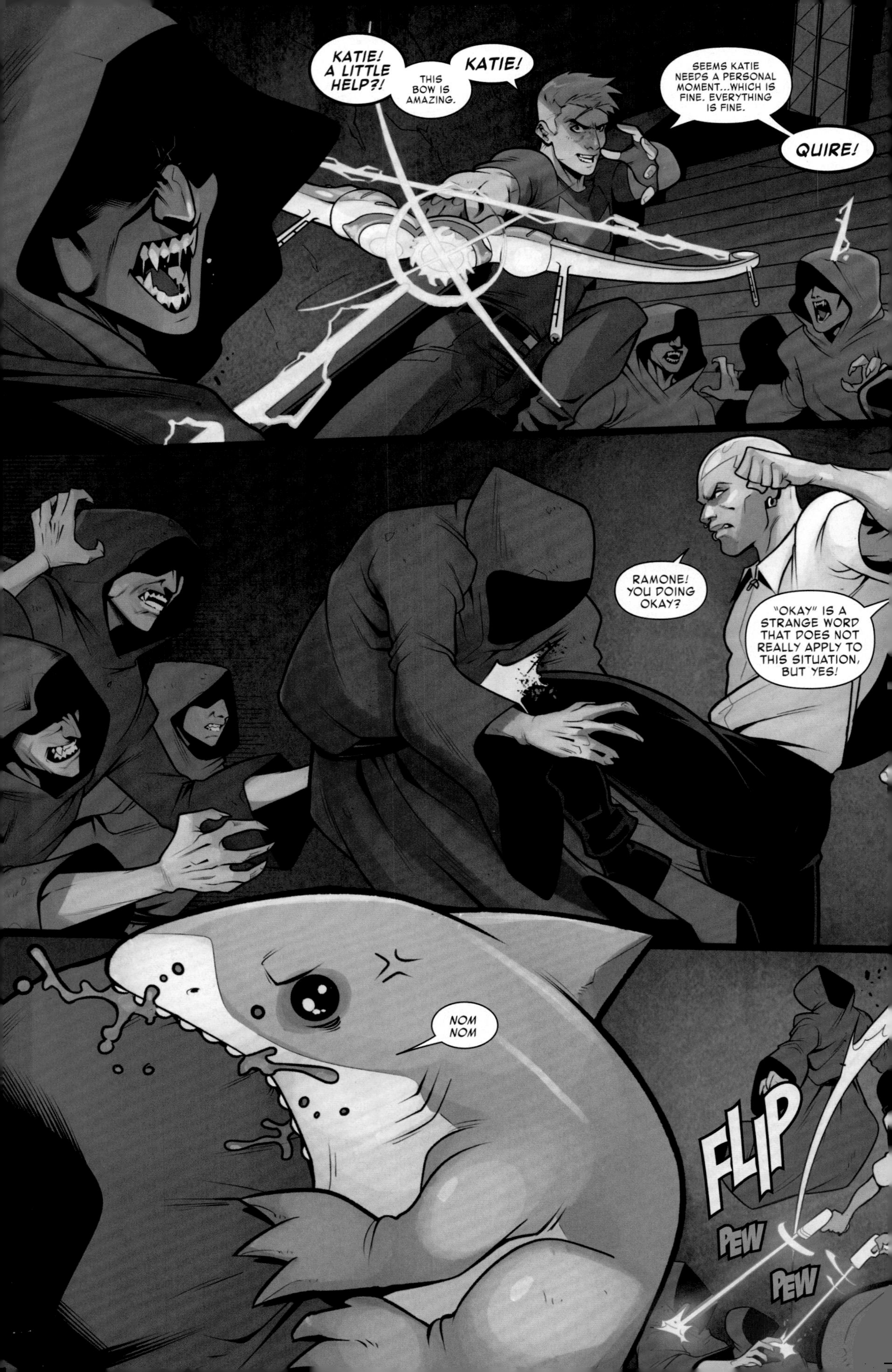
KATIE! A LITTLE HELP?!
THIS BOW IS AMAZING.
KATIE!
SEEMS KATIE NEEDS A PERSONAL MOMENT...WHICH IS FINE. EVERYTHING IS FINE.
QUIRE!
RAMONE! YOU DOING OKAY?
"OKAY" IS A STRANGE WORD THAT DOES NOT REALLY APPLY TO THIS SITUATION, BUT YES!
NOM NOM
FLIP
PEW
PEW

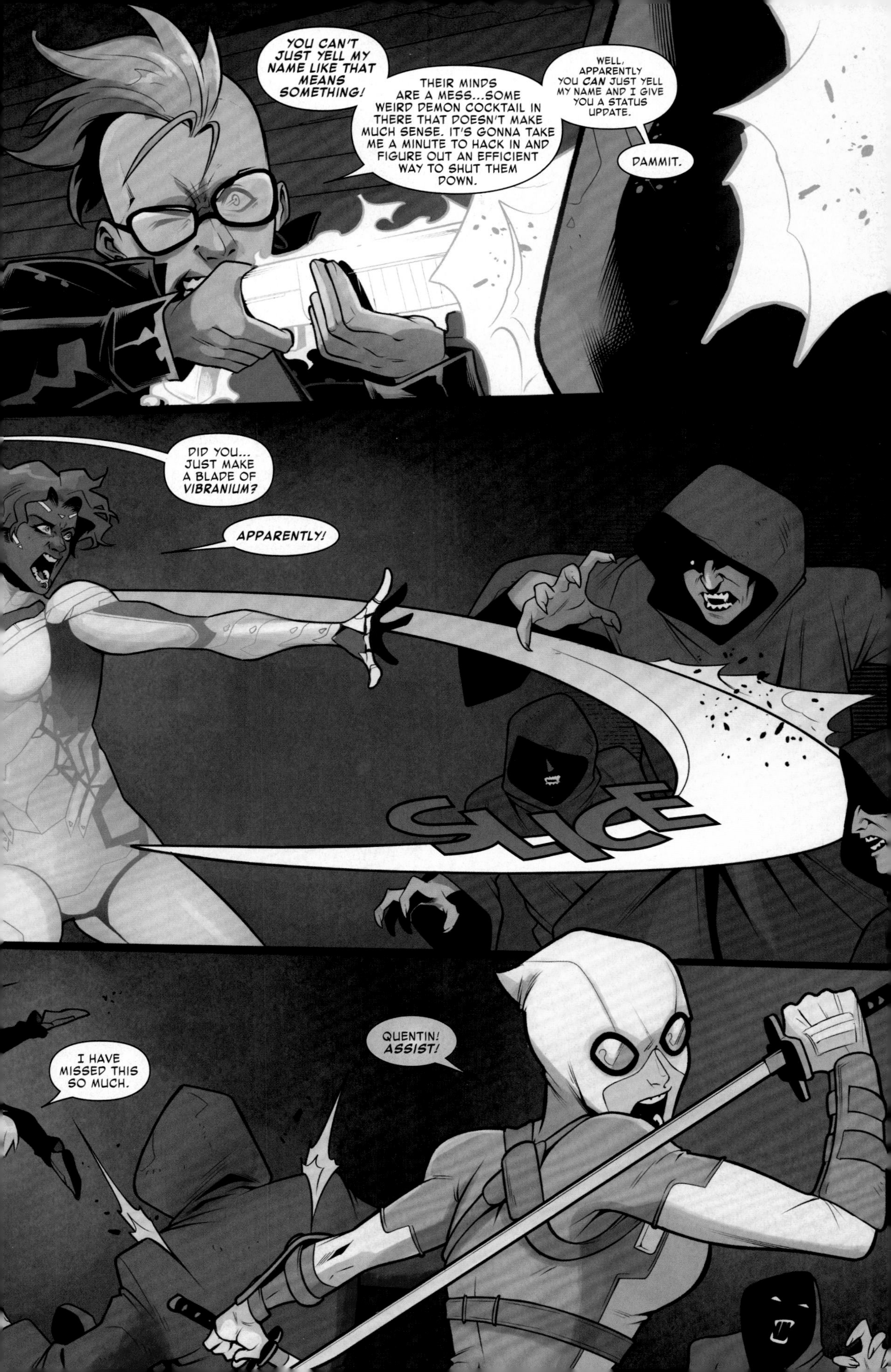
YOU CAN'T JUST YELL MY NAME LIKE THAT MEANS SOMETHING!
THEIR MINDS ARE A MESS...SOME WEIRD DEMON COCKTAIL IN THERE THAT DOESN'T MAKE MUCH SENSE. IT'S GONNA TAKE ME A MINUTE TO HACK IN AND FIGURE OUT AN EFFICIENT WAY TO SHUT THEM DOWN.
WELL, APPARENTLY YOU CAN JUST YELL MY NAME AND I GIVE YOU A STATUS UPDATE.
DAMMIT.
DID YOU... JUST MAKE A BLADE OF VIBRANIUM?
APPARENTLY!
SLICE
I HAVE MISSED THIS SO MUCH.
QUENTIN! ASSIST!

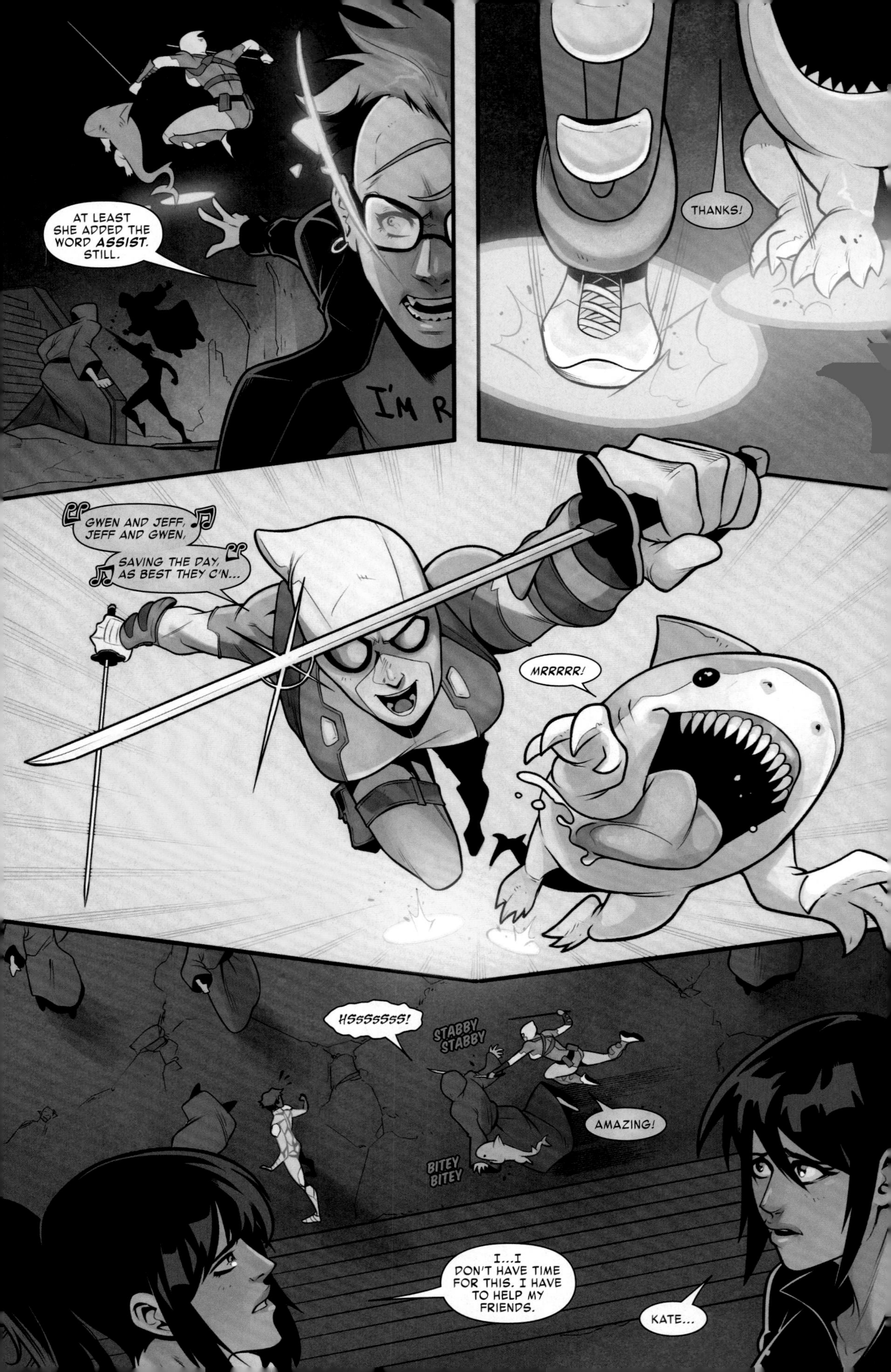
AT LEAST SHE ADDED THE WORD ASSIST. STILL.
I'M R
THANKS!
GWEN AND JEFF, JEFF AND GWEN,
SAVING THE DAY, AS BEST THEY C'N...
MRRRRR!
HSSSSSSS!
STABBY STABBY
AMAZING!
BITEY BITEY
I...I DON'T HAVE TIME FOR THIS. I HAVE TO HELP MY FRIENDS.
KATE...

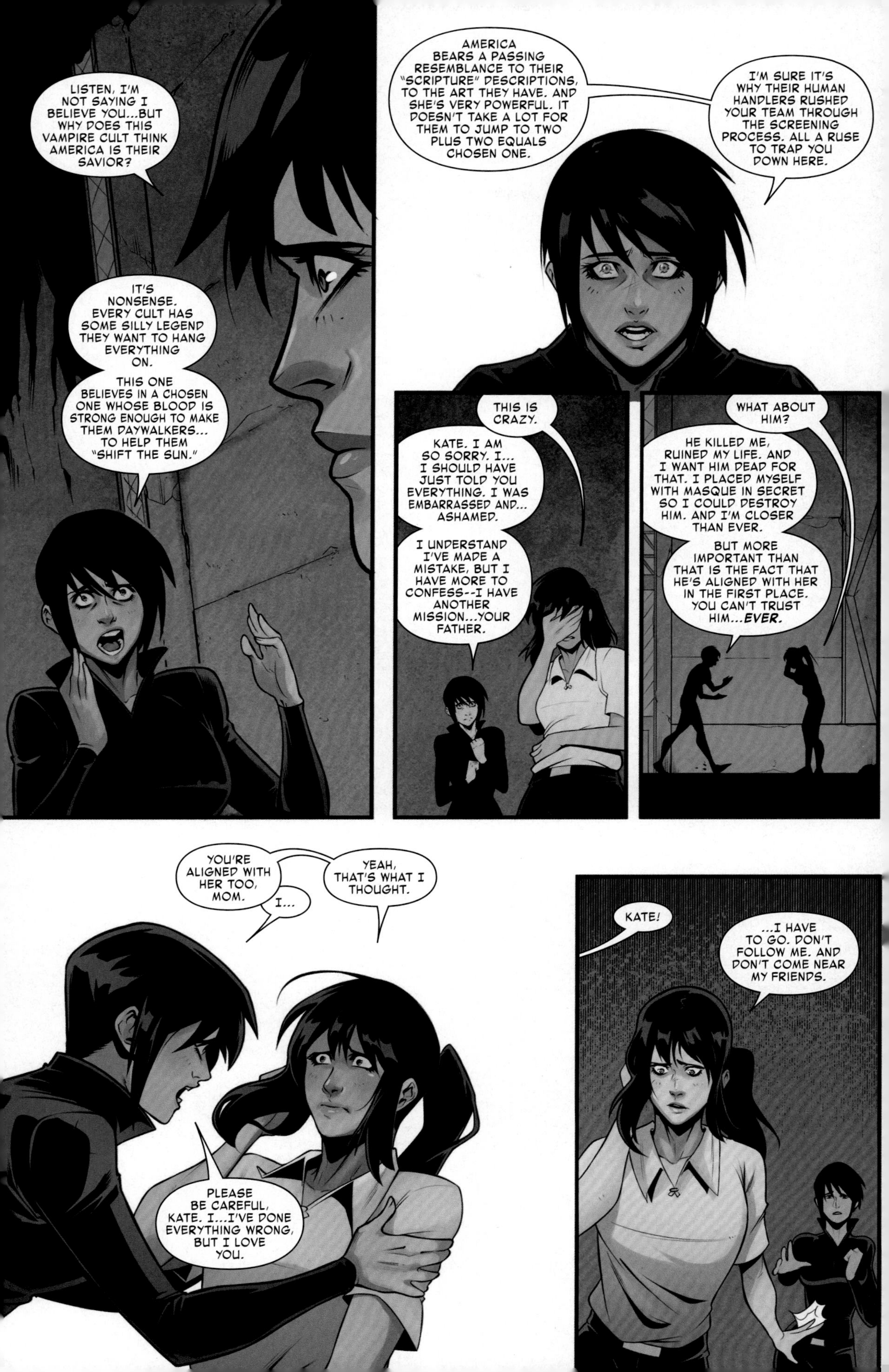
LISTEN, I'M NOT SAYING I BELIEVE YOU...BUT WHY DOES THIS VAMPIRE CULT THINK AMERICA IS THEIR SAVIOR?
IT'S NONSENSE. EVERY CULT HAS SOME SILLY LEGEND THEY WANT TO HANG EVERYTHING ON.
THIS ONE BELIEVES IN A CHOSEN ONE WHOSE BLOOD IS STRONG ENOUGH TO MAKE THEM DAYWALKERS... TO HELP THEM "SHIFT THE SUN."
AMERICA BEARS A PASSING RESEMBLANCE TO THEIR "SCRIPTURE" DESCRIPTIONS, TO THE ART THEY HAVE. AND SHE'S VERY POWERFUL. IT DOESN'T TAKE A LOT FOR THEM TO JUMP TO TWO PLUS TWO EQUALS CHOSEN ONE.
I'M SURE IT'S WHY THEIR HUMAN HANDLERS RUSHED YOUR TEAM THROUGH THE SCREENING PROCESS. ALL A RUSE TO TRAP YOU DOWN HERE.
THIS IS CRAZY.
KATE. I AM SO SORRY. I... I SHOULD HAVE JUST TOLD YOU EVERYTHING. I WAS EMBARRASSED AND... ASHAMED.
I UNDERSTAND I'VE MADE A MISTAKE, BUT I HAVE MORE TO CONFESS--I HAVE ANOTHER MISSION...YOUR FATHER.
WHAT ABOUT HIM?
HE KILLED ME, RUINED MY LIFE. AND I WANT HIM DEAD FOR THAT. I PLACED MYSELF WITH MASQUE IN SECRET SO I COULD DESTROY HIM. AND I'M CLOSER THAN EVER.
BUT MORE IMPORTANT THAN THAT IS THE FACT THAT HE'S ALIGNED WITH HER IN THE FIRST PLACE. YOU CAN'T TRUST HIM...EVER.
YOU'RE ALIGNED WITH HER TOO, MOM.
I...
YEAH, THAT'S WHAT I THOUGHT.
PLEASE BE CAREFUL, KATE. I...I'VE DONE EVERYTHING WRONG, BUT I LOVE YOU.
KATE!
...I HAVE TO GO. DON'T FOLLOW ME. AND DON'T COME NEAR MY FRIENDS.

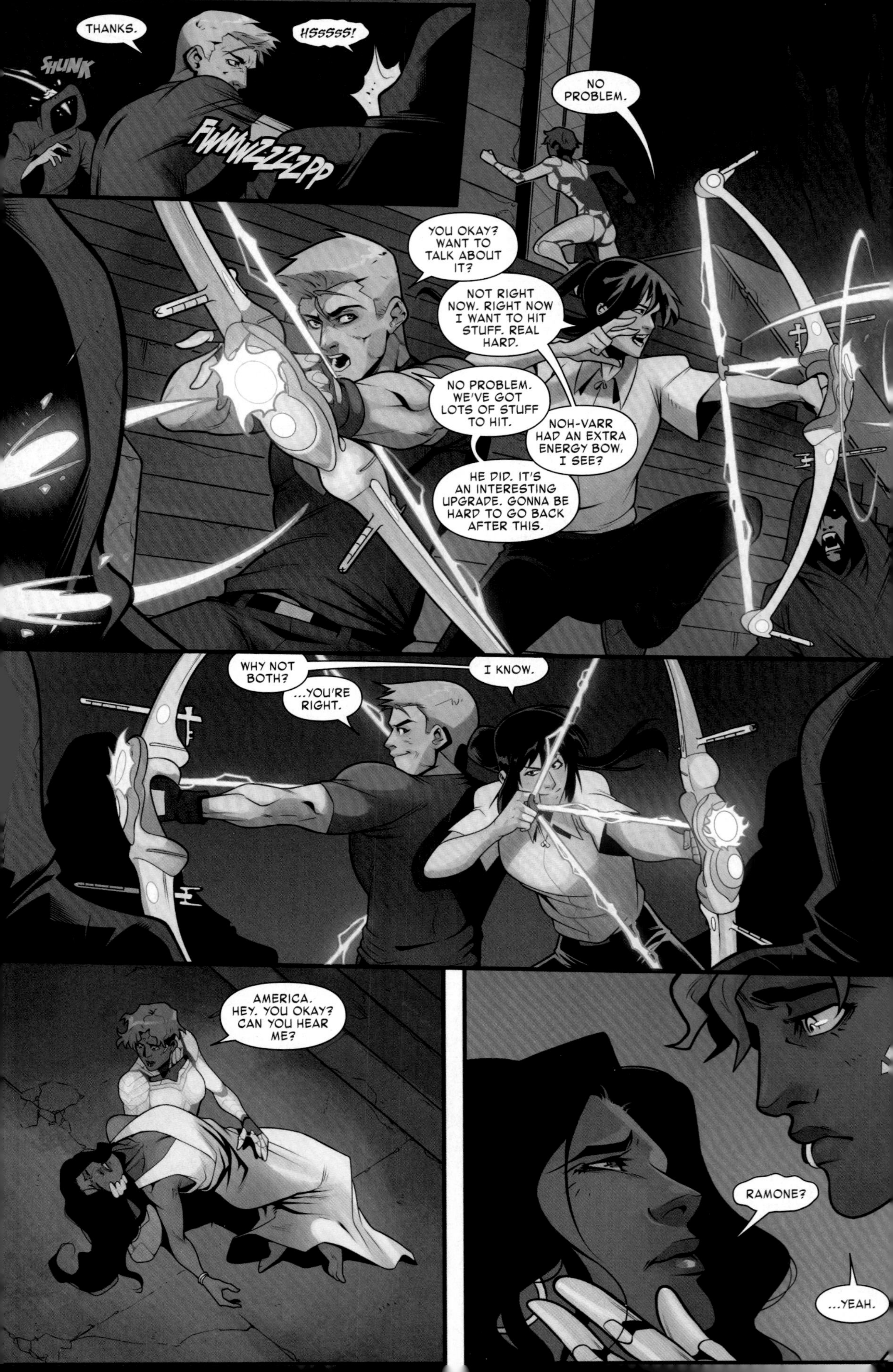
THANKS.
SHUNK
HSSSSS!
FWWWZZZZZPP
NO PROBLEM.
YOU OKAY? WANT TO TALK ABOUT IT?
NOT RIGHT NOW. RIGHT NOW I WANT TO HIT STUFF. REAL HARD.
NO PROBLEM. WE'VE GOT LOTS OF STUFF TO HIT.
NOH-VARR HAD AN EXTRA ENERGY BOW, I SEE?
HE DID. IT'S AN INTERESTING UPGRADE. GONNA BE HARD TO GO BACK AFTER THIS.
WHY NOT BOTH?
I KNOW.
...YOU'RE RIGHT.
AMERICA. HEY. YOU OKAY? CAN YOU HEAR ME?
RAMONE?
...YEAH.

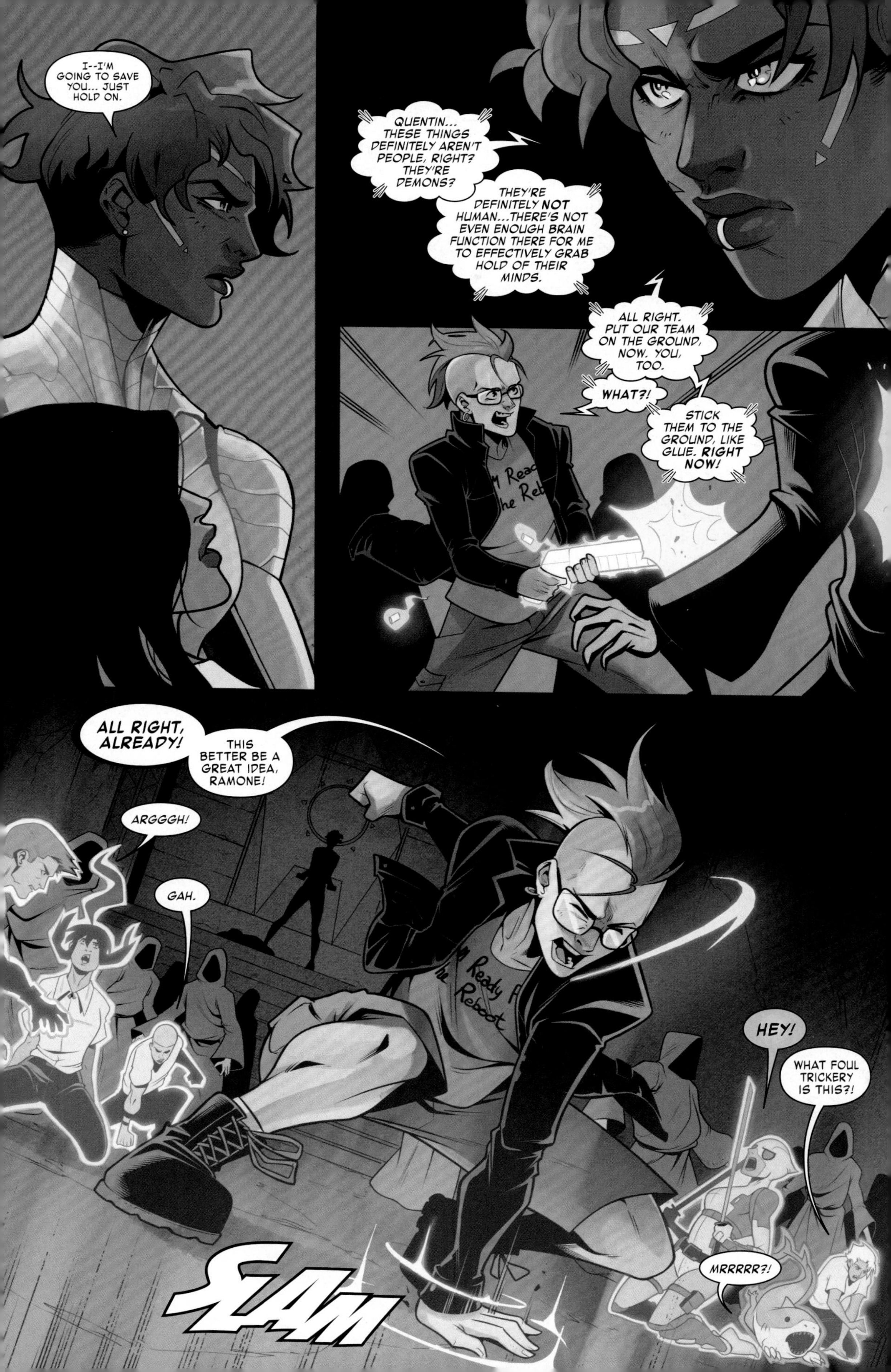
I--I'M GOING TO SAVE YOU... JUST HOLD ON.
QUENTIN... THESE THINGS DEFINITELY AREN'T PEOPLE, RIGHT? THEY'RE DEMONS?
THEY'RE DEFINITELY NOT HUMAN...THERE'S NOT EVEN ENOUGH BRAIN FUNCTION THERE FOR ME TO EFFECTIVELY GRAB HOLD OF THEIR MINDS.
ALL RIGHT. PUT OUR TEAM ON THE GROUND, NOW. YOU, TOO.
WHAT?!
STICK THEM TO THE GROUND, LIKE GLUE. RIGHT NOW!
ALL RIGHT, ALREADY!
THIS BETTER BE A GREAT IDEA, RAMONE!
ARGGGH!
GAH.
HEY!
WHAT FOUL TRICKERY IS THIS?!
MRRRRR?!
SLAM

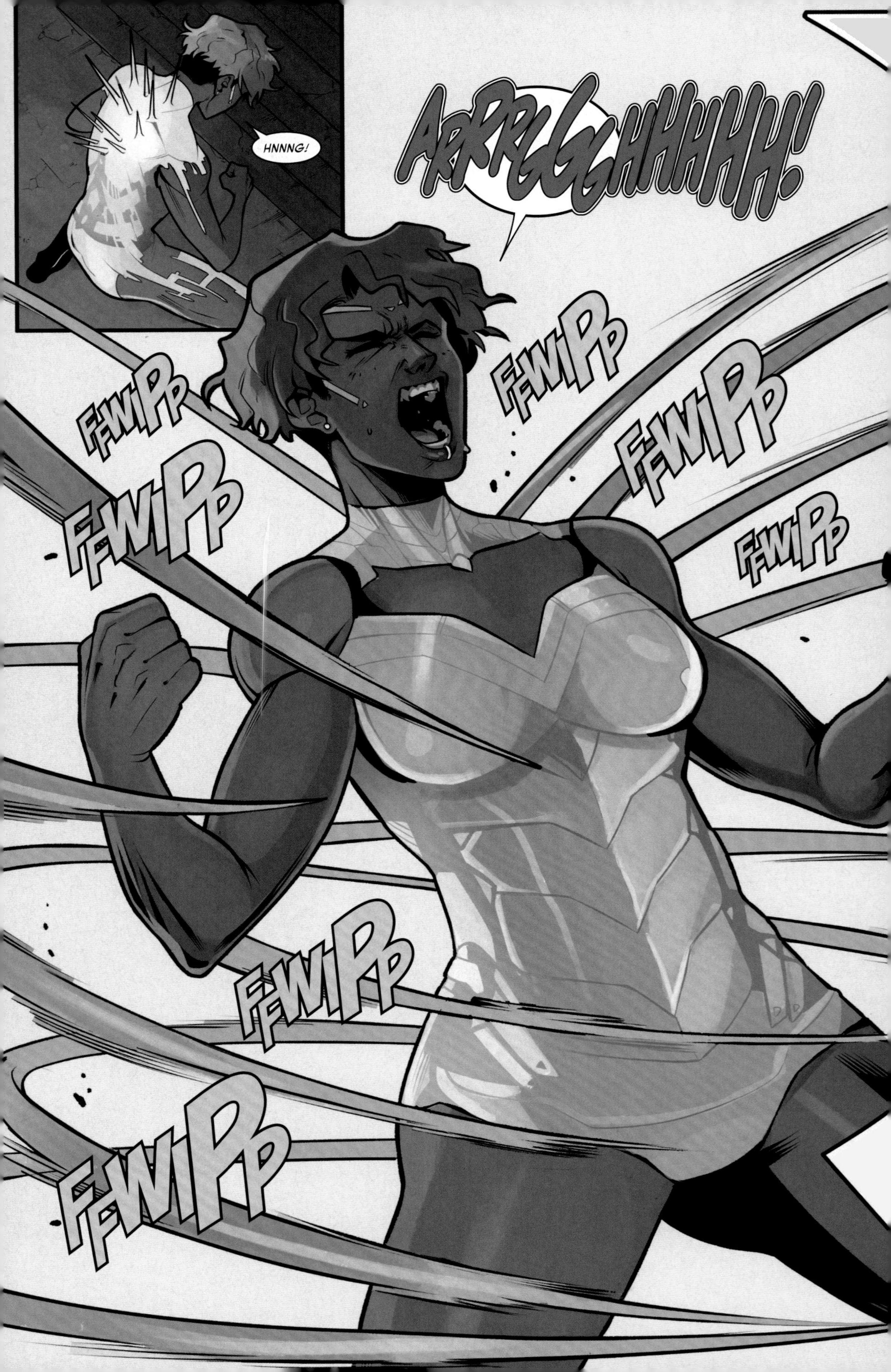
HNNNG!
ARRRGGGHHHHHH!
FFWIPP
FFWIPP
FFWIPP
FFWIPP
FFWIPP
FFWIPP
FFWIPP

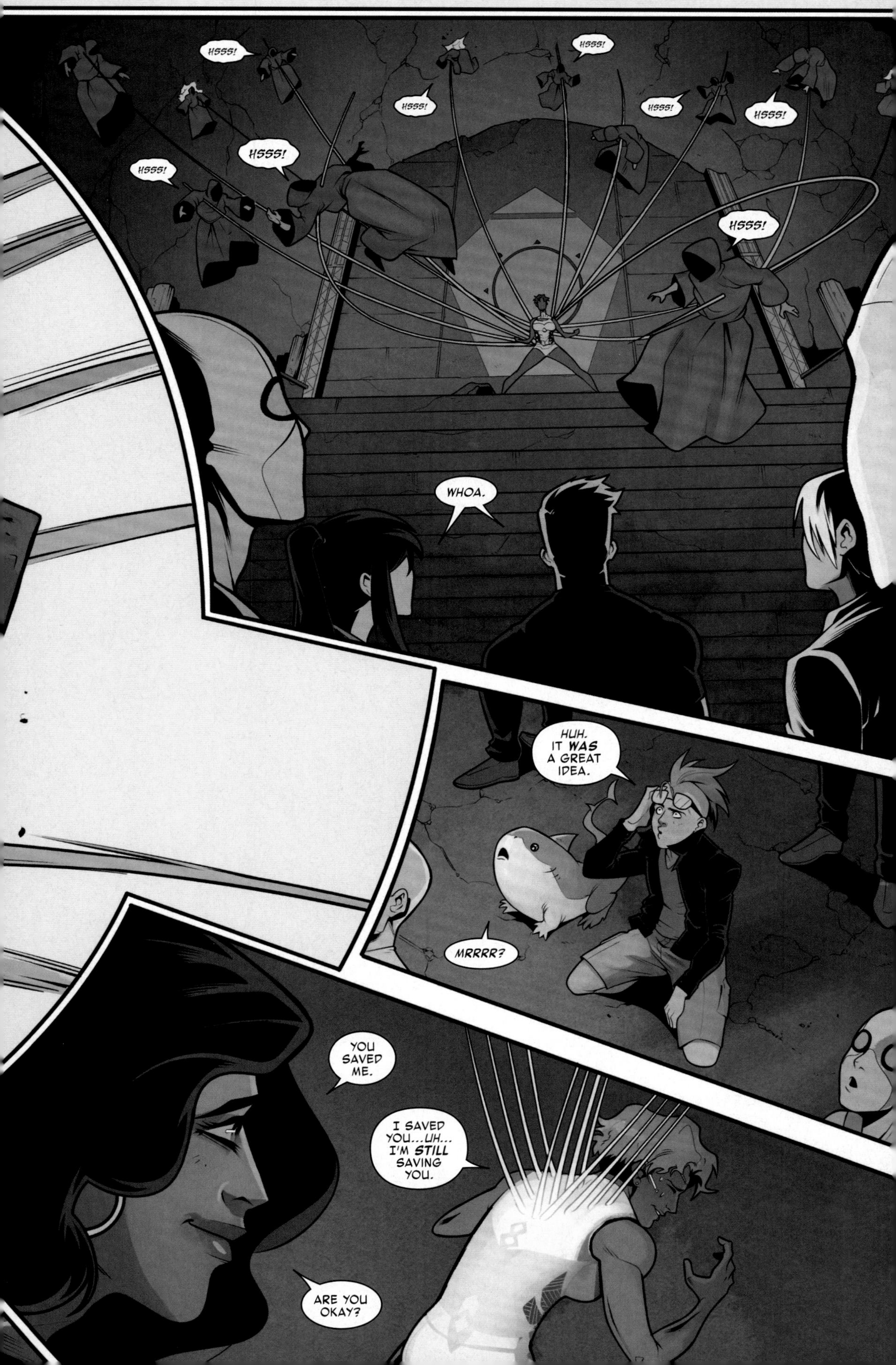
HSSS!
HSSS!
HSSS!
HSSS!
HSSS!
HSSS!
HSSS!
HSSS!
HSSS!
WHOA.
HUH. IT WAS A GREAT IDEA.
MRRRR?
YOU SAVED ME.
I SAVED YOU...UH... I'M STILL SAVING YOU.
ARE YOU OKAY?

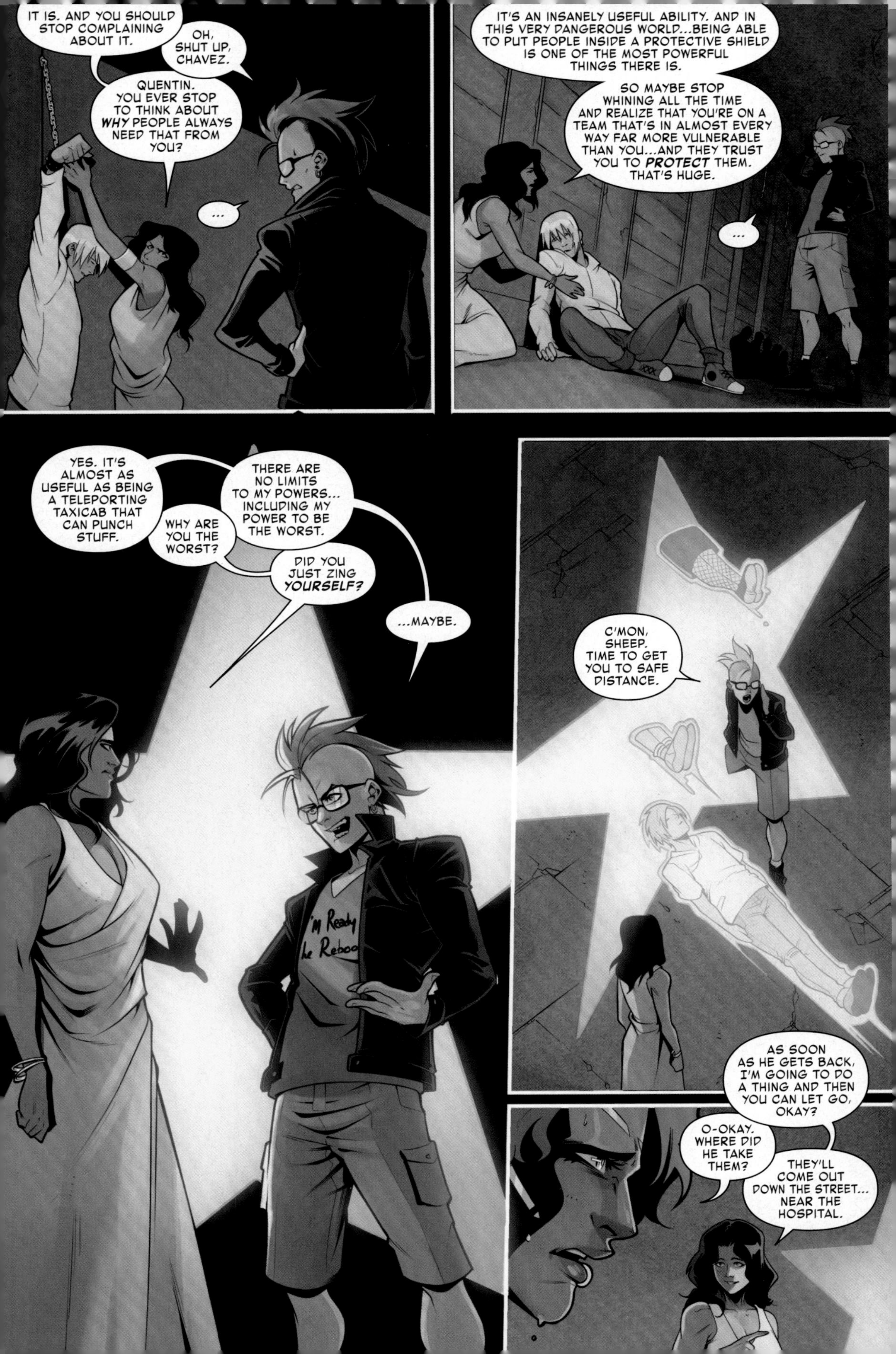

IT IS. AND YOU SHOULD STOP COMPLAINING ABOUT IT.
OH, SHUT UP, CHAVEZ.
QUENTIN. YOU EVER STOP TO THINK ABOUT *WHY* PEOPLE ALWAYS NEED THAT FROM YOU?
...
IT'S AN INSANELY USEFUL ABILITY. AND IN THIS VERY DANGEROUS WORLD...BEING ABLE TO PUT PEOPLE INSIDE A PROTECTIVE SHIELD IS ONE OF THE MOST POWERFUL THINGS THERE IS.
SO MAYBE STOP WHINING ALL THE TIME AND REALIZE THAT YOU'RE ON A TEAM THAT'S IN ALMOST EVERY WAY FAR MORE VULNERABLE THAN YOU...AND THEY TRUST YOU TO *PROTECT* THEM. THAT'S HUGE.
...
YES. IT'S ALMOST AS USEFUL AS BEING A TELEPORTING TAXICAB THAT CAN PUNCH STUFF.
THERE ARE NO LIMITS TO MY POWERS... INCLUDING MY POWER TO BE THE WORST.
WHY ARE YOU THE WORST?
DID YOU JUST ZING *YOURSELF?*
...MAYBE.
C'MON, SHEEP. TIME TO GET YOU TO SAFE DISTANCE.
AS SOON AS HE GETS BACK, I'M GOING TO DO A THING AND THEN YOU CAN LET GO, OKAY?
O-OKAY. WHERE DID HE TAKE THEM?
THEY'LL COME OUT DOWN THE STREET... NEAR THE HOSPITAL.

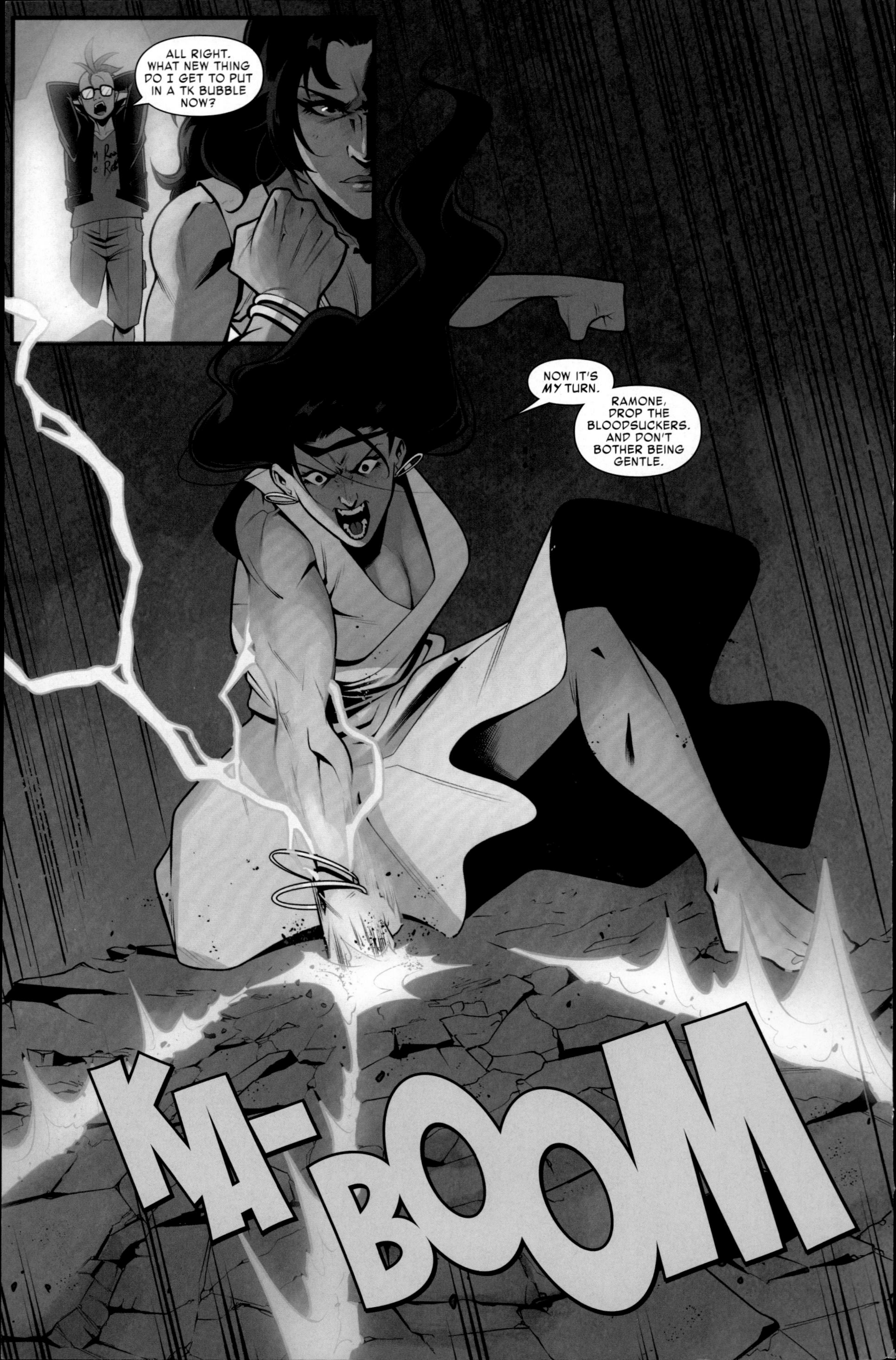
ALL RIGHT. WHAT NEW THING DO I GET TO PUT IN A TK BUBBLE NOW?
NOW IT'S MY TURN.
RAMONE, DROP THE BLOODSUCKERS. AND DON'T BOTHER BEING GENTLE.
KA-BOOM

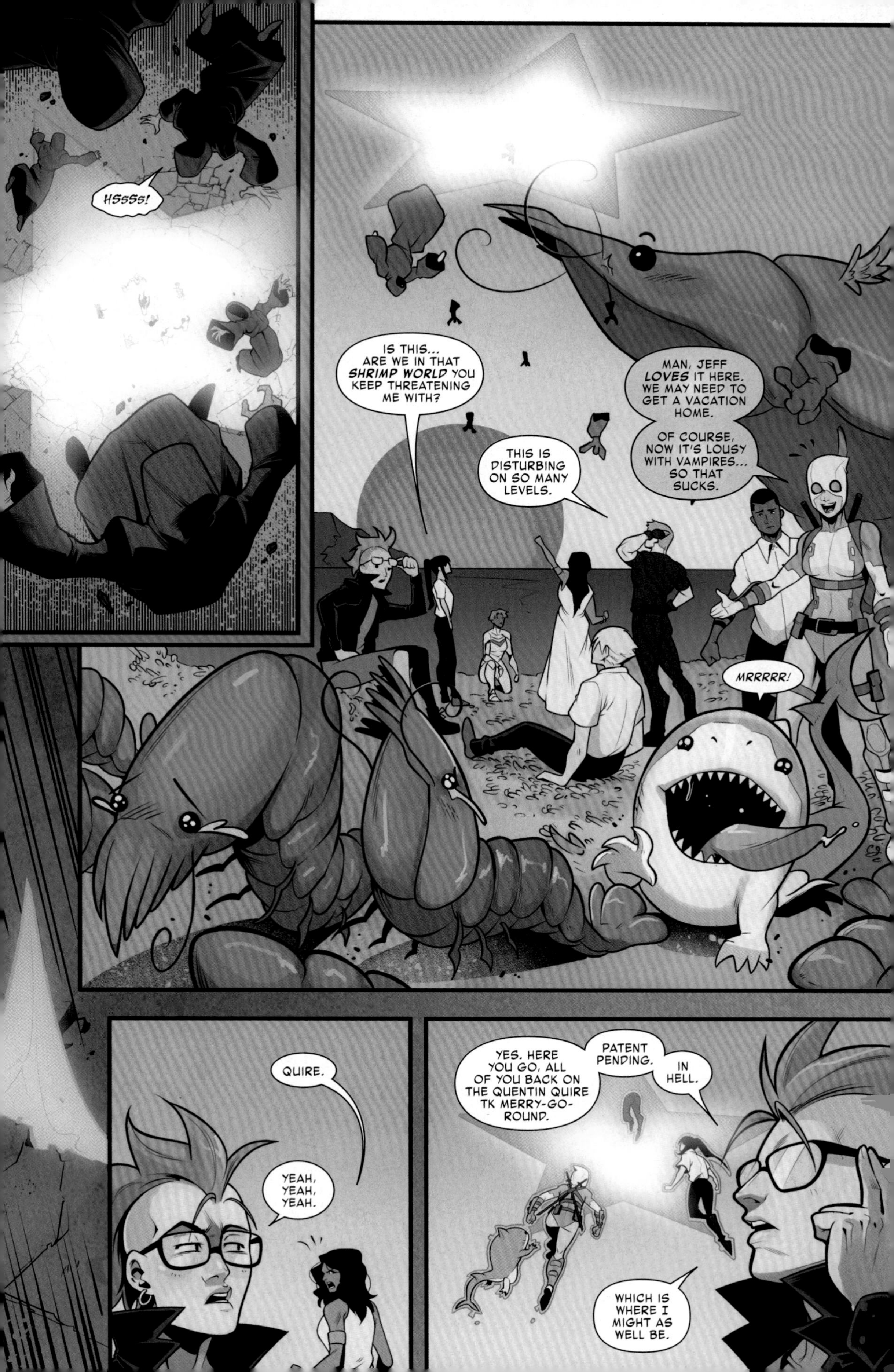
HSSSS!
IS THIS... ARE WE IN THAT SHRIMP WORLD YOU KEEP THREATENING ME WITH?
THIS IS DISTURBING ON SO MANY LEVELS.
MAN, JEFF LOVES IT HERE. WE MAY NEED TO GET A VACATION HOME.
OF COURSE, NOW IT'S LOUSY WITH VAMPIRES... SO THAT SUCKS.
MRRRRR!
QUIRE.
YEAH, YEAH, YEAH.
YES. HERE YOU GO, ALL OF YOU BACK ON THE QUENTIN QUIRE TK MERRY-GO-ROUND.
PATENT PENDING.
IN HELL.
WHICH IS WHERE I MIGHT AS WELL BE.

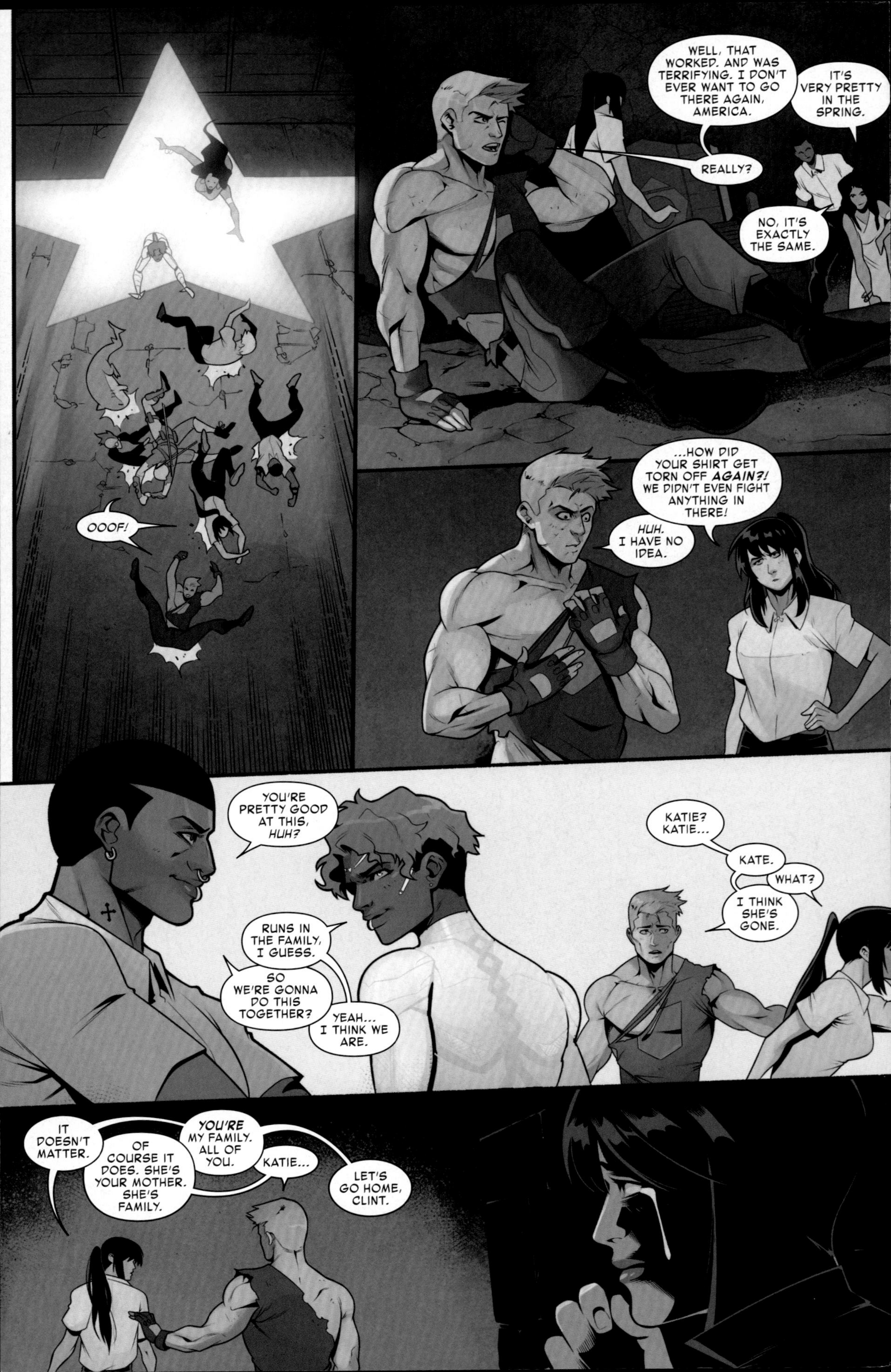
OOOF!
WELL, THAT WORKED. AND WAS TERRIFYING. I DON'T EVER WANT TO GO THERE AGAIN, AMERICA.
IT'S VERY PRETTY IN THE SPRING.
REALLY?
NO, IT'S EXACTLY THE SAME.
...HOW DID YOUR SHIRT GET TORN OFF AGAIN?! WE DIDN'T EVEN FIGHT ANYTHING IN THERE!
HUH. I HAVE NO IDEA.
YOU'RE PRETTY GOOD AT THIS, HUH?
RUNS IN THE FAMILY, I GUESS.
SO WE'RE GONNA DO THIS TOGETHER?
YEAH... I THINK WE ARE.
KATIE? KATIE...
KATE.
WHAT?
I THINK SHE'S GONE.
IT DOESN'T MATTER.
OF COURSE IT DOES. SHE'S YOUR MOTHER. SHE'S FAMILY.
YOU'RE MY FAMILY. ALL OF YOU.
KATIE...
LET'S GO HOME, CLINT.

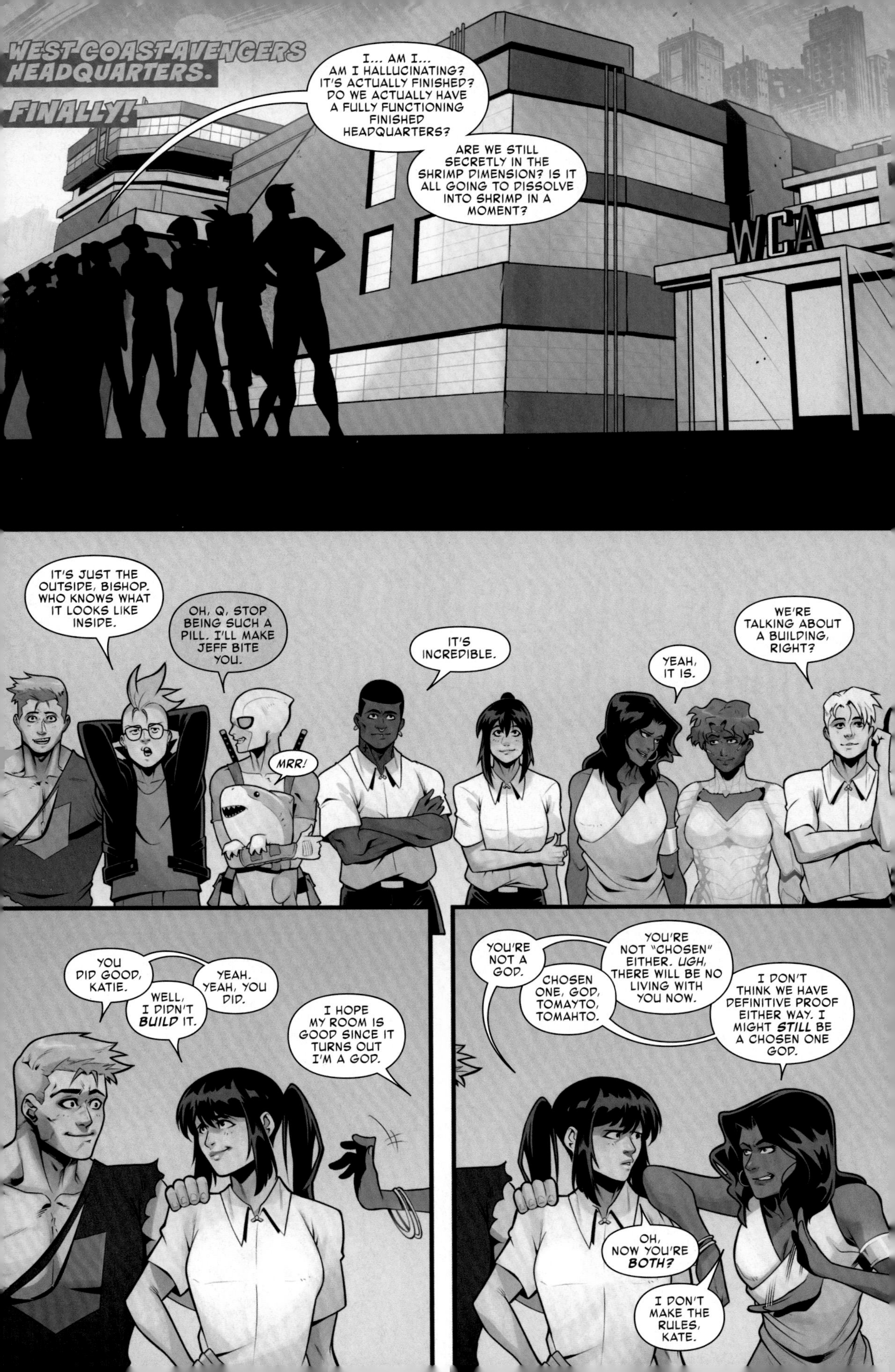
WEST COAST AVENGERS HEADQUARTERS.
FINALLY!
I... AM I... AM I HALLUCINATING? IT'S ACTUALLY FINISHED? DO WE ACTUALLY HAVE A FULLY FUNCTIONING FINISHED HEADQUARTERS?
ARE WE STILL SECRETLY IN THE SHRIMP DIMENSION? IS IT ALL GOING TO DISSOLVE INTO SHRIMP IN A MOMENT?
WCA
IT'S JUST THE OUTSIDE, BISHOP. WHO KNOWS WHAT IT LOOKS LIKE INSIDE.
OH, Q, STOP BEING SUCH A PILL. I'LL MAKE JEFF BITE YOU.
MRR!
IT'S INCREDIBLE.
YEAH, IT IS.
WE'RE TALKING ABOUT A BUILDING, RIGHT?
YOU DID GOOD, KATIE.
YEAH. YEAH, YOU DID.
WELL, I DIDN'T BUILD IT.
I HOPE MY ROOM IS GOOD SINCE IT TURNS OUT I'M A GOD.
YOU'RE NOT A GOD.
CHOSEN ONE, GOD, TOMAYTO, TOMAHTO.
YOU'RE NOT "CHOSEN" EITHER. UGH, THERE WILL BE NO LIVING WITH YOU NOW.
I DON'T THINK WE HAVE DEFINITIVE PROOF EITHER WAY. I MIGHT STILL BE A CHOSEN ONE GOD.
OH, NOW YOU'RE BOTH?
I DON'T MAKE THE RULES, KATE.

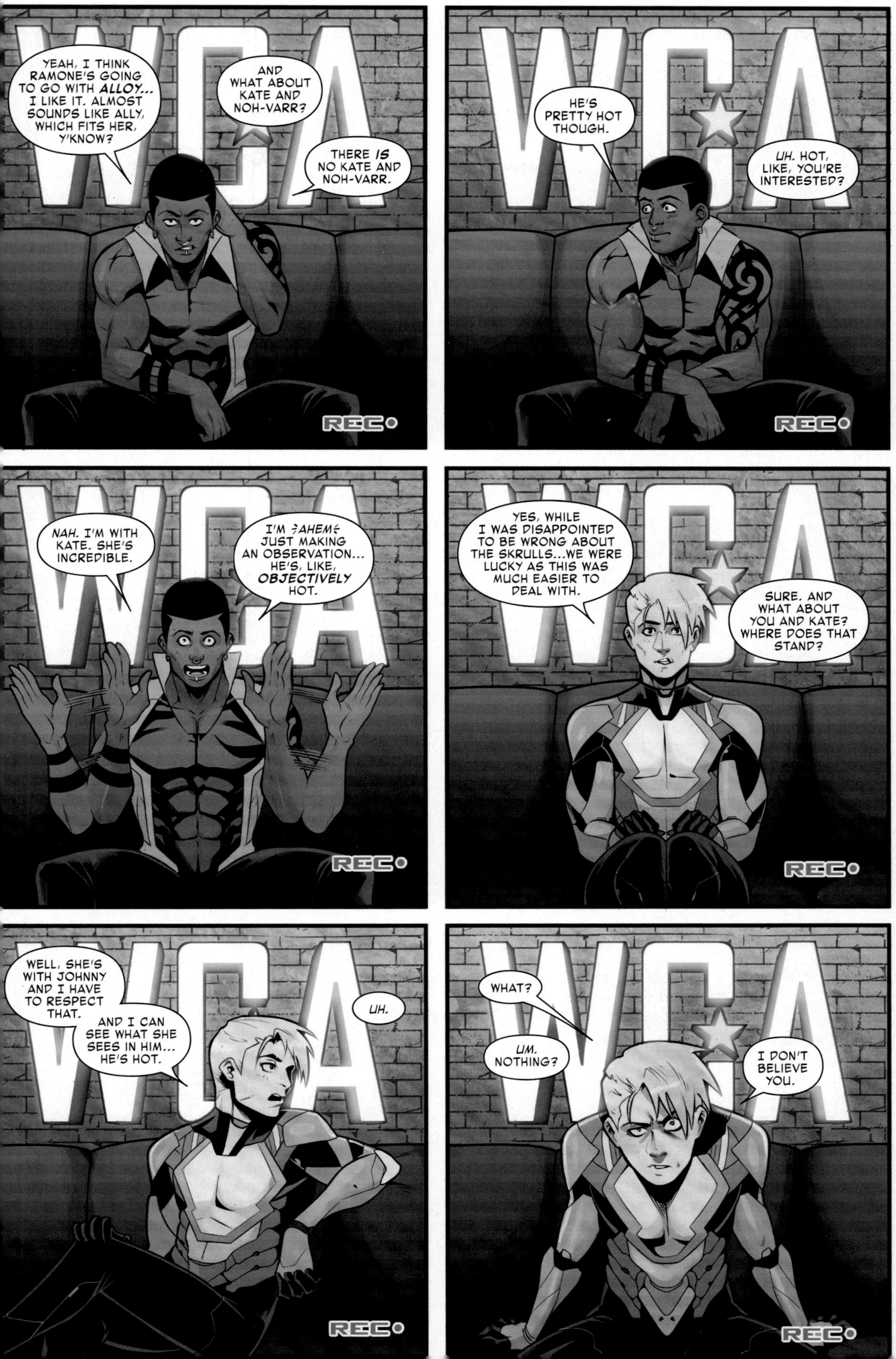
WCA
YEAH, I THINK RAMONE'S GOING TO GO WITH ALLOY... I LIKE IT. ALMOST SOUNDS LIKE ALLY, WHICH FITS HER, Y'KNOW?
AND WHAT ABOUT KATE AND NOH-VARR?
THERE IS NO KATE AND NOH-VARR.
REC
HE'S PRETTY HOT THOUGH.
UH. HOT, LIKE, YOU'RE INTERESTED?
REC
NAH. I'M WITH KATE. SHE'S INCREDIBLE.
I'M AHEM JUST MAKING AN OBSERVATION... HE'S, LIKE, OBJECTIVELY HOT.
REC
YES, WHILE I WAS DISAPPOINTED TO BE WRONG ABOUT THE SKRULLS...WE WERE LUCKY AS THIS WAS MUCH EASIER TO DEAL WITH.
SURE. AND WHAT ABOUT YOU AND KATE? WHERE DOES THAT STAND?
REC
WELL, SHE'S WITH JOHNNY AND I HAVE TO RESPECT THAT.
AND I CAN SEE WHAT SHE SEES IN HIM... HE'S HOT.
UH.
REC
WHAT?
UM. NOTHING?
I DON'T BELIEVE YOU.
REC

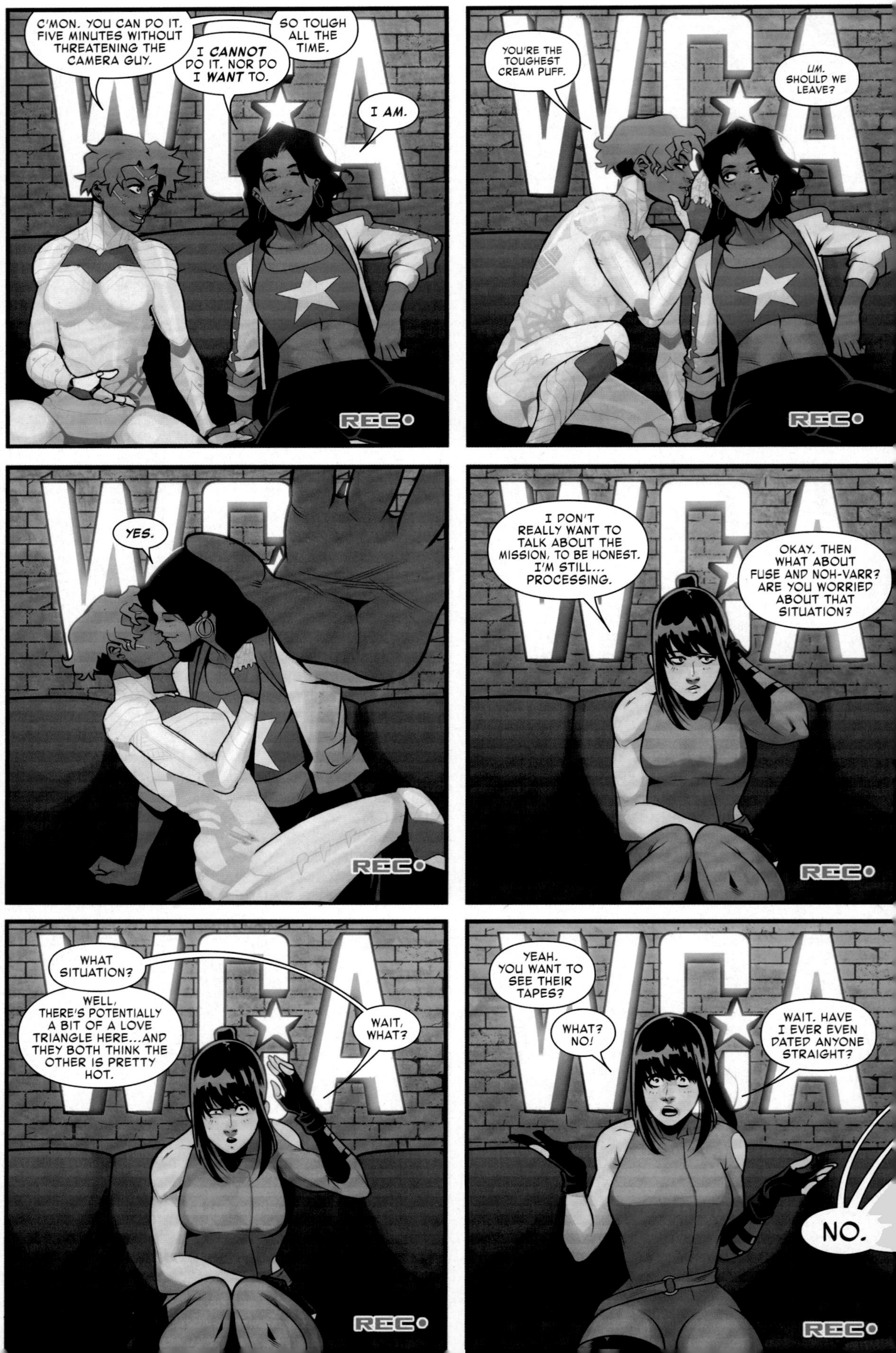
C'MON. YOU CAN DO IT. FIVE MINUTES WITHOUT THREATENING THE CAMERA GUY.
SO TOUGH ALL THE TIME.
I CANNOT DO IT. NOR DO I WANT TO.
I AM.
REC
YOU'RE THE TOUGHEST CREAM PUFF.
UM. SHOULD WE LEAVE?
REC
YES.
REC
I DON'T REALLY WANT TO TALK ABOUT THE MISSION, TO BE HONEST. I'M STILL... PROCESSING.
OKAY. THEN WHAT ABOUT FUSE AND NOH-VARR? ARE YOU WORRIED ABOUT THAT SITUATION?
REC
WHAT SITUATION?
WELL, THERE'S POTENTIALLY A BIT OF A LOVE TRIANGLE HERE...AND THEY BOTH THINK THE OTHER IS PRETTY HOT.
WAIT, WHAT?
REC
YEAH. YOU WANT TO SEE THEIR TAPES?
WHAT? NO!
WAIT. HAVE I EVER EVEN DATED ANYONE STRAIGHT?
NO.
REC

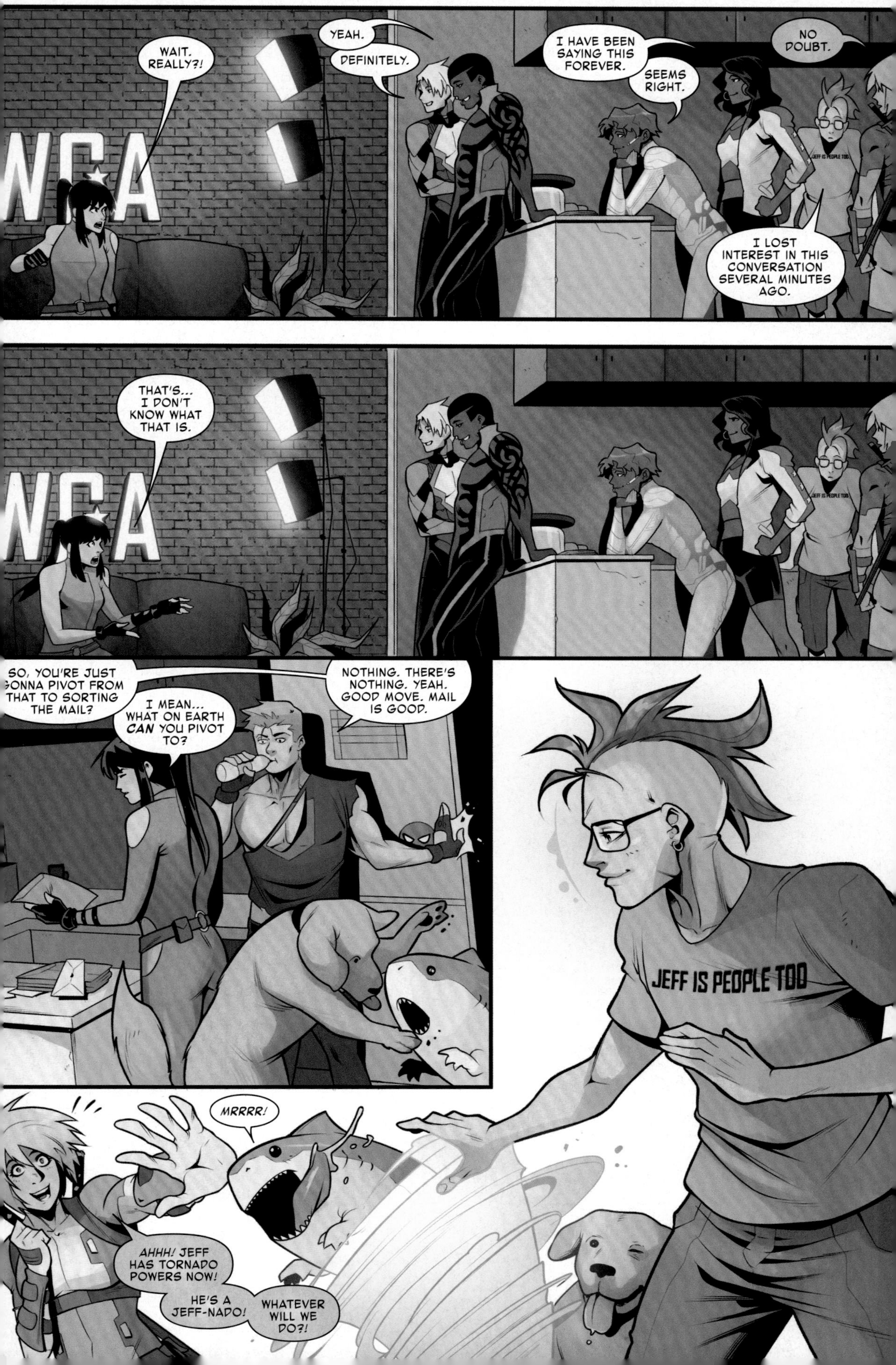
WAIT. REALLY?!
YEAH.
DEFINITELY.
I HAVE BEEN SAYING THIS FOREVER.
SEEMS RIGHT.
NO DOUBT.
JEFF IS PEOPLE TOO
I LOST INTEREST IN THIS CONVERSATION SEVERAL MINUTES AGO.
THAT'S... I DON'T KNOW WHAT THAT IS.
JEFF IS PEOPLE TOO
SO, YOU'RE JUST GONNA PIVOT FROM THAT TO SORTING THE MAIL?
I MEAN... WHAT ON EARTH **CAN** YOU PIVOT TO?
NOTHING. THERE'S NOTHING. YEAH. GOOD MOVE. MAIL IS GOOD.
JEFF IS PEOPLE TOO
!!
MRRRR!
AHHH! JEFF HAS TORNADO POWERS NOW!
HE'S A JEFF-NADO!
WHATEVER WILL WE DO?!

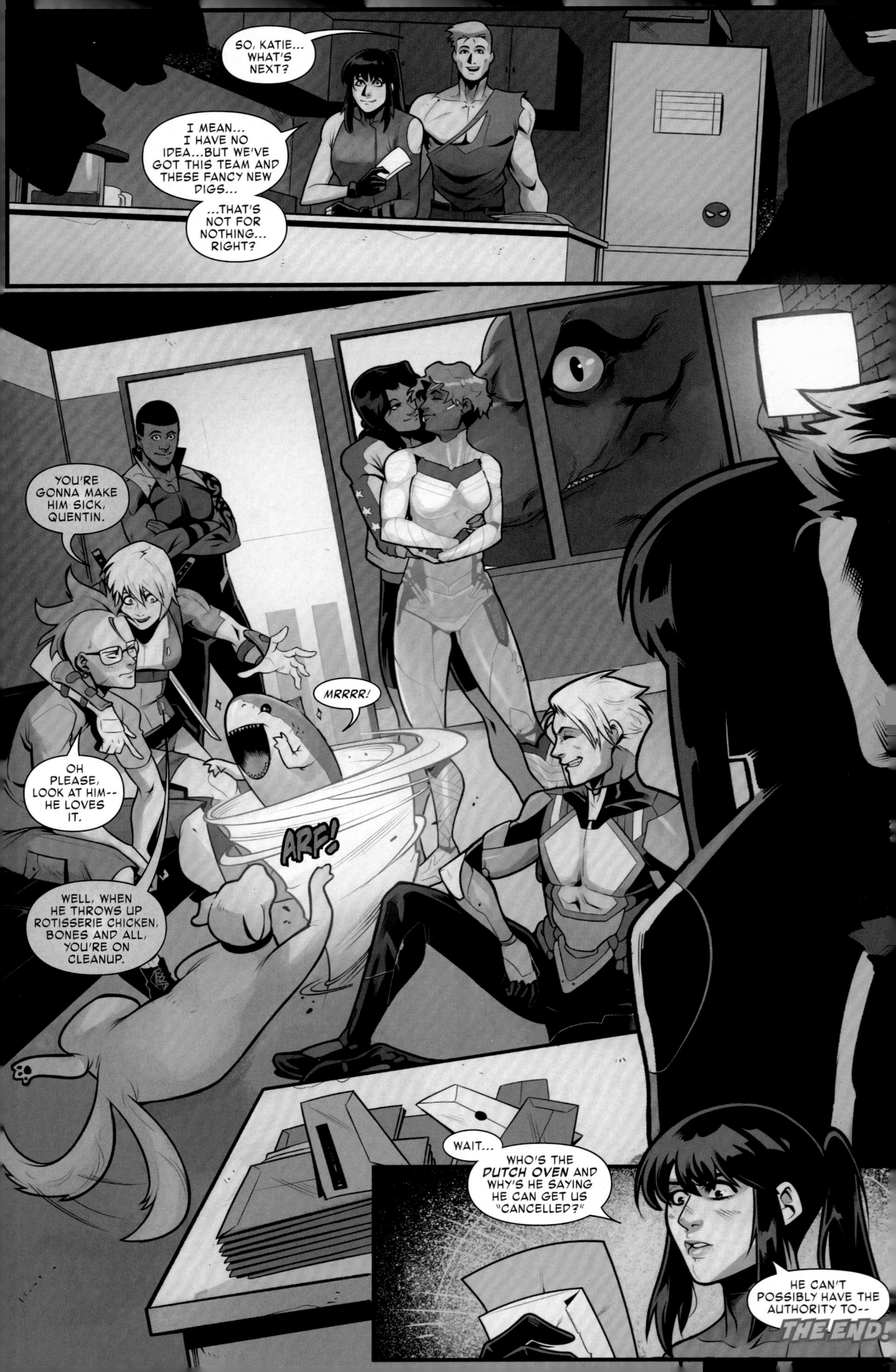

SO, KATIE... WHAT'S NEXT?
I MEAN... I HAVE NO IDEA...BUT WE'VE GOT THIS TEAM AND THESE FANCY NEW DIGS...
...THAT'S NOT FOR NOTHING... RIGHT?
YOU'RE GONNA MAKE HIM SICK, QUENTIN.
MRRRR!
OH PLEASE, LOOK AT HIM-- HE LOVES IT.
ARF!
WELL, WHEN HE THROWS UP ROTISSERIE CHICKEN, BONES AND ALL, YOU'RE ON CLEANUP.
WAIT...
WHO'S THE DUTCH OVEN AND WHY'S HE SAYING HE CAN GET US "CANCELLED?"
HE CAN'T POSSIBLY HAVE THE AUTHORITY TO--
THE END!

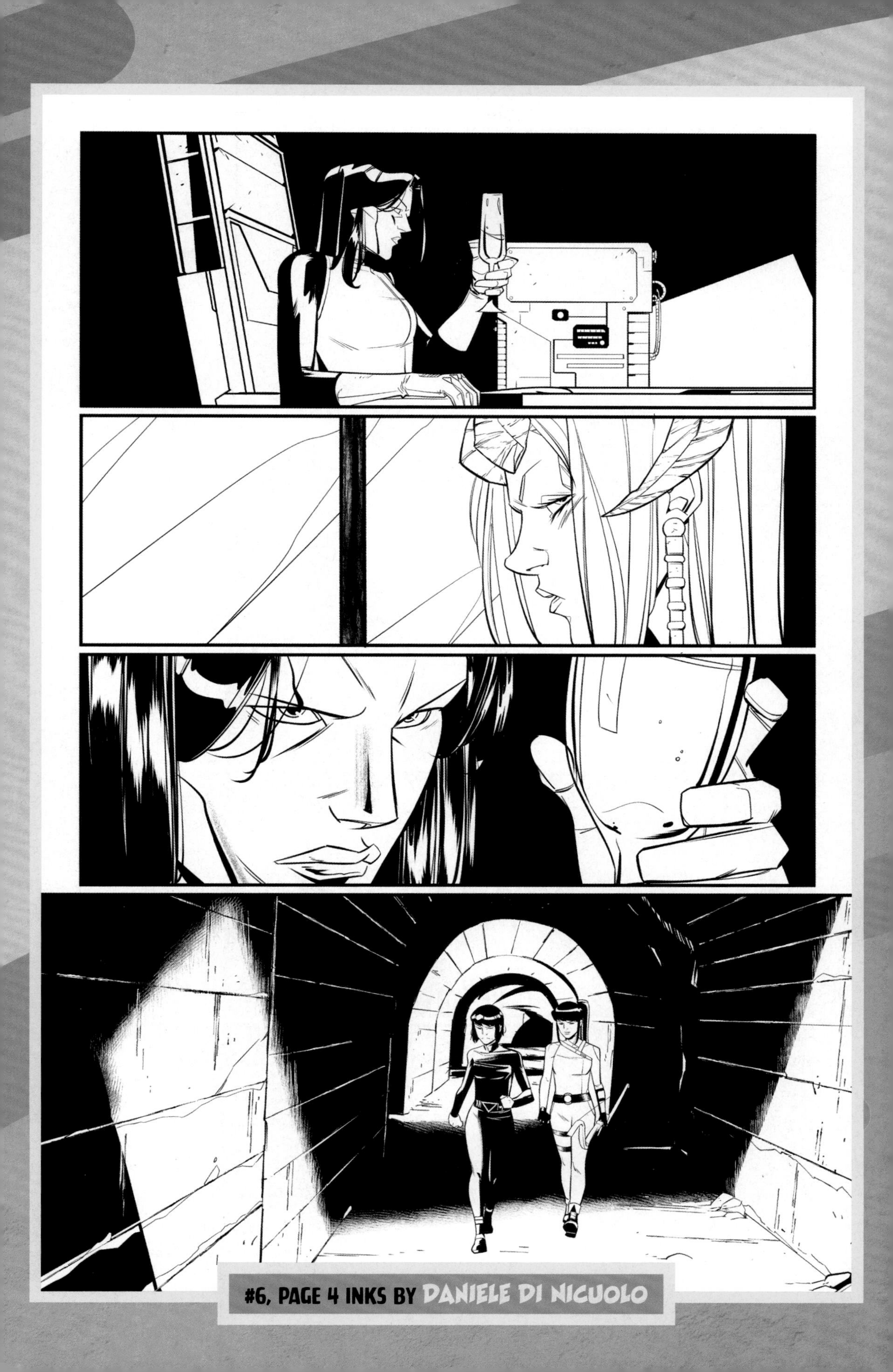

#6, PAGE 4 INKS BY DANIELE DI NICUOLO

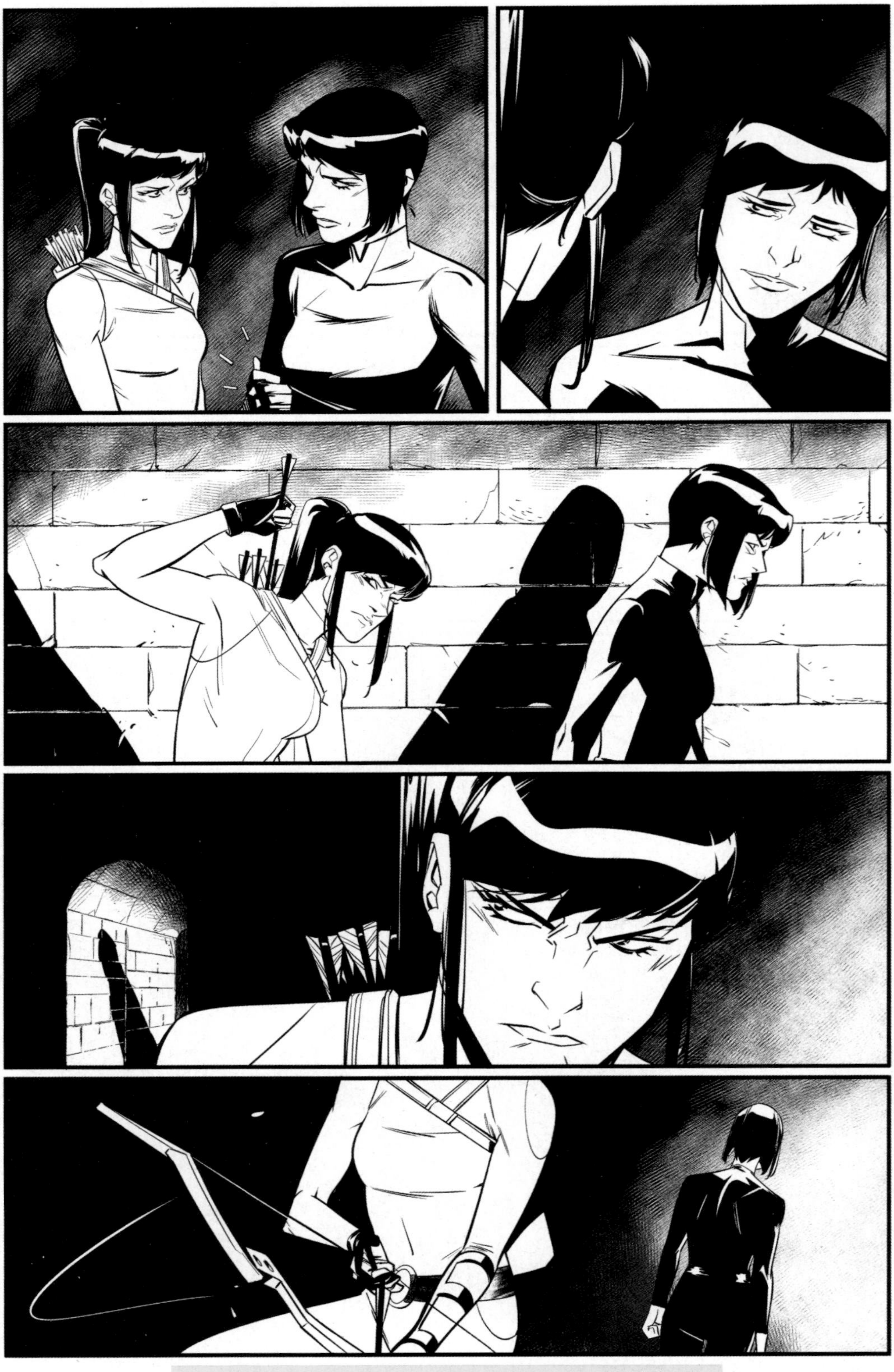

#6, PAGE 5 INKS BY DANIELE DI NICUOLO